SAFER
SANCTUARIES

Nurturing Trust within Faith Communities

A SAFE SANCTUARIES® RESOURCE

DISCIPLESHIP
RESOURCES
NASHVILLE

Contents

Foreword

by Joy Thornburg Melton

Dear Readers,

Welcome to the new resource *Safer Sanctuaries: Nurturing Trust within Faith Communities*. This resource follows in the tradition of other *Safe Sanctuaries* titles that have been published for more than twenty years. *Safer Sanctuaries* seeks to continue providing churches and ministries with support as they work to reduce the risk of abuse for children, youth, and vulnerable people in all ministry contexts while developing their congregations into safe and thriving communities.

At the 1996 General Conference, The United Methodist Church resolved to develop this type of resource to support not only all congregations, but also ministries beyond the local church. Since that time, our denomination has persistently sought to provide solid resources, foundational training, and quality leadership for all who engage with children, youth, and other vulnerable people. From my own experience and from the feedback that I have received from church leaders over the years, I believe that these efforts have been truly helpful. Nevertheless, the need still remains and requires the continuous and constant devotion of everyone in our congregations and various other ministries to protect all who seek inclusion in the community of faith.

I hope you will find this volume informative and helpful as you either begin or continue the work that you have done to provide safe sanctuaries for your community and continue to invite individuals to faith in our Lord and Savior, Jesus Christ.

Blessings,
Rev. Joy Thornburg Melton, J.D.

PART I
THE REASON

CHAPTER 1
Why Are You Here Really?

Bishop Peggy Johnson

Why are you here? Genuinely ask yourself that. Why are you reading these words right now? Most likely, you are a pastor, a lay leader, a teacher, or an administrator at your church. Taking on that role comes with certain responsibilities and obligations and, more likely than not, reading this book is part of fulfilling those responsibilities and obligations. You may even be here because of a mandate from denominational leadership.

Creating safe places for people to participate in Christian community, both in our buildings and in extended outreach locales, is an important part of our work. The work you are doing today is good. But, even though we know that this is true, we sometimes push back when asked to do this kind of work. It can feel inconvenient and time-consuming to undergo training. Implementing the kinds of policies we will discuss in this resource may come with financial implications for tight budgets when the protocols call for creating open spaces or putting windows in classroom doors. Perhaps you feel that this is common-sense information that we instinctively know how to handle without the need for more protocols. You may view this as one more task to check off on an already overloaded list of obligations. Simply put, it's understandable if your enthusiasm is limited despite the importance of the subject matter. It's understandable if you find yourself asking, "Why am I here?"

As humans, we are on a lifelong quest to answer one simple question, "Why?" As young children, my sons would instinctively respond with a litany of "why?" questions whenever I asked them to do any task. You know the kind of conversation that goes something like:

Me: "Take a bath!"

Son: "Why?"

Me: "Because you need one."

Son: "Why?"

Me: "Because you've been outside and have gotten dirty."

Son: "Why?"

_____

_____

_____

_____

_____

_____

_____

_____

_____

_____

_____

_____

In whatever role you've taken on that has led you here, you have chosen to make a covenant with God and those in your community to live according to the teachings of Jesus.

Me: "Because we don't go to bed dirty."

Son: "Why?"

This would go on and on until I finally said, with their first and middle names included, "Because I said so!" That was never a satisfactory answer for their inquiring minds, nor is it a satisfactory answer for you as we explore why you are here. As we get older, our need to know why becomes more nuanced, but no matter our age or station in life, our motivation for any task we undertake is grounded by our response to this important three-letter word.

There are obvious practical reasons to learn about shaping safer sanctuaries. We need to protect the vulnerable members of our communities from emotional and physical abuse. We need to protect everyone in our communities from harm. We need to protect leaders, community members, and even our organizations themselves from lawsuits, legal penalties, and reputational ruin. We need to build trust and faith with church members after trust has been lost. Those are all very practical reasons to do this work.

In my thirteen years serving as an episcopal leader in The United Methodist Church, I saw all these things firsthand. I also noticed, over time, the decreasing number of these incidents and the painful consequences that come with them as Safe Sanctuaries training events were offered and protocols were established. Risk management is important, but it is not the main reason we do this sacred ministry of establishment of protection protocols.

Earlier, I asked why you *are* here, but perhaps a more important question is why you *want* to be here. In whatever role you've taken on that has led you here, you have chosen to make a covenant with God and those in your community to live according to the teachings of Jesus. For Christians, resisting evil and working against injustice are part of living out our baptismal covenant to serve Jesus Christ, who is our Lord and Savior. You are here, we hope you *want* to be here, to be part of this work.

As people of faith, the most important whys are housed in a set of values that come from our relationship with God and with one another. These are the signposts that guide us in the way we should live. The scriptures remind believers that the rationale for everything we do stems from our love for God and commitment to obeying God's commandments as a demonstration of that love. When asked about the greatest commandment Jesus replied, "'You shall love the Lord your God with all your heart, with all your soul, and with all your mind. This is the first and great commandment. And the second is like it: 'You shall love your neighbor as yourself'" (Matthew 22:37-39 NKJV). Our love for God motivates us to do works of righteousness in the world. It is why God created us, as the letter to the Ephesians proclaims, "For we are His (God's) workmanship, created in Christ Jesus for good works, which God prepared beforehand that we should walk in them" (Ephesians 2:10 NKJV).

Reframing Safe Sanctuaries

Several years ago, I took on the task of reframing my diplomas and ordination credentials. For a long time, they were in inexpensive plastic frames held together with a cardboard backing. When I transferred these documents into attractive wooden frames with contrasting colored matting, it gave my credentials new life and enhanced visibility as they hung on my office wall.

In the same way, the ministry of Safe Sanctuaries needs to be reframed. It needs to be something we see as life-giving and community enhancing, first and foremost. Instead of viewing this as something we have to do, it can be something we are inspired to do, a proactive endeavor that enables flourishing ministry. Building safer sanctuaries can be an empowering, joyful way of being in community that promotes honesty, openness, and the safety and security of all people, rather than an obligation borne of fear and mandates.

In an article about reframing childhood adversity, Dr. Julie Sweetland, a sociolinguist, encourages people not to "use the scope or severity of the problem [of abuse] to engage people. Bleak facts and upsetting stories spark fatalistic attitudes or cause people to turn away to avoid discomfort."[1] She further explains that leaders in this work need to "show the futures we create by our choices to act or not act. Look for opportunities to contrast a gain scenario (in which action leads to a good thing) with a loss scenario in which delay or failure to act leads to undesirable outcomes."[2]

It is my hope that you, as a leader in your community, will frame the work of building safer sanctuaries as one of goodness and life-giving ministry. It is my hope that the tools provided by this resource support you in your work and help build a foundation for how your community can flourish and build trust with one another. We do this work because of our love for God and because of our love for our neighbor. We do this work in the context of community, which is found both within the walls of our buildings, and also outside those walls wherever we serve Christ. We do this work because it creates a bright future for all people.

Notes

1. Julie Sweetland, _Reframing Childhood Adversity: Promoting Upstream Approaches._ FrameWorks, (Washington, DC: FrameWorks Institute, March 2, 2021): 9, https://preventchildabuse.org/resources/frameworks-institute-reframing-childhood-adversity-promoting-upstream-approaches.
2. Sweetland, _Reframing Childhood Adversity_, 16.

> It is my hope that the tools provided by this resource support you in your work and help build a foundation for how your community can flourish and build trust with one another.

CHAPTER 2

Flourishing, Not Fear: A Theology of Safety and Sanctuary

Bishop Peggy Johnson

Choosing Flourishing over Fear

Fear and fear-mongering are rampant in the world today. There is no lack of worrisome things happening around us from climate change to pandemics to racism and xenophobia. There are endless stories in the news every day about political, social, and economic turmoil across every part of the globe. The world can be a scary place.

While the reality of the world can be frightening, we as God's people are not to be burdened with fear. We place our faith in God as the answer to the anxieties and worries of life. In the Gospel of John, Jesus tells his disciples, "In the world you will have tribulation; but be of good cheer, I have overcome the world" (John 16:33b, NKJV). The Apostle Paul likewise admonishes us, "Do not be anxious about anything, but in everything by prayer and supplication with thanksgiving let your requests be made known to God. And the peace of God, which surpasses all understanding, will guard your hearts and minds in Christ Jesus" (Philippians 4:6-7, NRSVUE). Connecting to the love of God guards us from fear.

Fear is a barrier to our well-being. It keeps us in its clutches and holds us back from thriving. There is a story of refugee children who were saved from the ravages of World War II and taken into an orphanage. At night, the children were unable to sleep because of their constant fear of hunger. Eventually, one wise caretaker at the orphanage decided to send the children to bed each night with a piece of bread. This bread, such a small and simple thing, was a "hands-on" assurance to the children that they would have enough food the next day. With that piece of bread held tightly in their hands, they were finally able to sleep soundly.[1]

As we approach the work of creating safer sanctuaries, we strive for flourishing, not fear, to always be first and foremost in our minds. The fear of abuse, the fear of harm, the fear of litigation, and the fear of all the negative outcomes that we are trying to avoid with this work is understandable. These threats are real. Nevertheless, the goal of establishing healthy relationships and healthy boundaries that nurture strong and growing faith communities is always our guiding principle. As Jesus wisely counseled us, "But seek first the kingdom of God and his righteousness, and all these things will be given to you as well" (Matthew 6:33 NRSVUE). As we focus on the life-giving, nurturing work of God's righteousness, our work and this ministry will become a source of joy. In return, God promises to fulfill all our needs, and this includes vanquishing our fears.

The apostle Paul reiterates this message to his young mentee Timothy when he writes, "For God has not given us a spirit of fear, but of power and of love and of a sound mind" (2 Timothy 1:7, NKJV). We must choose this spirit of power and love, this spirit of flourishing, instead of fear. Think of it like a switch mechanism on a train that allows us to go down one track or the other. Christian writer and spiritual director MaryKate Morse explains, "One track is safe and clear and allows the train to steam ahead. The other leads it toward collision. God gave us a switch that does not lead us down a track to fear, isolation, despair, anger and self-interest, but one that leads towards something completely different: power, love and a sound mind."[2]

Our approach to this work is a choice. That choice is based on our faith in the eternal goodness of God, who wants health, wholeness, and life for all of creation. My personal ministry journey included serving for many years as the pastor of a congregation comprised almost exclusively of people who were deaf and deaf-blind. One would think that communication barriers and isolation would be a dismal and fearful reality in the lives of these church members. However, while there were certainly challenges at times, the overwhelming spirit in their lives was one of joy, love, and nurture. On a daily basis, we witnessed people overcoming barriers of discrimination and rejection. They responded to life's fears with dependance on God. These were choices of the heart, dependent not on circumstance, but on faith in God's abundant goodness.

Likewise, as we begin the task of arranging safety and accountability training for our congregations and establishing boundary policies for our ministries, we must choose to keep the goal of flourishing before us, knowing that it comes from the heart of God whose purpose is good will for all of creation. We do this together, as a community, knowing that God is with us and emboldening our spirit as we proceed.

Thriving through Communities

The Triune God, Father, Son, and Holy Spirit, models community for us in its very essence. God is forever three and forever one. The Trinity is simultaneously the synergy of creation, redemption, and sustenance. In a similar way, the church, the body of Christ, is a diverse community that functions as one body with many members. It thrives when each part of the community uses their God-given gifts to improve the whole. The Apostle Paul explains this to the contentious Corinthian church saying, "To each is given the manifestation of the Spirit for the common good" (1 Corinthians 12:7 NRSVUE).

The work of building safer sanctuaries can be accomplished only in community. Each part of the church must use its unique gifts and sensitivities to carry out the

Notes

Our approach to this work is a choice. That choice is based on our faith in the eternal goodness of God, who wants health, wholeness, and life for all of creation.

Notes

_____

_____

_____

_____

_____

_____

_____

_____

_____

_____

_____

_____

_____

Establishing boundaries and providing protection allows room for everyone to grow and flourish. Boundaries protect everyone.

work. Everyone does the work, and everyone benefits. This includes agreeing, as one body, to enforce the boundaries and protocols that are established.

A few years ago, I visited the home of an old college friend. In her back yard, she had a thriving vegetable garden. I noticed tall fences surrounding the garden and inquired about their exceptional height. She explained that there were a lot of deer in the area and that the towering fences had to be erected to keep them from eating all the crops. Deer are naturally skilled jumpers, and short fences would not suffice. These barriers were quite effective, and because they were protecting the garden so well, I came home that day with a basket of ripe summer vegetables.

Interestingly, these fences were also good for the deer. According to wildlife experts, deer can suffer harm when they feed on sources of food that aren't naturally occurring or when they are fed by well-meaning but misguided people. It is better for the deer that they find their food in the wild. Access to a well-supplied garden creates habits that impede their normal feeding cycles and can result in starvation or aggressive behaviors later on.[3] These barriers protected everyone, both the garden and the deer, and as a result, both flourished.

While our churches are both more valuable and more complex than a vegetable garden, the principle remains the same. Establishing boundaries and providing protection allows room for everyone to grow and flourish. Boundaries protect everyone. They protect the church, the people who would suffer harm, the people who would be doing that harm, and even people who are simply ignorant of the ways that certain behaviors may harm others. When faith communities establish Safe Sanctuaries protocols, everyone enjoys safety, and everyone plays a part in the work of accountability. Joy Melton and Michelle L. Foster, authors of *Safe Sanctuaries in a Virtual World*, remind us, "The work of being the church also means clearly establishing boundaries, principles and guidelines by which we will hold one another accountable to the unity of the Spirit of God."[4]

When everyone takes responsibility for this ministry of protection, then it becomes a natural part of church life.

Keeping Our Baptismal Identity

The practice of keeping boundaries is closely tied to our baptismal vows. When we bind ourselves to Christ through the sacrament of baptism, we commit to renounce the spiritual forces of wickedness, reject the evil powers of this world, repent of sin, accept the freedom and power God gives to resist evil, injustice and oppression in whatever forms they present themselves, confess Jesus Christ as Savior, put our whole trust in his grace, promise to serve him as Lord in union with the church, which Christ has opened to people of all ages, nations and races, and promise to remain a faithful member of Christ's holy church and to serve as Christ's representatives in the world.[5] This is the bedrock faith commitment we make to God through our baptism.

Embedded in these vows is our promise to faithfully engage in the work of justice. We do this by renouncing evil and pushing toward the goal that all people will experience the wholeness of new life in Jesus Christ. Boundary setting and accountability protocols are an integral part of this work and therefore an integral part of our commitment to God as a disciple of our Lord and Savior.

At the conclusion of a baptismal service, the congregation is called upon to reaffirm their commitment to these vows and to promise to nurture and care for the new member of the body of Christ. Together, we say, "With God's help we will so order our lives after the example of Christ that, surrounded by steadfast love, you may be established in the faith, and confirmed and strengthened in the way that leads to life eternal."[6] We are all in this together. This is a mutual commitment to nurture and protect. Our baptism and its promises shape our identity.

Years ago, I was involved in a community food ministry that delivered groceries to a high-rise apartment building in our city. Our congregation participated in this work as an outgrowth of our commitment to Christ, the same commitment set forth in our baptismal vows. One day when I arrived at the front of the apartment building with groceries in both hands, a young child who was standing in the lobby exclaimed to all the bystanders, "Here comes the church!" It was the greatest compliment one could ever receive. The food delivery and the church were synonymous in his young mind. Our identity as disciples of Christ was tied directly to what we did in the community.

Likewise, boundary-keeping is an important part of a church's identity, and it is vital that we make this identity clear to the community both in and outside of the church. Keeping people safe is as important as all the other ministries we do because it enables us to be church in concrete ways and it empowers other ministries to thrive. It requires discipline to keep our identity centered in Christ, to stay focused on the work of Christ, and not to get side-tracked by other identities.

In their book, *The Integrity of the Body of Christ: Boundary Keeping as Shared Responsibility*, Arden Mahlberg and Craig Nessan state:

> One constant temptation in the life of the church is to substitute some other identity to replace core Christian identity. Thereby the church serves as a social outlet for the enjoyment of the members, or as an organization to provide services for those who pay their dues. Or the church gets construed as a business venture that only has value when it makes a profit. Or the church exists primarily to perpetuate the building and provide a cemetery. So many false identities threaten to overtake the church's identity as the people of God in Christ Jesus. Good boundaries clarify, protect and preserve the true nature of church so that it can fulfill its mission of living the Great Commandment.[7]

When we place safety and boundaries at the core of our collective identity, we work together to take responsibility for one another in tangible ways. This is how we support one another as the body of Christ.

Notes

> We are all in this together. This is a mutual commitment to nurture and protect. Our baptism and its promises shape our identity.

_____

_____

_____

_____

_____

_____

_____

_____

_____

_____

_____

_____

> **This is a call to action. It's a call to get busy and do the work.**

Action Required

One of my professors in seminary once said that every sermon needs to call the congregation to put on their roller skates. This professor meant that sermons should inspire the hearer to get busy and *do* something out in the world. I was never very good at roller skating, but with a skilled skater holding my hand, I could do quite well. As the body of Christ, we support one another in the ministry. Think of the work of building safer sanctuaries as an invitation to put on your skates, an invitation to get out and do something, to create a flourishing, safe environment, that incorporates the entire congregation and is fundamentally a ministry that stems from our commitment to Christ as set forth in our baptism vows.

This is a call to action. It's a call to get busy and do the work. As you do, keep in mind The General Rules of the Methodist Church. These rules, as expressed long ago by the founder of the Methodist movement, John Wesley, are as follows:

1. "Doing no harm, by avoiding evil or every kind . . ."
2. "Doing good; by being in every kind merciful after their power as they have opportunity, doing good of every possible sort and as far as possible to all men . . ."
3. "Attending upon all the ordinances of God."[8]

In recent years, this fundamental rubric has been popularized as the "Three Simple Rules." Bishop Rueben Job authored a book with this title and celebrated the timeless relevance of this wise guidance. In his book, Bishop Job writes, "The three simple rules in themselves are contemporary and exceptionally well-suited to our times, our culture and our needs today."[9]

These rules are helpful guides as we engage in Safer Sanctuaries ministries. In an effort to do no harm, we must consciously ask ourselves if someone else is being harmed by either our action or inaction. In her book, *Love Does No Harm: Sexual Ethics for the Rest of Us*, Marie Fortune writes, "Doing the least harm is a realistic and tangible goal to set for ourselves. Avoiding harm is also one of the oldest stated ethical expectations for those in the helping professions. The Hippocratic Oath (fifth century BCE) requires physicians to 'keep [patients] from harm and injustice.'"[10]

The practice of ministry, no less than the practice of medicine, presents us with challenging dilemmas in which there are no easy answers. However, the imperative to avoid both harm and injustice can be our guide.

Doing good also comes with nuances. Doing good is a call to follow the Golden Rule and to treat others as we would want to be treated. The Book of James reminds us, "If you really fulfill the royal law according to the scripture, 'You shall love your neighbor as yourself,' you do well" (James 2:8 NRSVUE). The way you love yourself provides a reference for what is pleasing and life-giving. Extending that out to others and treating them in ways that gives them life makes decisions about doing good easier to discern.

Once, when I was serving as the pastor of a local church, there was a debate about whether the church should build a wheelchair ramp. Some on the board of trustees objected because of the cost and the fact that no one attending at the time had a mobility challenge. They ultimately decided not to build the ramp. Soon after, one of the prominent members of the church had a fall and required the use of a wheelchair for several months. A ramp was hastily erected. That member began to think about the Golden Rule. He began to think about accessibility through his own experience and how he should want the same for all people. This recognition led the church to the begin the good work of focusing on other issues of accessibility such as large-print bulletins, listening devices, and dietary sensitivity at the regular potluck dinners. This is the same mindset we should take on when determining what good we should be doing while building safer sanctuaries. This work requires us to ask ourselves what we would like for ourselves in terms of safety and respect.

Finally, when we attend to the "ordinances of God," those spiritual disciplines of prayer, study of scripture, worship, Sabbath-keeping, partaking of the Lord's Supper, and fasting, to name a few, we avail ourselves of the Spirit's power to avoid evil and do good in the world. Moreover, these disciplines, especially prayer and study of scripture, give us guidance and wisdom for what we should do in the moment, especially when decisions are difficult.

In *The Book of Joy: Lasting Happiness in a Changing World,* Douglas Abram threads together a dialogue between the Dalai Lama and the late Archbishop Desmond Tutu. In the book, Abram tells of a time when he challenged the archbishop about making an apology to someone. He writes, "As my verbal assault became more pointed and challenging, I saw his head draw back in reaction and perhaps some defensiveness . . . it was as if I could see the archbishop—in a split-second pause—collect his consciousness, reflect on his options, and choose his response, one that was thoughtful and engaged rather than reactive and rejecting. It was one of the most profound examples of what a prayerful and meditative life can give us—that pause, the freedom to respond instead of react."[11]

Attending to the spiritual disciplines of our faith gives us that "still small voice" from above that guides us in how to speak and act. Prayer requires us to stop and listen to God as we make plans to build safer sanctuaries and respond to situations that arise. This ministry involves a vast array of decisions, and we must have God's guidance to succeed.

Pray, plan, and dream. Work together with your community to create and craft a church that protects its people, that is a flourishing beacon of light for all. Remember your baptism and be thankful that it shapes your identity for ministry. Do this work in the strength of the God that guides and directs. In all things, be an agent for good and do no harm in your church, your community, and the world.

Notes

Prayer requires us to stop and listen to God as we make plans to build safer sanctuaries and respond to situations that arise.

Notes

_____

_____

_____

_____

_____

_____

_____

_____

_____

_____

_____

_____

Work together with your community to create and craft a church that protects its people, that is a flourishing beacon of light for all.

Notes

1. Dennis Linn, Sheila Fabricant Linn, Matthew Linn, *Sleeping with Bread: Holding What Gives You Life* (Mahwah: Paulist Press, 1995).

2. MaryKate Morse, "Flourishing, Not Fear: The Gift of Power" (Part II). *The Well, InterVarsity Women Scholars and Professionals*, May 19, 2009, https://thewell .intervarsity.org/spiritual-formation/flourishing-not-fear-gift-power-part-ii.

3. New Hampshire Fish and Game Department, "More Harm Than Good: Here's Why the New Hampshire Fish and Game Department Urges You to NOT Feed the Deer." https://www.wildlife.state.nh.us/wildlife/documents/more-harm.pdf.

4. Joy Thornburg Melton and Michelle L. Foster, *Safe Sanctuaries in a Virtual World* (Nashville: Discipleship Resources, 2014), 11.

5. *The Baptismal Covenant IV, The United Methodist Hymnal* (Nashville: The United Methodist Publishing House), 50.

6. The Baptismal Covenant III, *The United Methodist Hymnal* (Nashville: The United Methodist Publishing House), 48.

7. Arden F. Mahlberg, Craig L. Nessan, *The Integrity of the Body of Christ: Boundary Keeping as Shared Responsibility* (Eugene: Cascade Books, 2016), 22.

8. *The Book of Discipline of The United Methodist Church 2016* (Nashville: The United Methodist Publishing House, 2016), 78–79.

9. Rueben P. Job, *Three Simple Rules: A Wesleyan Way of Living* (Nashville: Abingdon Press, 2007), 17.

10. Marie M. Fortune, *Love Does No Harm: Sexual Ethics for the Rest of Us* (New York: Continuum, 2006), 34.

11. Dalai Lama and Desmond Tutu with Douglas Abrams, *The Book of Joy: Lasting Happiness in a Changing World* (New York: Avery, 2016), 181.

CHAPTER 3
The Effects, Known and Unknown

Bishop Peggy Johnson

The need for safer communities may seem abstract to some in your congregation. Some may even deem it unnecessary, believing that the church is already safe enough. In my early years of ministry, when safety protocols like these were first being established in the annual conference where I served, the initial attempts were not well-received by some teachers at my local church. At the time, we were simply asking Sunday school teachers and youth workers to sign a statement affirming that they had never been associated with child abuse. It felt like an easy enough ask, but a few of our teachers immediately resigned in protest. They viewed this requirement as an insult. They believed that everyone at the church was trustworthy and that this need for further confirmation was something only necessary in the secular world.

Sadly, would-be abusers are often permitted to act in churches without hindrance because of this kind of attitude. While the church is the body of Christ and is filled with people made in the image of God, these same people are also fallible humans. The same people who do kindness with one hand, do selfish acts with the other. The same people who offer healing one day, hurt others the next. Safety protocols are therefore even more important in a place that proclaims itself to be a haven for God's people, full of goodness and love. We are only as trustworthy as we show ourselves to be with systems put in place to protect the vulnerable. Goodness and love thrive in places of safety.

For some, the church is the only place where they experience relationships of grace and integrity. When their trust is violated in the church, it can be even more devastating than usual. Even well-meaning people can unknowingly cause harm when they aren't thinking about how their actions affect others. Not every harmful action rises to the level of a crime; sometimes it's simply careless or selfish.

When I was a child growing up in The United Methodist Church, there was a long-time member at my local church who made it his practice to hug all the girls on Sunday morning. In those days, this kind of thing was never challenged by any of the adults standing nearby, and as teenagers, we never thought we had the agency to refuse his advances, even though we did not like it. There were no *Safe Sanctuary* protocols back then. One girl stopped coming to church entirely because these hugs were a trigger for her and reminded her of the abuse she experienced at home.

_____

_____

_____

_____

_____

_____

_____

_____

_____

_____

_____

These are neon signs that shout, "We care about you, we want you safe, we hide nothing here."

The man in question wasn't trying to hurt anyone. I'm sure he had good intentions, but we didn't want his hugs. We didn't want to be touched like that. And for that one girl, it drove her away, away from a place where she could find safety and refuge. This is simply how things were years ago.

Today, this same church is a protected place, a safer place, because of the policies and procedures put in place, the training events they've held, and the vigilant work they've done to create a safe sanctuary. People ask about giving hugs before they assume that everyone wants one. There is so much good that comes from this safer environment, both known and unknown.

Known Effects

The benefits of Safe Sanctuaries ministry are not always found in the harms prevented, but also in the visible benefits safety and conscientious action can bring to a community. When churches take this work seriously, when they post their protocols and expectations on their websites, the walls of their classrooms, and in their newsletters and bulletins, people who are looking for a church will know that this is a place of caring and safety. In turn, they will be more likely to become a part of this congregation. In some ways, Safe Sanctuaries ministry is an evangelism tool that celebrates community care while promoting trust, compassion, and unity around the issue of safety for all. It reflects the support and care we all want from a church.

In *The Book of Joy*, the Dalai Lama celebrates this gift of trust in a community:

> When there is trust, people are brought together—whole nations are brought together. When you have a more compassionate mind and cultivate warm heartedness, the whole atmosphere around you becomes more positive and friendlier. You see friends everywhere. If you feel fear and distrust, then other people will distance themselves. They will also feel cautious, suspicious and distrustful.[1]

The personality of a church is shown through the way people interact, the care they have for one another, the nurturing fellowship, and the sweet fragrance of respect that permeates everything. Even the architecture, windows in every classroom, open spaces in the pastor's study with an administrative office nearby, speaks to openness and honesty. The presence of two teachers in every classroom, the sign-in and sign-out sheets for parents with children in the nursery speak to accountability. These are neon signs that shout, "We care about you, we want you safe, we hide nothing here." This is the kind of church people want to join because there is a promise of openness and honesty, a promise of boundaries and safety.

Unknown Effects

While there are many visible effects on the community, most of the results that come from building safer sanctuaries will not be visible. In this way, they are like the largest part of an iceberg, unseen, hidden in the deep Arctic waters. These unknown effects are the result of the catastrophes that were avoided, the abuse that didn't happen, the pain that wasn't caused, and the fears that were never allowed to take root and grow. These unknown effects, which are the direct result of the work we do, cannot be measured, but they are the fruits of our ministry, the fruits of the policies, procedures, trainings, and diligence that we employ to firm up the foundations of our communities.

From time to time, we may learn about an incident that our protocols prevented, a close call that might not have been avoided otherwise. Once, when I was serving a congregation, a convicted child sex offender began attending worship. We presented this man with our "covenant of safety." In order to continue attending, the man was required to sign this covenant and agree to several rules of conduct. The rules included restrictions like avoiding all contact with children or youth, staying with a shepherd in the congregation, and continuing to attend regular counseling sessions with his therapist.

He initially agreed to the covenant, but soon he stopped coming to the church. I found out later that he began attending another church. He abused someone at this congregation and ended up in prison again. We may never know the amount of the pain and misery that will be avoided in our communities because of the careful work we do.

Peace of mind and a sense of personal security is another unknown benefit of building safer sanctuaries. People don't often verbalize their fears and apprehensions about being at church. These are deeply personal feelings and self-disclosure can be painful or even risky. For example, some people do not feel comfortable being in a bathroom with others because of safety concerns. When a church has a secure family or unisex bathroom available, there is no need for an explanation; anyone can use it with complete privacy. This can bring peace of mind to someone that we will never hear about, but it will mean something to them.

The lives of the people in our communities are complicated; their history can be fraught, and they may carry wounds from their past. Both the foundational principles found in this resource and the protocols covered here and laid out in Safe Sanctuary ministries across the country are meant to help vulnerable people be a part of community without fear. We desire to build communities where people are free from fear of new hurts or of triggering past wounds. We also hope to protect everyone from misunderstandings and actions that unknowingly cause harm when these measures are not in place.

We desire to build communities where people are free from fear of new hurts or of triggering past wounds.

Notes

_____
_____
_____
_____
_____
_____
_____
_____
_____
_____
_____
_____
_____
_____

There is no way to measure how far this culture will reach as it spreads through the work of a church whose members are passionate about safety for everyone, everywhere.

Like leaven in a lump of dough, when Safe Sanctuary practices become a regular part of "being church," they help create a culture of safety. Like any culture, Safe Sanctuaries has its own unique language, history, traditions, and values that are internal to the community. Over time these same values, this same culture, becomes hard-coded into your church.

More importantly, these cultural expectations are not bound by the church's walls. The life-giving, community-building principles lived out in this community become a part of the people, and the people spread these values throughout the rest of their lives, no matter where they may go. Whether in school boards, shopping centers, community garden clubs, or any place where people gather together, people trained and shaped by the principles of Safe Sanctuaries carry these values and this culture into the rest of the world. This is faith in action. This is what it looks like for people to live out the principles of faith and share the fruit of ministry beyond the walls of the church. There is no way to measure how far this culture will reach as it spreads through the work of a church whose members are passionate about safety for everyone, everywhere.

Finally, the most difficult effects to fathom are the long-term effects that won't be seen until far in the future. Vast and immeasurable in their scope, these effects are often unimaginable. In his essay, "Remember the Future, Bishop Robert Schnase reminds us, "In every discussion, deliberation, discernment and decision, a leader must give deep and conscientious consideration to the future—to the future of the mission, to future contexts to future generations to a future with hope."[2] When we keep the future in mind, it makes this work even more important, even more sacred. Long after our time on earth is over, what we do now will echo in the generations that follow us.

My sister, a retired elementary school teacher, has long been passionate about protecting the environment and planting trees. During her long tenure as a teacher, she taught children about the benefits of planting trees in urban areas. But she didn't only talk about it, she also worked with the students to plant and care for trees themselves. One year, a large number of saplings were donated to the school. She and the students were given permission to plant them on the school property. They undertook this project with considerable pride, but unfortunately, a new groundskeeper, who had not been advised about the project, mowed down all the trees by mistake. My sister was devastated, but then a member of the county forestry board consoled her, "Don't worry about the trees, we can always get new ones, but the most important thing cannot be destroyed with a lawn mower. These children learned about trees, and they will carry that with them and plant their own trees in the future."

This is a wise lesson for all of us as we engage in important work. The lessons we teach our children, the work we do, and the culture we create are what shape the future. Even when it is hard, even when we feel like failures, we are moving forward and building a safer, healthier, thriving community for all involved. What we do today is important because it lives on through word and deed in the lives of those who have learned about this work from us. We simply need to have faith where we cannot see and not grow weary of doing good.

As we embark on this journey, may we work to create safe communities as a way of showing care and love for others that reflects our love for God. May we do this work for the seen and unseen benefits, and may we trust that every work we do for the Lord will reap a harvest.

Notes

1. Dalai Lama and Tutu, *The Book of Joy,* 129.
2. Robert Schnase,. "Remember the Future," *Ministry Matters* (February 19, 2012), https://ministrymatters.com/all/entry/2140/rememberthefuture.

Notes

The lessons we teach our children, the work we do, and the culture we create are what shape the future.

PART II
THE REALITY

CHAPTER 4
Awareness of Reality

Angela D. Schaffner, Ph.D.

We aim for flourishing. We aim for ministries that inspire, support, and protect our children and the vulnerable among us. That's the goal of *Safer Sanctuaries*. But the reality we face still induces fear. We look at the children in our lives, the children we know and love, and witness the kind of trust they put in others, a trust that comes much more readily than it does to us as adults. We see their desire to please, their needs and vulnerability. We see their dependency upon their caregivers.

Children depend on the village of adults surrounding them in a host of ways. Their brains are not yet fully developed. They are learning, growing, and experiencing many parts of life for the first time. They need a safe place to continue this growth, to develop into the people they have been created to be, and it is our task to provide them with this sanctuary, this place of safety. This task is also not limited to children. It extends to all people, all ages, those who view themselves as vulnerable and those who view themselves as strong. My dream is that the church fully embraces this call, this challenge, and becomes the type of place that is so safe, so supportive, and so inclusive, that it is a place people run to in times of suffering.

However, if we fail in this task, we contribute to an already devastating problem. Too often, people do not feel safe venturing inside the walls of a church. They feel the need to cover up their imperfections, to put on their finest version of themselves and arrive at their best. They arrive hoping to please and adapt and be accepted for who they appear to be rather than who they are. In recent years, I sit across from more and more clients who are disappointed and saddened by their church experiences. Some feel invalidated. Some feel excluded. Others have been judged harshly. Some have had their voices silenced or have been treated unfairly by those more privileged and powerful than they. Many simply have questions about faith and theology that they wish they could ask inside the walls of the church, that they wish they felt safer to ask within the walls of the church. While the central task of this resource is to help prevent abuse in the church, this aim is also part of a much greater challenge we face. Our ultimate challenge is to build a culture, a community, and a church that is known for the safety of its sanctuaries, the unmatched love and support it provides to all, rather than a system that minimizes and silences voices to protect reputations, avoid conflicts, and maintain existing power structures.

We can do so much better! We begin with a theological foundation that emphasizes flourishing over fear. Much of the time, fear keeps us boxed into spaces that don't allow us room to breathe, that don't allow

_____

_____

_____

_____

_____

_____

_____

_____

_____

_____

_____

Our communities deserve our best selves, grounded in the present, willing to hear the details of the difficult truth.

room for difficult and complex conversations. So many times, we read about Jesus urging his disciples not to be afraid (Matthew 28:10, Mark 6:50). Yet, we also know that fear is a normal feeling, a normal experience in the range of human emotions. Fear can even be a life-saving gift in a moment of danger when our bodies instinctively respond to protect us from harm.[1] In other instances, however, fear can be imagined or remembered, a feeling based more on what has happened to us in the past rather than what is happening in the present moment. For us to achieve the goals we have set, we must learn discernment. We must learn to distinguish between different types of fear so that we can be alert in the present moment.

We must learn to discern when true fear tells us that there is a real threat to a child or vulnerable adult. In these situations, listen to your true fear! Your true fear may be a gift that keeps someone safe. Many of us have experienced church as a safe place, and we have internalized well-established scripts about what life in church should be, scripts filled with heartfelt hymns, nourishing dinners, trusted leaders, and skilled, inspiring preachers. If that has been our experience, we may dismiss true fear when we most need to listen to it. We must remember that even our safest havens can still house dangerous people who seek to take advantage of others. Fear can be useful.

In contrast to true fear, however, we can have remembered fears. Our bodies may recall a familiar scent, a familiar sound, or a familiar situation that sparks a memory of a time when we were not safe.[2] These memories can make us feel like we're re-experiencing the traumatic event all over again. We may become hypervigilant, panicked, or emotionally overwhelmed. But this type of fear is not about the present; it is a sign that we need support, we deserve support, but it should not be the basis for how we respond to or perceive others. Fear can be an illusion.

Part of creating a safer sanctuary is learning how to create a trauma-informed environment. We need to know that when faced with scary feelings and situations, there are ways to help us tolerate distress, feel more emotionally grounded, and provide the necessary help for those who have been harmed. Our communities deserve our best selves, grounded in the present, willing to hear the details of the difficult truth.

The difficult truth is that there would not be a need for this resource if adverse childhood experiences and harmful incidents of all kinds did not occur on a regular basis within our Christian communities. Christians, like all people, are capable of inflicting harm and are vulnerable to being harmed. Even in the spaces that we want to believe are the safest and most secure, trusted leaders, friends, and family members have inflicted harm, are inflicting harm, and will inflict harm on the most vulnerable among us.

Take a deep breath and sit with this reality for a moment. What feelings do you notice in your body as you consider this statement? It's understandable that the topic of abuse and neglect occurring in our church communities would raise anxiety. In many of these situations, we have incomplete knowledge about what has happened. There may be conflicting stories from different people and unanswered questions. Anxiety escalates in the face of uncertainty, and in the face of anxiety, we can tend to become avoidant. We may be tempted, as a result, to avert our eyes from what we most need to see. We may be tempted to find a false sense of peace that is not peace at all, but avoidance from an anxiety-producing reality.

If we retreat from this reality, if we minimize or deny the fact that abuse, neglect, and other adverse childhood experiences not only happen, but often happen in our church communities, then our anxiety and fear will only increase the next time we confront those realities. Speaking about the process of making difficult decisions, Dr. Hillary McBride, a psychologist and expert on embodiment, emphasized that we need to be able to stay with the sadness, grief, and fear in our bodies in order to make courageous decisions.[3] She added that some choices are right even if they are painful to make. Remember this when you're dealing with a tough situation involving an allegation or witnessing a behavior that makes you uncomfortable or violates the Safe Sanctuaries policies your church has put in place. Remember to act in ways that are courageous rather than pursuing the relief that comes from avoidance. Doing the hard, but right thing may not leave you with a sense of peace. I'm not sure anyone has a sense of peace while facing these tragic, disturbing realities, but we can still act in ways that reflect our commitment to do no harm, to do good, and to show our love for God and for all people.

Adverse Childhood Experiences

While it's difficult to think and talk about specific traumatic events, it's infinitely more difficult to be the person who experiences and survives that trauma. By developing a basic awareness about different types of abuse, we are better equipped to recognize abuse that is occurring and intervene to advocate for someone's safety and protection. When we know what is happening, we are more likely to pay attention and recognize potentially harmful behaviors or notice signs that harmful behaviors are occurring. With this knowledge, we hope to prevent more trauma from occurring and to respond in healing ways even when a traumatic event has already happened.

In the field of psychology, the term "adverse childhood experiences," also abbreviated as "ACEs," refers to harmful events in the lives of children under the age of eighteen. Based on a study conducted by Kaiser in the late nineties and data from 17,000 residents of Southern California, we know that ACEs fall into three broad categories: abuse, neglect, and household difficulties.[4] It's essential that we have accurate definitions and understand what types of behavior fall into these categories. We may minimize or dismiss behaviors if we don't realize that they are included within the categories of abuse, neglect, and other adverse childhood experiences.

In churches and ministry settings, take note of ACEs you witness or hear children referencing. A child may mention a family member or another adult swearing at or

Notes

_____

_____

_____

_____

_____

_____

_____

_____

_____

_____

> When we know what is happening, we are more likely to pay attention and recognize potentially harmful behaviors or notice signs that harmful behaviors are occurring.

_____

_____

_____

_____

_____

_____

_____

_____

_____

_____

_____

According to one survey, three out of every five adults reported that they had experienced at least one type of ACE, and nearly one in six reported they had experienced four or more.

insulting them, or making them feel physically threatened. They may share that an adult pushed or grabbed them or hurt them physically in some other way that left a mark or injury. A child or vulnerable adult may mention or reference someone touching or fondling them or attempting to engage them sexually in some other way. These are all examples of ACEs to watch and listen for in your day-to-day ministry experiences. Even a casual reference or something that sounds initially like a joke or dismissive comment could be important to follow up on.

Similarly, you will want to follow up with a child if the child talks about not having enough to eat, you see him or her regularly wearing dirty or seasonally inappropriate clothing, or if the child needs to see a doctor. A child may mention not feeling loved, important, or special, or not having a sense of closeness with family. These are potential signs of emotional or physical neglect. Children may also indicate they are experiencing challenges in their homes. Maybe a parent has been violent, aggressive, or threatening to their partner. Maybe a parent is frequently abusing alcohol or drugs. Parents may be going through a separation or divorce, incarceration, or coping with a mental illness. It is important to tune into these challenges and pursue more information to determine whether further steps should be taken to keep children safe.

Earlier we talked about the importance of acknowledging uncomfortable truths. One such truth is that these adverse childhood experiences, including abuse and neglect, happen on a regular basis. ACEs are very common. According to one survey, three out of every five adults reported that they had experienced at least one type of ACE, and nearly one in six reported they had experienced four or more.[5]

ACEs contribute to a host of negative consequences related to health and well-being. For example, ACEs are linked to alcoholism, drug abuse, depression, suicide attempts, high-risk sexual behavior, heart disease, and cancer.[6] Some prevention efforts have focused specifically on solutions within communities and teaching social-emotional and relationship skills to help those who have experienced these events and foster healthier communities moving forward. One example of these practices includes fostering a culture of consent. For instance, asking children if they would like a hug rather than assuming they do. This extends to other types of physical contact as well and brings clarity regarding a person's boundaries and comfort level with physical contact. If someone is feeling coerced or obligated to have any kind of physical contact, that person is not experiencing the kind of safety that we are aiming to provide.

It's important to note that the examples identified in these few paragraphs, and in fact the examples identified in ACE studies themselves, do not represent an exhaustive list of adverse childhood experiences. While definitions of abuse and neglect can be quite specific, they can also be limiting and exclude variations of events that can be equally harmful, with long-term consequences that are just as serious.[7]

There are also a number of traumatic experiences not highlighted specifically under these adverse childhood experiences that can occur in church environments and among church members. Racism, xenophobia, homophobia, ableism, transphobia, and many other attitudes that result in stereotyping, discrimination, and harm run rampant in church environments. These attitudes and behaviors may be overt and easily observed, or they many occur in more subtle and hushed ways. Either way, they have an impact and do harm. An important part of creating safer sanctuaries includes educating the entire community on how to include and show God's love for all those who are part of the body of Christ.

As you read about these different types of adverse childhood experiences, you may recognize some of them in your own life. If you have known any of these experiences personally, take note of how you are feeling right now. Consider some of the effects that these events have had on your life now or in the recent past. The work of building safer sanctuaries is important, but do not let the importance of your current task negate your own feelings in this moment. It is vitally important that you can take of yourself as you do this work, and part of this is considering your own history. If you are a trauma survivor and feel you may benefit from talking more about what you've experienced, please take the time to call someone and seek help. You may consider talking with a pastor or trusted friend or church member about counseling resources in the community and getting connected with more support. One helpful resource is psychologytoday.com, a website where you can look up profiles of therapists in your area, find out which therapists will be covered by your insurance plan, and get contact information to set up a free phone consultation or to schedule a first appointment. If you didn't go through any of these experiences as a child but still find that some feelings have come up for you around this topic, you also may benefit from talking with someone, so please don't hesitate to reach out for more support.

We all need love, support, and protection. We need it just as much as those we are seeking to help and minister to in our communities. When we are wounded through trauma, we can feel fragmented. We can feel as if we lack a sense of wholeness that would otherwise allow us to thrive. The more work we do to know ourselves, to deal with our own experiences and struggles, and to find love, support, and protection in our communities, the more loving, supportive, and available we can be to others. When we do our own work, everyone around us benefits.

Misconceptions About Abuse and Neglect

Beyond facing hard truths, discerning our fears, and identifying common adverse childhood experiences, it's also necessary for us to deconstruct some mistaken ideas about abuse and neglect, particularly regarding sexual abuse. For instance, many operate under the assumption, either spoken or unspoken, that certain types of abuse could never in happen in their community. Unfortunately, this simply isn't true. While rates of physical abuse may be affected by socioeconomic status,

> We all need love, support, and protection. We need it just as much as those we are seeking to help and minister to in our communities.

Be willing to embrace your most courageous self and move toward your discomfort rather than away from it.

The National Children's Advocacy Center reported in 2018 that child sexual abuse occurs in all parts of society.[8]

Another common misconception is that children are primarily abused by strangers. However, the facts are that nine out of ten survivors of abuse (of all types) were abused by either one or both parents. Similarly, nine out of ten survivors of sexual abuse specifically knew their perpetrator. It is often hard to reconcile this reality with the way we would prefer the world to be, but it does not change the reality.

Additionally, we must deconstruct the mistaken belief that children would certainly tell someone if they were experiencing something traumatic like sexual abuse. Once again, this is not the case. Most children delay telling anyone about their experience or simply never disclose child sexual abuse to anyone. This painful truth is compounded by the fact that many mistakenly overestimate the number of false allegations made by children. In reality, only two to ten percent of allegations are ultimately found to be false.

Furthermore, many people mistakenly assume that the perpetrators of sexual abuse are almost always men. While it is true that most instances of sexual abuse are perpetrated by men, the perpetrator is female in one out of every five cases.

Confronting the harsh reality of abuse is challenging. It forces us to ask uncomfortable questions about ourselves, the communities we live in, and society in general. But we also know that as we confront the realities of harm that have occurred in our communities and that have affected those we know and love, there is also light ahead. The harsh reality is not the end of our work; it is the beginning. It is the opening into which we begin to pour hope and love and dedication as we work to provide safety and healing.

You can and will play an important part in strengthening and healing our faith communities. If you are willing to take a wise, honest, and informed look within yourself and at the people and events surrounding you every day, you will be an agent of change; you will be doing God's work in the world. Be willing to embrace your most courageous self and move toward your discomfort rather than away from it. Though it sounds counterintuitive, when we sit in our discomfort and become familiar with it, we learn how to live with discomfort rather than deny or minimize it. This is when we all become our strongest and most capable selves.

Consider yourself courageous already for confronting uncomfortable realities; know that it is okay if you feel discomfort around the topics in this chapter. Try to challenge yourself to move forward, unpacking your feelings of fear and discomfort with gentle curiosity. Seek prayerful understanding, with the hope that you will be part of shaping our faith communities into places of safety, where members of the church are aware, pay attention, and make courageous decisions. As we pause to acknowledge and hold the troubling reality of abuse and neglect in one hand, let's hold hope and empowerment in the other and sit with both at the same time. This knowledge and awareness of troubling realities helps open our eyes to the truth so that we are better able to prevent harm, respond lovingly when harm occurs, and provide safety and support in our communities.

Notes

1. Gavin de Becker, *The Gift of Fear: Survival Signals that Protect Us from Violence* (New York: Dell Publishing, 1997), 194–203.

2. Bessel Van Der Kolk, *The Body Keeps the Score: Brain, Mind, and Body in the Healing of Trauma* (New York: Penguin Books, 2014).

3. Emily P. Freeman, interview with Hillary L. McBride, *The Next Right Thing*, podcast audio (February 15, 2022), https://emilypfreeman.com/podcast/213.

4. "About the CDC-Kaiser Case Study," Centers for Disease Control (April 6, 2021), https://www.cdc.gov/violenceprevention/aces/about.html.

5. "Fast Facts: Preventing Adverse Childhood Experiences," Centers for Disease Control website (April 6, 2021), https://www.cdc.gov/violenceprevention/aces/fastfact.html.

6. V. j. Felitti, R.F. Anda, D. Nordenberg, D.F. Williamson, A.M. Spitz, V. Edwards, M.P. Koss, and J.S. Marks, "Relationship of Childhood Abuse and Household Dysfunction to Many of the Leading Causes of Death in Adults. The Adverse Childhood Experiences (ACE) Study. *American Journal of Preventive Medicine* (1998), 14(4), 245–258.

7. Robyn A. Dolson, Diana M. Morelen, Julia C. Dodd, & Andrea D. Clements. "Pocket ACE: Child Abuse Survivors Missed by the ACEs Study Questionnaire," *Child Abuse and Neglect* (July 2021), DOI: 10.1016. https://pubmed.ncbi.nlm.nih.gov/33862525.

8. "10 Common Myths About Child Abuse," National Children's Advocacy Center (April 1, 2022), https://nationalcac.org/wp-content/uploads/2018/02/FINAL-10-Common -Myths-with-References.pdf.

Notes

As we pause to acknowledge and hold the troubling reality of abuse and neglect in one hand, let's hold hope and empowerment in the other and sit with both at the same time.

CHAPTER 5

Valuing Safety in the Church

Angela D. Schaffner, Ph.D.

Acquiring knowledge is a strong start. It's good for us to attend a training, learn some new skills, and feel like we're building a culture that is dedicated to loving and protecting the most vulnerable among us. However, we must remember that this is just the beginning. Sooner or later, the work of creating safer sanctuaries becomes less a generally good, but unspecific idea and more of a personal challenge. Eventually, a close friend will do something questionable. Eventually, a trusted church leader will make a remark that doesn't sit well with you. Eventually, a child you love will share something deeply unsettling that they've witnessed or experienced.

Eventually, the work will move from theory to practice, and you will face a choice. You'll need to make a quick and potentially difficult decision. Your mind will race, and you'll ask yourself, "Am I going to dismiss this and minimize what I'm seeing for the sake of keeping the peace and maintaining relationships?" You're going to wonder if it's worth the risk to bring issues into the light. You're going to wonder if the allegations are true. You will question if you really saw what you think you saw. You will wonder if you are willing to do what's necessary to protect others who need your help and advocacy, or if you will succumb to inaction, silence, and personal comfort. You will wonder if you can actually do the things you confidently believe that you will be able to do today.

When these thoughts come up, and they will, understand that they are not unusual. The work we are doing here is hard and challenging. It takes courage. My hope is that when these thoughts come up, you will remember this training, dig deep within yourself, and stand behind the values you profess as a Christian to do no harm, to protect, and to love.

If we value safety in our sanctuaries, we must embrace goals, commitments, and practices that go beyond statements of belief and demonstrate a willingness to stand behind those statements in a powerful way to protect all the members of our communities. We must hold church members and leaders accountable for their behaviors. We must not excuse, minimize, or dismiss an allegation or an observation that something seems off. We do not do these things to punish, but to show our love, to show our seriousness and our dedication to the safety of the entire community.

It takes tremendous courage for those affected to give voice to their experiences. The voices of those reporting harm should always be taken seriously and treated with great care. Start by believing those who come forward with an allegation. Starting from belief, rather than adversarial questioning, is an act of love and validation to someone who has been courageous enough to speak up rather than remain silent. There will be time to search for the truth, time to learn the whole story, but a fragile trust can be shattered in an instant and trust is essential to provide safety and support.

Recognizing and Acknowledging Problems

The first step to recognizing and acknowledging potential problems is to pay attention to the relationships in your community. Notice what happens before, during, and after church events. Pay close attention to who seems connected to others and who seems isolated. Be on the lookout for who seems calm and who seems nervous. Are some in the community more detached than others? These nonverbal cues can be as important as the words people speak out loud. Also, while your intuition is not infallible, your gut instincts can be quite informative. When you feel like something is off, it is wise to seek out more information.

Trauma survivors who suffer from post-traumatic stress can experience highly distressing symptoms that result in them feeling less emotionally regulated and present, putting them at further risk. Be aware of these common signs of post-traumatic stress:

- Avoiding situations and events that remind them of the trauma.
- Re-experiencing emotions related to the trauma.
- Showing a general sense of hypervigilance
- Appearing panicky, or having an exaggerated startle response.

Awareness of these signs may help you recognize those who are at risk and may need your advocacy. It is always okay to check in with people and ask simple questions like, "Are you doing okay? You seem a little down." When they respond, simply listen and provide what support that you can.

Trauma survivors often experience pervasive shame and self-doubt. As a result, many hesitate to talk about their trauma and often do not disclose it at all. I've met with many clients who seek to minimize or dismiss the obvious forms of abuse that they have experienced. For a variety of reasons, they convince themselves their lived experience "doesn't count" or "isn't that bad." This is why it is so important for us to pay attention and believe people when they speak about harm they've either observed or experienced. Simply saying the words out loud is a major hurdle to clear.

Notes

It is always okay to check in with people and ask simple questions like, "Are you doing okay? You seem a little down."

Allegations of abuse may also force us to hold two seemingly contradictory truths at once. For instance, a person can be both a gifted ministry leader *and* a perpetrator inflicting harm in the community. An allegation against a skilled preacher or a beloved community member must be taken as seriously as an allegation against anyone else. Ministry experience does not negate an allegation, nor does observed trustworthiness. People are complicated. The same person can be both kind in one situation and abusive in another. Holding these two truths at once may be distressing, but that distress cannot lead us to either dismiss or minimize an allegation. You can play a significant role in preventing further harm by moving toward the discomfort within yourself, holding space for hard realities, and having hard, but necessary conversations. In contrast, when you dismiss uncomfortable allegations, you contribute to a culture of silence and open the door for more harm.

All of this requires discernment, honesty, and balance. While we should trust our intuition and investigate when something seems off, we should not trust our desire to make things easier or make them go away by not addressing a difficult situation. For instance, it's never acceptable to act on a gut instinct that someone would be good at working with children without going through the steps of having a background check and reference check. There should be no exceptions to the processes and rules put in place to protect the members of our communities. Otherwise, we are not truly creating safer sanctuaries.

Legal and Moral Issues

When it comes to reporting abuse and neglect, many of us occupy roles that make us mandated reporters. Mandated reporters are people who hold a professional position that requires them to report child abuse to the appropriate state authorities when there is reasonable cause to suspect that abuse is going on. When we are unsure if a particular situation needs to be reported, we can always call Child Protective Services, state the situation, and find out whether a report needs to be made. Some examples of mandated reporters are psychologists, social workers, counselors, physicians, and teachers. Clergy are also often included in the list of mandated reporters, though this varies somewhat state by state. However, anyone can and should make a report if they suspect child abuse.

Since the legal process can itself be either traumatizing or re-traumatizing for both children and adults, it is essential to connect those involved with trauma-informed legal advocacy. Once the legal process is under way, they will need to find someone to represent them who is familiar with the signs and symptoms of trauma, who facilitates resilience and empowerment in the process, who prioritizes physical and psychological safety, who takes steps to minimize re-traumatization by involvement in court proceedings, and who recognizes when the client may be having a trauma-related response.[1]

As a psychologist, I have ethical requirements in addition to legal ones. The general ethical principles for psychologists are aspirational and meant to guide

> There should be no exceptions to the processes and rules put in place to protect the members of our communities.

psychologists toward the highest ideal, much like a statement of faith might for clergy or church members. Professionally, my principles include beneficence and nonmaleficence (seeking to benefit those I work with and do no harm), fidelity and responsibility (establishing trust and coordinating care), integrity, justice, and respect for people's rights and dignity.[2] Many specific rules, ethical guidelines, policies, and practices fall under these general principles, but embracing the principles as overarching ideals allows me to revisit what is central to my work in the midst of complex scenarios. I would hope the same is true for the beliefs we hold in our communities of faith.

While reporting abuse can be a legal requirement for many in the church, all Christians have the moral obligation to both do no harm and protect those in our communities. Throughout this resource, we will explore the specific guidelines and practices necessary to create safer sanctuaries, but let us also aspire to higher ideals and general principles.

In his book *Three Simple Rules*, Reuben Job addresses our three essential moral obligations for us as Christians: do no harm, do good, and stay in love with God.[3] Job's take on doing no harm addresses the general climate of our communities. When we establish a culture and make a collective commitment to do no harm, we will approach conflict with an entirely different mindset. Silence, dismissing the words of others, and disbelief when an allegation is shared are all examples of how we do harm to our communities. In contrast, we do good when we believe, support, provide safety, and advocate for those who are vulnerable. The practices, policies, and procedures that we value are important, but alone they are not enough. We need self-examination. We need to adopt a mindset that is both inclusive of all people and willing to advocate for those being harmed. We need to acknowledge and call out harm when it occurs and hold perpetrators accountable so that we don't contribute to further harm with silence or minimizing behavior.

Responding to an Incident

While later chapters will cover the specific steps to take when responding to allegations and revelations of abuse, let me take this opportunity to highlight some guidelines on how to provide emotional support to those involved in an abusive situation. As mentioned earlier, it's vital that we emphasize listening, believing the person making the allegation, and taking action to protect and heal those involved.

When you encounter someone who has experienced a traumatic incident, be mindful of the need to address it effectively in the moment, but also remember that recovery will take time. When therapists help clients recover from trauma, there are typically three stages of recovery that survivors progress through at their own pace. The work is usually long-term, intense, and complex. The process begins with education, working to establish safety for the individuals, and stabilizing them by addressing any self-destructive symptoms and behaviors that may be present. Secondly, survivors will process memories and mourn the losses involved in the

Notes

> We need to adopt a mindset that is both inclusive of all people and willing to advocate for those being harmed.

39

_____

_____

_____

_____

_____

_____

_____

_____

_____

_____

_____

_____

Remain mindful of the value of sitting with others in their pain rather than trying to fix it to soothe our own anxiety in the presence of suffering and disturbing truths.

traumatic experience. Finally, survivors work to find meaning and connection by leaning into their communities with a renewed and more integrated sense of self.[4]

Trauma tends to fragment us into parts with each separate part doing its best to help us survive. Healing involves a reintegration of these parts into the whole and building an identity of one who is loved and valued. The overall focus throughout therapy moves from safety to integration to reconnection, and the process can take years.

As a person providing emotional support, it's important to note that you cannot and should not attempt to be someone's therapist. However, it helps to know the basics about what is involved in recovery from trauma and how you can help someone connect with a therapist, if needed, when the person is ready. You can support people in this process and hold a deep respect and appreciation for the scope and intensity of the journey toward recovery. Trauma survivors can feel isolated and fearful. Your calm and steady presence can be soothing and regulating. This can make a huge difference, even if (maybe especially if) you never suggest one tip, Bible verse, coping strategy, or solution. There is no easy path or quick fix for trauma, but support goes a long way.

Keeping in mind what a person who has just experienced a trauma is likely to be navigating, here are some ways to offer immediate practical support:

- Saying something like, "Let me know if you need anything," may not feel helpful or specific enough to those who are emotionally overwhelmed. Instead, offer specific actions of practical support. Ask if you can organize a meal team over the next few weeks, offer to make grocery runs, or offer to help coordinating appointments or handling other regularly occurring obligations like yard work.

- Emotional support is essential. In the wake of trauma, we can feel disconnected, disengaged, and fragmented. Send a card, text, or care package as a way of showing support. Offer to go on a walk, spend time over tea or coffee, or find time to be available by phone if the person you're supporting would like to talk. The person may feel supported and soothed by any type of conversation; it may not need to be specific to the traumatic event.

- If you're not sure what to offer in terms of emotional support, you can always ask and give an option like, "Would it help if I'm just here with you and we talk about other things?" or "Would you like to talk more about what happened?" Always respect people's boundaries. If they'd rather not talk at all, that is okay too.

- Remain mindful of the value of sitting with others in their pain rather than trying to fix it to soothe our own anxiety in the presence of suffering and disturbing truths. At the same time, take the steps that are in your control to advocate for those who are hurting.

These strategies can help you provide practical and emotional support both immediately following the event and going forward, especially around high-stress times like trial dates. Another important way to support someone is by protecting privacy.

It should be clear what will and will not be shared with church staff, with congregants, and with members of the larger community. Trauma survivors have been jolted into a new sense of themselves, other people, God, and the world around them. When people feel unsafe, panicked, or emotionally overwhelmed, they often feel a lack of control. By protecting sensitive information, we offer them some sense of control during a trying time. Sharing information that is not yours to share makes the sanctuary unsafe, so it is important to do your part and report what needs to be known while keeping other sensitive information private. Whenever you are sharing private information, consider your motivation and return to the moral of doing no harm.

Notes

1. "Trauma-Informed Legal Advocacy: A Resource for Juvenile Defense Attorneys," National Child Traumatic Stress Network, Justice Consortium Attorney Workgroup Subcommittee, National Center for Child Traumatic Stress, 2018, https://www.americanbar.org/content/dam/aba/administrative/child_law/trauma-informed-legal-advocacy-juv-defense.pdf.

2. "Ethical Principles of Psychologists and Code of Conduct," American Psychological Association, 2022, https://www.apa.org/ethics/code.

3. Reuben P. Job, *Three Simple Rules: A Wesleyan Way of Living* (Nashville, TN: Abingdon Press, 2007), 21–32.

4. Judith Herman. *Trauma and Recovery: The Aftermath of Violence—From Domestic Abuse to Political Terror* (New York: Basic Books) 1997, 155–213.

Notes

> It should be clear what will and will not be shared with church staff, with congregants, and with members of the larger community.

CHAPTER 6
Taking Collective Responsibility

Angela D. Schaffner, Ph.D.

The collective task of creating a safe sanctuary is an ambitious one. It requires boldness to build a community where faith can reside and grow within boundaries that increase feelings of safety and security. While this is a collective task, it is also one best approached by assuming each individual plays a vital role. In this chapter, we'll explore this individual role further. First, we'll begin by considering why we avoid feelings of discomfort and how to confront these feelings. Then, we'll look at how to take responsible action, practice openness, and consider forgiveness as we work toward building a healthier, vibrant community.

Confronting Our Discomfort

One reason we tend to overlook abuse it that its very existence cuts to the core of our deepest and most troubling questions. These can be questions about God, about our community, and even about ourselves. Abuse can make us wonder why God allows bad things to happen to vulnerable people. It can make us wonder why, despite our best efforts, our sacred communities, our sanctuaries, remain unsafe. It can force us to consider what role we play in these ongoing problems. It is hard to confront these troubling realities. It is hard to consider that those we love and admire may be either inflicting harm or experiencing harm. Confronting this can make us feel out of control, and these traumatic events may stir up memories from our own lives that we'd rather forget.

At its root, confronting uncomfortable topics is a theological challenge. If we are going to seek the truth as Christians, let us acknowledge all the information life presents to us. When we look through a lens that allows us to see only what we want to see, we turn our eyes away from the complete truth, including the parts that are hardest to accept. In his account of the gospel, John writes, "When the Spirit of truth comes, he will guide you into all the truth, for he will not speak on his own, but will speak whatever he hears, and he will declare to you the things that are to come" (John 16:13, NRSVUE). The Spirit leads us into *all* the truth, not just the comfortable parts. This means that our collective goal of embracing flourishing instead of fear requires that we move toward and through our fears so that we can establish and maintain the flourishing communities and ministries we desire.

Humanity includes the capacity for great love and great harm. It's disturbing to sit with the possibility that someone you know and love as a neighbor, church member, or friend could be responsible for harming someone else, especially a child. But it happens. No one benefits from avoiding this truth. Avoidance perpetuates shame and secrecy and allows abuse and neglect to go undetected, minimized, or denied. The challenge is to find a balance. Living with excessive fear and suspicion doesn't work, nor does living in a false, checked-out state of toxic positivity. Instead, we need to be equipped with knowledge, willing to trust our intuition, and open to facing hard truths.

When something seems off, we must move toward the situation, pay attention, and investigate instead of rationalizing and dismissing a potentially harmful interaction or situation. Over time, this will help us develop better discernment skills as part of our work in ministry. Likewise, we must remain aware that it is a natural and normal tendency to become defensive when someone brings an allegation to our attention, particularly if it is an allegation against someone we know. This reminder allows us to acknowledge the discomfort and take active steps to protect people anyway.

When we avoid a topic or a situation, several things happen. First, if there is any fear or anxiety about that topic or situation, it tends to grow more intense with continued avoidance. Only when we open ourselves up and make space for uncomfortable feelings to be discussed can healing and progress occur. Secondly, reality does not change simply because we avoid dealing with it. Acknowledging the truth does not make it truer, it just moves us from a place of denial to a place where we can more effectively make a difference and handle a situation openly.

Understanding how our brains function can also help us put our desire for truth, safety, and action into practice. In simple terms, we have a "thinking brain" that allows us to do our best problem-solving and planning work, and we have more primitive parts of our brain where our traumatic experiences are embedded and remembered in the form of feelings and body sensations. When we are in a highly anxious state, we are using the more primitive parts of our brain and don't have access to our best problem-solving abilities in the moment.

There are several skills we can learn to help us regain access to the thinking brain so we can feel our emotions *and* solve problems. This state, called our "window of tolerance," is an internal state where we do our best and wisest healing work.[1] When we are outside this window of tolerance, we are either too keyed up to access our thinking brain or we shut down entirely. In anxious states, we typically engage a fight-or-flight response and become primarily concerned with escaping danger. Conversely, we may enter a shut-down state. A shut-down state is another attempt to survive by freezing all activity. In either case, we're not at our best when it comes to thinking and problem-solving.

When we understand these brain processes better, it allows us to realize that the anxiety we feel in these difficult situations is not a character flaw, but a physical

Notes

> **Only when we open ourselves up and make space for uncomfortable feelings to be discussed can healing and progress occur.**

_____

_____

_____

_____

_____

_____

_____

_____

_____

_____

_____

experience in our bodies that prompts us to avoid addressing complex and unsettling truths. If we learn how to shift out of these hyperanxious or checked-out states, we can be more fully present and problem-solve much more effectively. When we have access to our thinking brains, we can combat the negative thought streams that encourage us to avoid painful truths and more calmly address these important situations with openness and honesty.

Taking Collective Responsibility

We all play a part. To understand the systemic problems surrounding abuse, particularly the culture of minimization and silence that we often encounter, it helps to start with a discussion about some basic human tendencies that have been observed in the field of social psychology.

For instance, our brains tend to take shortcuts when we process information. Especially in situations where we have limited information, our brains will interpret events based on what seems likely based on our prior experience. This is useful in a lot of situations, but unfortunately it can be unhelpful when it comes to recognizing abuse. We may be confronted with an incomplete story and a difficult question like, "Would a trusted church member harm a child?" Our brain then wants to fill in the gaps with our own experience of that person. We may be tempted to rationalize or explain away this behavior by thinking something like "He doesn't seem likely to do that. He gave a great sermon on loving our neighbor recently." In this way, we short circuit the work we should be doing. Similarly, we may fill in these gaps by trying to think of comparable situations. This leads us to dismiss concerns about abuse because we don't know of any previous examples of the accused treating someone poorly or simply because we have never heard of any incidents of abuse in our church.[2]

Another basic human tendency is the bystander effect. This happens we witness something as part of a group. Because we are not the only ones to see what happened, we tend to accept less responsibility for what occurred and to either dismiss the event or our responsibility to respond, especially when those around us seem calm or dismissive. In these scenarios, it is easy to believe that it is someone else's responsibility to respond, or we may experience confusion when others do not react as we would expect. To counter the bystander effect, it's important to describe what you see happening, take responsibility based on what you have witnessed, and not allow the response of others to guide yours. Then, help the child or other person involved move to a safer situation and report what you have seen.[3]

One final tendency to be aware of is what Melvin J. Lerner, a professor of social psychology, describes as our "belief in a just world." This is our inherent need to perceive the world as a controllable environment where good things happen to good people and bad things happen to bad people. This belief helps us deal with potential threats to ourselves. If we believe that a good person would not be victimized at random, then we can convince ourselves that we are a good person

If we learn how to shift out of these hyperanxious or checked-out states, we can be more fully present and problem-solve much more effectively.

and therefore safe. This is obviously untrue, but it can be scary to confront the frightening reality that many things are outside our control. Unfortunately, this tendency often results is people blaming victims for the acts that are committed against them. It is essential that we do not blame the victim and remind ourselves that our instinctive rationalizations are not synonymous with the truth.[4]

It can be challenging to confront these instinctive tendencies. In many cases, these tendencies serve us well, but when confronting the painful realities of abuse, they can often lead us astray. Therefore, it is important to know about these social tendencies, to acknowledge them when they happen, and then to slow down, think about what we are witnessing, and act to protect others anyway. This is an essential part of establishing a safe, healthy community, and of creating safer sanctuaries.

Ways to Play an Active Role in Healing

1. Prioritize safety, trust, and transparency.
2. Talk openly about bodies, sex, and boundaries.
3. Build a culture of support.
4. Practice voicing concerns.

1) Prioritize Safety, Trust, and Transparency

For a system to be trauma-informed, it must provide an environment of safety, trust, and transparency. We build trust by providing trainings that address challenging topics, having open and frequent conversations about concrete steps we are taking to make our environments safer, and by explicitly stating our values. Additionally, when we consistently abide by the guidelines and standards our communities have established, adhering to practices like the two-deep rule and regular background checks, we contribute to both the physical and psychological safety of the community.

Second, peer support provides connection and reinforces the culture of our communities. As an example, I once led a retreat focused on destigmatizing mental health for a congregation. At one point, members stood and shared stories about their mental health struggles and experiences with trauma. As they shared, they provided one another guidance and support.

We should also strive to support the voices and choices of those who have survived trauma. When trauma survivors trust us with their story, we help best by listening, believing, and tuning into specific needs, rather than by jumping in to fix things. We should seek ways to encourage empowerment and self-advocacy among survivors. This collaboration builds relational bonds and a sense of mutuality. We all have more wisdom than we realize and can help one another find healing.

Notes

> We should also strive to support the voices and choices of those who have survived trauma.

_____

_____

_____

_____

_____

_____

_____

_____

_____

_____

_____

Embracing trauma-informed values helps us all play an active role in healing. These values of safety, trust, and transparency should be identified, communicated to leaders, staff, and members of the community, and then reviewed regularly. Consider what may be needed in your community to ensure that everyone feels they can live into these values.

2) Talk Openly About Bodies, Sex, and Boundaries

A lot of the pain associated with abuse comes from a fundamental discomfort with conversations about our bodies, our boundaries, and about sex in general. In keeping with the value of transparency mentioned earlier, open conversation about these topics can help to create a healthier environment where those who have been harmed can heal and those at risk feel free to share and communicate their experience.

Discussions and questions about sex, sexuality, and our physical bodies are complex and too often we force these conversations into an oversimplified list of internalized behavioral rules. Many of us have been in environments that were unsafe because discussions about sex were largely negative, presented in a fear-inducing or shaming way, or were omitted altogether. The reality is that sex can be an experience of joy and connection, or it can result in harm.

Matthias Roberts captured the complexity of sexual relationships by noting and discussing five paradoxes in sex: 1) sex is both healthy _and_ it involves risk, 2) sex makes us vulnerable _and_ can be used to avoid vulnerability, 3) sex requires safety _and_ safety cannot be guaranteed, 4) we will get things wrong _and_ right at the same time during sex, and 5) to get beyond shame surrounding our sexual experiences, we need to name and embrace it.[5] Roberts presents these concepts in a refreshingly clear way that allows for the complexity of our lived experience. Rarely do our developing identities and unique experiences and orientations fit neatly into categories and boxes or lend themselves to a concise list of rules. We're better off embracing the paradoxes that can both free us and provide guidance and boundaries in our own unique relationship dynamics and scenarios.

Wonderfully Made is a curriculum for older children and youth that educates about changes to expect during puberty and how to feel confident in their bodies and with sexuality.[6] When my son Caleb was eleven, he attended the program at our church, held from 9:00 a.m. until 4:00 p.m. on a Saturday. He sat around a table with other boys and girls and listened as our pastor welcomed everyone and emphasized that our bodies and our sexuality are good. A nurse practitioner at our church presented the program.

The first activity involved a body tracing on a large sheet of paper with a peer. Students wrote qualities they like about themselves on the drawings and decorated

> **The reality is that sex can be an experience of joy and connection, or it can result in harm.**

them. This activity encouraged self-expression and self-acceptance and a general tone of positivity as the topic shifted to diagrams, biology, vocabulary about the changes that occur in our bodies during puberty, and the correct vocabulary for various body parts, sexual terms, gender identities, and sexual orientations.

Throughout the day, students had many opportunities to write an anonymous question on a note card and put it in the "question box." The leader pulled questions from the box and answered them for everyone. Questions ranged from, "Does it hurt to wear a tampon?" to "Why do people like having sex?" to "Do I have to have sex?" I felt deeply grateful for my son being able to attend this program and for the foundation it provided for future questions and conversations. When I asked Caleb several months later what the best part of the program was, Caleb said the question box, because he and everyone else could ask questions without feeling embarrassed.

Conversations like this may seem awkward, but they also help to build a foundation of trust, openness, and confidence that can create healthier environments for everyone in the long run.

3) Build a Culture of Support

We also contribute to safety in our sanctuaries when we build a culture of support for all identities and orientations. Knowledge and awareness allow us to welcome all members of our congregations with warmth and kindness. A basic knowledge of sexual orientation and gender identity is essential to welcoming people into inclusive environments as participants, members, and leaders. While sexual orientation refers to which gender a person finds sexually attractive, gender identity refers to an internal sense of one's gender that may or may not correlate (cisgender/transgender) with the person's assigned sex. When we request both names and pronouns on nametags or in online meetings, we communicate openness and validation of all gender identities. When we do this, our sanctuaries become safer.

Finally, trauma-informed churches actively address historical, cultural, and gender-based issues. When we actively value different cultural practices and traditions, we create a safe space for everyone. In contrast, racism, xenophobia, homophobia, ableism, transphobia, and other attitudes that result in stereotyping and discrimination tear apart the sense of safety in our sanctuaries. These attitudes and behaviors may be overt and easily observed, or they many occur in more subtle ways. Either way, they have an impact and do substantial harm. Education and inclusion are an important part of creating safe sanctuaries. As we establish safe, trauma-informed environments, people will know they can attend church and be themselves. Then, we can welcome people into spaces where we hear and believe their voices, advocate for their needs, and protect and support them.

Notes

When we actively value different cultural practices and traditions, we create a safe space for everyone.

_____

_____

_____

_____

_____

_____

_____

_____

_____

_____

_____

_____

Forgiveness is not a superficial act, nor does it lack a commitment to justice. Forgiveness does not mean that we condone or excuse the harm that has been done.

4) Practice Voicing Concerns

Like any skill, we get better at voicing our concerns when we practice. However, we don't have to wait for a worrying event to occur to practice getting more comfortable with the conversation about safety in our faith communities. Work together with those in your community to learn and use a common vocabulary to practice expressing concerns. For instance, when you use the word, "abuse," what kind of behavior does this include? This helps prepare everyone to have clear lines of communication in the future.

Beyond a common language, practice discussing your feelings, concerns, and observations about safety with your team using brief, but detailed descriptions. Consider who was present, what time you made your observation, and what you observed. Practice sharing exactly what you have observed without guessing at the motivations of others or making immediate judgments. Instead, simply describe what you saw, heard, and felt. For instance, "Tonight, I saw a youth volunteer give a lot of hugs that seemed unwelcome by several of the youth," or, "I felt uncomfortable with the way one of the volunteers was approaching another volunteer tonight." Pay attention to when something seems off and say something.

Additionally, make sure that the congregation is regularly informed by printing the name and contact information of the Child Safety Officer in any bulletins and e-newsletters and regularly informing congregants about the Child Safety Officer's role. For those who may already be experiencing fear, ambivalence, or hesitation to speak up, we should work as a community to make it as easy as possible to report concerns and take them seriously.

A Note About Forgiveness

As Christians, we are called to consider forgiveness when harm is done (Colossians 3:13, Ephesians 4:32). When doing so, remain mindful of what forgiveness is and what it is not. Forgiveness is not a superficial act, nor does it lack a commitment to justice. Forgiveness does not mean that we condone or excuse the harm that has been done. It does not require reconciliation with the person who harmed you.

That said, thoughtful engagement with the process of forgiveness can be an important part of healing from trauma. When approached in a sensitive way, with plenty of space to work at one's own pace, it can provide a measure of peace and resolution. Dr. Robert Enright proposed a model of forgiveness that progresses through several distinct stages. This makes it more of a general practice and a lifestyle rather than an isolated, one-off event. None of us, especially trauma survivors, need to rush toward forgiveness. None of us will work through the process perfectly. In a collection of studies on forgiveness therapy, Enright discovered that people who were helped by forgiveness therapy did not necessarily become skilled forgivers. Even people who went from low to average on measures of forgiveness enjoyed great mental health benefits. They tended to be less anxious and depressed after the process and to have higher self-esteem and hope for the future.[7]

From this, we can conclude that forgiveness is an important part of healing, but we can also rest assured that it doesn't need to be done perfectly. Especially when trauma is involved, forgiveness may be best viewed as a practice that continues to evolve over the various stages of our healing journeys. If you are supporting people who have been through a trauma and they want to move toward forgiveness, encourage them to give themselves permission to be bad at it and to make plenty of space for all the feelings they will have during the process. Let them know that it is okay if they are not yet ready to forgive. Premature forgiveness may be more accurately described as avoidance or spiritual bypassing. Avoiding the truth about distressing events and painful emotions is not a virtue, so let's embrace a longer-term process of forgiveness as a community. Letting ourselves and others arrive at forgiveness at our own pace creates a safe sanctuary where we can be at any place in that process and still be supported.

Notes

1. Elizabeth A. Stanley, *Widen the Window: Training your Brain and Body to Thrive During Stress and Recover from Trauma* (New York: Avery) 2019.

2. Susan T. Fiske and Shelley E. Taylor. *Social Cognition*, 2nd Ed. (New York: McGraw-Hill, Inc. 1991), 382–386.

3. *Darkness to Light's Stewards of Children* (Charleston, SC: Darkness to Light, 2013)

4. Susan T. Fiske and Shelley E. Taylor, 86.

5. Matthias Roberts, *Beyond Shame: Creating a Healthy Sex Life on Your Own Terms* (Minneapolis, MN: Fortress Press, 2020), 99–176.

6. Heather Gottas Moore. "Wonderfully Made: A Ministry of Holistic Human Sexuality" (April 22, 2022), https://www.ministryofholistichumansexuality.org/wonderfully-made.html.

7. Robert D. Enright. *The Forgiving Life: A Pathway to Overcoming Resentment and Creating a Legacy of Love* (Washington, D.C.: American Psychological Association, 2012), 26–31; 37–38; 49–50.

Notes

> Especially when trauma is involved, forgiveness may be best viewed as a practice that continues to evolve over the various stages of our healing journeys.

CHAPTER 7

Trust Yourself and Support Others in Trusting Themselves

Angela D. Schaffner, Ph.D.

Situations involving abuse are difficult to navigate. Our best efforts at wisdom and discernment emerge when we combine our intuitive, emotional insights with our rational and logical analytical skills. Similarly, we make our best decisions when we are calm, connected, and curious all at once. We are at our best when we are present in our bodies and our minds are focused. However, when abuse happens, it can be incredibly difficult to find these equilibriums and respond in the best way possible.

We all have inner conflicts and emotions that can be activated during intense and challenging situations. It is important that we are aware of these inner conflicts and emotions so that we can work through them and provide the support victims of abuse need when they come to us.

When they come forward, victims of abuse are confronting and talking about uncomfortable truths that they'd most likely rather avoid. We know that feeling safe, remembering and sharing trauma stories, and integrating these stories are key components of trauma recovery. Therefore, when a trauma survivor chooses to speak up, it's important for us to listen. It's also important that we be willing to talk about these uncomfortable truths with the person instead of immediately challenging that person's story. Minimizing a story when someone chooses to share can have potentially devastating and life-altering effects for that person.

The best way to be there for someone in the moment of need is to be in a healthy place yourself. In order to this, we must think about our own internal dynamics. We must recognize the wisdom we already possess based on our lived experiences, feelings, and knowledge, and we must learn how to utilize these tools for those in need of our support.

Internal Dynamics

Think about the internal dialogues you have with yourself every day, the type of internal conflicts that come up over and over. For instance, think about this series of thoughts about getting up in the morning:

- "Why are you still in bed and not getting up? Your children need to leave for school in thirty minutes."
- "This bed is so comfy! Just one more snooze."
- "Ok, we made it on time yesterday, and we will likely make it again today."

In those three thoughts, you see someone who is frustrated by the inability to do something they know is right, someone expressing a desire for comfort, and someone using past experience to analyze the situation and reassure himself/herself. And all three of these thoughts come from the same person, one right after another.

We all have different parts of our personality. There are times when we feel more like a child, times we feel more like a professional, times when we're more nurturing or more assertive, times when we're angry or stressed or excited. These internal dynamics are part of our psychological system, and all the parts interact with one another.[1]

Each aspect of our selves has its own goals and needs. Consider this story from a therapy session with a client of mine. In our session, I used a sand tray filled with several figurines and asked the client to identify the different parts of her personality and use the toys as a visual reference. First, she chose a robot figurine to represent the protector part of herself that over-functions in an intellectual way so that she can feel a sense of control in her life. Next, she chose a child figurine to represent a more hurt and vulnerable part of herself. Then, she chose a polar bear figurine to represent the part of her that can be impulsive and self-destructive, a part of her identity that seeks to quickly address and relieve painful emotions. In the center of the sand tray, she chose an object that represented her core self, the part that she can trust the most, the part that is in tune with both intuitive, emotional information and rational, logical information.

This client knew that tuning in to information from every part of her would lead her to wiser choices. Understanding and processing these different internal dynamics in our sessions helped her gain more awareness of how she approaches relationships and helped highlight areas where she is working toward more self-compassion.

The more lovingly we can respond to each part of ourselves, the better we can understand and respond to our needs without unconsciously replaying behaviors that do not serve us well. We can listen to the input from each of our parts and then decide how to act lovingly to ourselves and others to minimize and prevent harm. Then, we can go on to do all the good we can and stay in love with God.[2]

When examining our internal dynamics, we do not label the individual parts as good or bad.[3] Instead, we seek to understand what each part provides to the system, how it functions, and how together they can all integrate to form a core self" that makes the wisest decisions possible in any given scenario.

If you are a church member and you witness an interaction between an adult and a teenager in your church that makes you uncomfortable, you will likely have several

Notes

The more lovingly we can respond to each part of ourselves, the better we can understand and respond to our needs without unconsciously replaying behaviors that do not serve us well.

51

different kinds of reactions and responses. It will be important in that moment to tune into the information you are hearing from each part of yourself, and to tune into your wisest, most integrated sense of what is going on. If the part of you who wants to avoid conflict says, "It's probably nothing. He's a great guy and youth leader," but an emotional, more intuitive part of you feels something is off and hears alarm bells going off, you will need to tune into both parts to access the wisest course of action.

At the same time, another part of you may be stirred up emotionally and feel distress if you've been through an adverse childhood experience and sense danger when you witness potential harm. If you are uncertain, err on the side of talking with someone about the situation. Do not allow silence or inaction to become your default response.

A skilled therapist can also help you determine what to do. There is no need to try and understand complex situations and how internal dynamics work in isolation. A great resource for learning more about internal parts of the self is Richard Schwartz's *Greater than the Sum of Our Parts: Discovering Your True Self through Internal Family Systems Therapy*.[4]

Access All of Your Wisdom

When we have more awareness of ourselves and our internal psychological landscape, our emotional responses to all kinds of situations begin to make more sense. We learn that our emotions provide us with helpful information enabling us to make wiser, more well-informed decisions about how to respond to what we observe in our faith communities.

Know yourself well enough to be aware of the internal dynamics you are responding to in various situations. Tune in and embrace the parts of you that act to decrease discomfort, the parts that seek to protect you, the parts of you that feel vulnerable, and, most importantly, your core integrated self that hears from all your parts and is most equipped and capable of wise decisions. Each of our parts offers both emotional and logical information to us in our decision-making process. The place within us where logic and emotion overlap is usually where we can find our wisest courses of action.[5] Decision-making that relies on both logic and emotion has been scientifically shown to be more accurate than decision-making that relies on logic alone.[6]

An emotion like fear, especially the true fear that alerts us when danger is present, is reliable and life-saving.[7] It's helpful therefore to distinguish true fear from perceived fear and remembered fear. For instance, when a trauma survivors develop post-traumatic stress as a result of adverse childhood experiences, they may re-experience the remembered fear from a past event in the present moment. This happens because trauma memories are stored differently in the brain than other, less emotionally laden memories from our life narratives. Our bodies re-experience traumatic events when we remember them.

Decision-making that relies on both logic and emotion has been scientifically shown to be more accurate than decision-making that relies on logic alone.

Learn What Helps You Stay Calm

Regardless of what has happened in our lives or the degree of trauma we've experienced, we all have moments of heightened anxiety. Anxiety is not all bad. Moderate levels of anxiety actually help us perform better. Anxiety shows that we are invested, that we care about what is happening around us.

However, since it is so common for us to become emotionally activated during stressful situations, we need skills to help us reconnect with our most calm, rational self in these moments of heightened anxiety. By returning to this calm, connected, curious state, we have access to our best self, our best wisdom, and our best problem-solving abilities.

During stressful situations, we tend to move away from this calm, curious state in one of two ways. First, we may enter into a state of heightened anxiety that leaves us frazzled and panicked. Alternatively, we may temporarily check out and shut down.

If we need to move from a state of heightened anxiety to a more calm, curious state where we have better access to the parts of our brain engaged in problem-solving, we can do things like taking deep breaths and engaging the five senses by taking note of our immediate surroundings. We may need to simply catalog the things that we can see, hear, touch, smell, and taste. We may also try saying a positive affirmation to ourselves, listening to soothing music, moving to a sacred safe space, or squeezing a stress ball.

On the other hand, if we find ourselves shutting down emotionally or checking out, we may need to try something like holding something cold like an ice pack, listening to upbeat music, taking a brief nap, or simply moving our bodies.

Know How to Tolerate Distress

Beyond knowing how to calm yourself in stressful situations, there are also skills and tools that can help you tolerate distress and regulate emotions. A few simple strategies can provide a great deal of relief when we are facing stressful situations and complex, conflicting, or overwhelming feelings as we encounter the inevitable stress life presents in our faith communities.

In order to build healthy, loving, and safe communities, it's important that we build confidence in our ability to sit with difficult situations, confront others when needed, and share hard truths out loud. We can do this by learning some go-to skills for tolerating the distress we will experience when conversations get intense and our own fear and discomfort arises.

Skills for tolerating distress include using cold temperatures (holding an ice cube, taking a cold shower, splashing cold water on your face), deep breathing, and

Notes

In order to build healthy, loving, and safe communities, it's important that we build confidence in our ability to sit with difficult situations, confront others when needed, and share hard truths out loud.

intense exercise to shift your body into a less distressed state. Additionally, skills for regulating emotion include pausing to take a breath and allowing space for emotion, practicing a curious rather than judgmental response to our emotional states, noticing where in our bodies we experience emotion, and knowing how to self-soothe to reduce the intensity. Taking care of our bodies with balanced eating, regular sleep, movement, and good hygiene also helps prepare us to respond to highly stressful situations.

Concluding Main Points

The bottom line is that we must accept that we will encounter the full scope of humanity in our faith communities. This is true both for better and for worse. However, we are best prepared to deal with complex and overwhelming scenarios when we know ourselves, trust ourselves, and accept reality.

Adverse experiences can have a lifelong impact, and these adverse experiences can happen in faith communities just as much as they can anywhere else. By taking steps to inform ourselves and remain attentive, learning to communicate effectively with a common language, creating a culture of openness and dialogue about concerning behaviors, and offering clear guidelines regarding boundaries and appropriate behavior, we can collectively and effectively reduce the number of adverse childhood experiences that occur in our communities.

In our culture, where certain bodies are given more power because of size, race, sexual orientation, gender, and physical ability, we can level the playing field by actively choosing to value and advocate for all bodies, inviting diversity into our leadership and decision-making. We can dramatically decrease harm by breaking the silence and shame surrounding difficult, traumatic experiences. We can contribute instead to a trauma-informed approach to maintaining safe communities.

> **We can dramatically decrease harm by breaking the silence and shame surrounding difficult, traumatic experiences.**

You play an important role in a system that can either help or harm, and you can count on facing decisions and situations at some point that require you to make the wisest choice you can. Equip yourself. Talk with a trusted mentor or therapist if you're uncertain or uncomfortable about something you feel or notice in your faith community. You can make a substantial difference in someone's life when you tune in and act courageously to shine a light on the whole truth, not just parts of the truth.

Notes

1. Richard C. Schwartz, Martha Sweezy, and Brian Arens, *Internal Family Systems Therapy: Second Edition* (New York: Guilford, 2019).
2. Reuben P. Job, *Three Simple Rules: A Wesleyan Way of Living* (Nashville, TN: Abingdon Press, 2007), 21–32.

3. Richard C. Schwartz and Alanis Morissette. *No Bad Parts: Healing Trauma and Restoring Wholeness with the Internal Family Systems Model* (Louisville, CO: Sounds True, 2021).

4. Richard C. Schwartz, *Greater Than the Sum of Our Parts: Discovering Your True Self Through Internal Family Systems Therapy* (Sounds True, 2018).

5. Marsha Linehan, *DBT Skills Training Manual: Second Edition* (New York: Guilford, 2014).

6. Emily P. Freeman, interview with Hillary L. McBride, *The Next Right Thing*, podcast audio (February 15, 2022), https://emilypfreeman.com/podcast/213.

7. Gavin de Becker, *The Gift of Fear: Survival Signals that Protect Us from Violence* (New York: Dell Publishing, 1997), 194–203.

Notes

Talk with a trusted mentor or therapist if you're uncertain or uncomfortable about something you feel or notice in your faith community.

PART III

THE FOUNDATIONS

CHAPTER 8

General Rules of Safer Sanctuaries

Bonnie L. Bevers

There is a lot to learn when it comes to building safer sanctuaries and preventing abuse in our churches and communities. Even in this resource, you'll be hearing from many different voices about definitions of abuse, why it is crucial work for us as ministry leaders, and a variety of ideas, tips, and guidelines for how to put this information into practice. It can feel a little bit like drinking from a fire hose.

With that in mind, let's take a moment to step back and focus on the fundamentals. What are the concepts you most need to remember? What can you share with a person who is brand new to all this and say, "Here's what you need to know," to help that person get started? In my years of work creating healthy environments for our congregations and training others to do the same, I've found it important to focus on the following ten simple rules when creating a safer sanctuary.

1. All people working with vulnerable people should pass a background check before beginning work or volunteering.
2. No adult should ever be alone with a vulnerable person. Alone means being out of sight and sound range of other adults. We call this the "two-deep rule."
3. Supervising adults should not be related.
4. An appropriate and safe ratio of adults to vulnerable people should always be maintained.
5. When ministering and working with vulnerable people, ensure that doors are open and sight and sound lines are unobstructed.
6. When working with minors, the supervising adult should always be five years older than the oldest participant.
7. All release forms, including medical, transportation, photo/video, and communication releases, should be kept up to date for all participants.
8. Separate shower and bathroom facilities should be maintained for each gender.
9. Separate sleeping quarters should be provided for each gender.
10. Each person should have his or her own space for rest. Beds should not be shared.

Notes

_____

_____

_____

_____

_____

_____

_____

_____

_____

_____

_____

Many of these ten simple rules may appear obvious, but they lay the groundwork for establishing healthy and safe boundaries that can build trust and encourage flourishing in our communities. Let's look at each of these guidelines one at a time to explore why they are so important to safe ministry spaces.

1) All people working with vulnerable people should pass a background check before beginning work or volunteering.

Each of us has parts of our histories that we would rather not share with others. We all have things that we don't walk to talk about. This is perfectly understandable. For most people, a background check is little more than a formality, but in some circumstances, it can be a vital piece of information that can keep our communities safe. Simply put, we do not always know the people around us as well as we might believe. It is essential for the safety of our communities that we know if a person has been accused or convicted of a crime that could put members of our ministry in danger.

In an earlier chapter, Bishop Peggy Johnson shared a story about a man who signed a covenant with his congregation stating that he would be accompanied by a shepherd when attending church events. When this grew tiresome for the individual, he left that church and began attending elsewhere. Unfortunately, this man abused someone at this new church and ended up returning to prison. This was a terrible outcome for all involved, especially the person who suffered the abuse, and it is the kind of situation that can be avoided when we do background checks and put appropriate boundaries in place.

You may be thinking to yourself, "Isn't the church intended to be a place of forgiveness for all?" I have heard this argument before from many in your position right now. And the honest answer, is, yes, it is! Jesus ate with sinners and spent time with those who society deemed unfit or unworthy. However, we must balance this openness and hospitality with vigilance in our ministry spaces. There are many ways that a church can offer a safe space for all people, including both the vulnerable and those with checkered pasts. We can provide people in this situation a different opportunity to volunteer, ask them to sign a covenant appropriate to the concerns that have been brought forward, and we can work with these individuals to find a place in the community for them.

A few years ago, a man with whom I had done ministry for many years went through a rough patch in his life. He made several poor decisions and ended up getting arrested. As part of his sentence, he was placed on the sex-offender registry. In the wake of this, he left the church for a while, ashamed of his actions. When he was ready to return and begin volunteering again, we were forced to have a challenging conversation. The man could no longer work with students, even though it was where he found his passion for ministry. However, after an honest and open

> Jesus ate with sinners and spent time with those who society deemed unfit or unworthy. However, we must balance this openness and hospitality with vigilance in our ministry spaces.

dialogue, he understood that there were consequences to his choices and that we had to keep everyone involved safe, including him.

These conversations are not easy, but they are necessary. We can create safe spaces for all people with open and honest communication. This begins with having all the information necessary to make appropriate decisions.

2) No adult should ever be alone with a vulnerable person while out of sight and sound range of other adults. We call this the "two-deep rule."

The two-deep rule is one of the most important rules we follow in ministry. It is said that there is safety in numbers. This phrase definitely applies when it comes to doing ministry. There are a number of reasons why it's essential for more than one adult to be around when we are doing ministry. First and foremost, emergencies happen. If someone falls and gets hurt, or if someone gets sick, then an adult needs to respond to this situation. If there is only one adult present to supervise all participants, then that adult cannot leave to handle the situation. Similarly, if one adult is not feeling one hundred percent, then the other can step in to help where needed. Most everyone has volunteered or worked with a headache or something that causes them to be off their game.

Second, adults working together can keep each other in check. If one adult gets carried away while joking or playing with students, another can intervene and calm the situation down. We all get carried away sometimes. Furthermore, if there is a question that one adult is struggling to answer, another can help handle the question and find an appropriate answer. It's always good to know that you're not alone.

Having two adults around also means there will be witnesses if any issues or allegations arise. If a participant or another adult alleges that inappropriate behavior has occurred, it will be essential to have multiple adults in the area to either handle the situation or to report on what they have witnessed. This not only keeps participants safe, but also keeps adult supervisors safe. Safe Sanctuaries ministry is about creating spaces where all people feel comfortable being themselves. Having multiple adults present fosters this environment.

3) Supervising adults should not be related.

This general rule builds from the previous rule that we discussed. While it is essential to always have more than one adult present, it is important that these two adults are not related. This includes biological and married relationships. Spouses,

Notes

It's always good to know that you're not alone.

61

_____

_____

_____

_____

_____

_____

_____

_____

_____

_____

_____

> As has been stated before, creating a safe sanctuary means not only protecting participants but also protecting those working and volunteering in our ministries.

parents and children, siblings, and in-laws are all included within this definition. The best practice is to extend this even to those who are cohabitating, whether roommates or romantically involved.

There are a few reasons to follow this rule. First, it is hard for people to speak against those they love. If a situation were to arise where an adult acted or attempted to act inappropriately, having an intimate relationship can make it difficult for the other adult present to speak out against the accused or stop that person in the moment. As has been stated before, creating a safe sanctuary means not only protecting participants but also protecting those working and volunteering in our ministries. Placing people in a position where they may be asked to speak against someone they love can create a space that feels unsafe and unwelcoming.

There is also a legal component to this. A spouse cannot be compelled to testify against a partner in a court of law. According to the Legal Information Institute at Cornell Law School, "Spousal privilege . . . includes two types of privileges: the spousal communications privilege and the spousal testimonial privilege. The spousal communications privilege . . . shields communications made in confidence. The purpose of the privilege is to provide assurance that all private statements between spouses will be free from public exposure . . . The spousal testimonial privilege precludes one spouse from testifying against the other spouse in criminal or related proceedings. Either spouse can invoke the privilege to prevent the testimony."

The best practice is simply to avoid placing anyone in this difficult-to-navigate situation and refrain from having two related adults working alone as ministry leaders.

4) An appropriate and safe ratio of adults to vulnerable people should be consistently maintained.

This rule exists for the safety of all participants and adults. The ratio can vary based on age, as younger children often require more adult supervision than older teenagers or vulnerable adults. A good rule of thumb is one adult for every eight participants. This allows the participants the ability to interact with one another without feeling overwhelmed by adult supervision but also provides for enough adults to see anything that might occur, such as a participant falling or an argument breaking out among friends.

Maintaining this kind of ratio can also be helpful when it comes to finding volunteers to help with events. You can assure potential volunteers that no person will ever be expected to supervise a group alone. They will always have adequate help to keep everyone safe. It also means that when following the two-deep rule, you are always prepared for up to sixteen participants. Depending on the size of the group with which you are working, this allows for a bit of leeway with the number of participants.

One additional suggestion to help you maintain this ratio is create a list of backup volunteers and staff. If more people attend than you anticipated, you will already have a list of people you can call and ask to help. This also helps if an adult gets sick or has an emergency and needs to leave early or cancel at the last minute. Things happen in people's lives and in ministry, there should always be a plan B, just in case.

5) When ministering and working with vulnerable persons, ensure that doors are open and sight and sound lines are unobstructed.

Instinctually, we may view quiet spaces and closed doors as the proper setting for having hard conversations, but it is vital that those working with vulnerable people keep sight and sound lines open to other supervising adults. In fact, this is a rule best followed in all ministries regardless of the participant with whom one is working. This keeps all people involved safe and free from uncomfortable situations.

When doors are closed, there is an implied intimacy to a situation that does not necessarily belong in a ministry setting. It also creates an expectation of privacy that may not be able to be maintained depending on the topic of a conversation.

Private conversations are, however, an important part of ministry. They can be held in safe environments that protect all those involved. If a participant is most comfortable talking to a specific adult, it can be suggested that a second adult be there for support. If the person would prefer to speak to only one person, then space should allow another certified adult to be nearby observing what transpires during the conversation. This allows the individuals wishing to talk to feel they have the full attention of their companion and the privacy they seek while maintaining a safe situation for both parties.

If a conversation gets intense or if the listener is uncomfortable with what is being said, another adult is there to witness what is happening and step in. This also helps the speaker if the listener acts or speaks in a way that makes the speaker uncomfortable.

Something to remember about this rule is that it does not only apply to physical spaces. We live in a digital world. The COVID-19 pandemic created even more digital spaces, particularly in ministry settings. We must remember to be visible in these online spaces as well as physical spaces. When holding a meeting or gathering, the digital space should be open to certified adults, and the rule of two should always be followed.

Whether it is a ministry meeting or a text message, the idea of open doors and windows should always be followed. Be sure that another adult is a part of the space.

Notes

> Things happen in people's lives and in ministry, there should always be a plan B, just in case.

_____

_____

_____

_____

_____

_____

_____

_____

_____

_____

_____

6) When working with minors, the supervising adult should always be five years older than the oldest participant.

This suggestion is often met with resistance. Some see this as excluding young adults and college-aged people from participating in ministry. While it can be interpreted that way, it is not the intention of the rule. Instead, this rule is intended to protect students and volunteers from gray areas that can be hard to navigate. The role of ministry volunteers is to help minister to those around them through mentorship and example. At certain ages, the line between mentor and friend can easily blur, even unintentionally.

For instance, if you have an eighteen-year-old high school senior being mentored by a twenty-year-old volunteer, it is not unreasonable for an emotional connection to develop beyond what is intended or desired. In another setting, these two people might find it normal to interact socially or romantically. However, in a ministry setting, this can cause significant damage to a program and to the trust that has developed within that environment.

This rule does not mean that young adults should not be allowed to volunteer in youth ministry or that youth cannot help in children's ministry. This rule simply states that this young person should not be the supervising adult in a space. For instance, if you have a seventh-grade student volunteering to help with a children's event, that student should not be considered a "supervising adult" for a group of upper elementary students. The middle schooler is welcome to be present and to assist an adult leader, but the middle schooler should not be left alone with the students or counted as one of the two adults to satisfy the two-deep rule.

Let me be clear that many of the best volunteers I have worked with in youth ministry over the years have been college-aged young adults. The students in my various churches have responded to these people in ways that they simply do not with me. These younger volunteers also speak a language that becomes less familiar to me as I age. These young adults are a vital part of the ministries I have served. Because of this, I strive to protect them and the students so that powerful ministry can continue.

> The role of ministry volunteers is to help minister to those around them through mentorship and example.

7) Release forms for medical, transportation, photo and video use, and communication should be kept up-to-date for all participants.

Release forms are an integral part of creating safe spaces. As a ministry leader, it is crucial to know all the pertinent information regarding the participants with whom we are working. There is often information that will not be communicated if not directly asked about. We should never assume that we know all there is to know about others.

Medical release forms allow leaders to know pertinent medical information regarding their participants. This includes allergies, medications, and other such information. It is also crucial that these forms stay updated as medical situations change and new allergies develop while others become less severe.

This form also lets leaders know what over-the-counter medications they can provide a participant if needed. It is important not to give participants any medication, including basic over-the-counter medication, without written permission from their legal caretaker. A participant could have an allergy about which the leaders are unaware or be taking another medication that can cause negative side effects.

The form can also grant permission for the supervising adult to work with medical personnel if needed. For example, if a participant falls and breaks a bone, the medical release form instructs the leaders on how to proceed. If a participant must be taken to the hospital, for instance, it is important to know if a staff member has permission to work with the doctor until the guardian arrives or if they should wait for the caregiver to come before any decisions are made.

In my own ministry, a medical release permitted me to take a sick student to the doctor and have a prescription filled while on a trip. I spoke with the student's parents during the process and showed the release forms to the doctor and pharmacy to take care of the student without being the legal guardian.

Transportation release forms permit a participant to ride in a vehicle with an adult other than the legal guardian. This can include traveling to an event with the ministry staff or being picked up after an event by another adult. Ministry leaders must pay close attention to who has permission to take a person from the site of ministry.

Photo and video release forms should be required for all ministry participants, regardless of age. These forms give a ministry permission to take photos or videos of a person and use them within their spaces. A photo and video release form should also include language allowing the media to be used internally and externally.

In the situation that a person or the caregivers of a participant do not want to sign this release, then no image of that person or participant can be used on social media, websites, internal fliers, advertisements posted internally or externally, or displayed in any manner. This is another area that can seem more or less important to the safety of different participants, but it is an important question to ask.

There are many circumstances when a leader might be unaware that a person's image should not be used. In many states, for instance, it is illegal for pictures of children in foster care to be displayed. Other situations, such as adoption or child removal, can cause a family to be cautious about posting pictures of their loved ones online.

Notes

There is often information that will not be communicated if not directly asked about. We should never assume that we know all there is to know about others.

Photo use can also be a personal preference. Some families choose not to post photos of themselves or their members in the public domain. Using images they do not wish published would create an unsafe space for those individuals. Asking for a release and following the terms of that release protects both the student and the family.

Communication release forms are also crucial in safe ministry settings. It is up to the guardian of a vulnerable person to determine with whom that person may interact. A communication release form should note who in a ministry the participant is allowed to communicate with and in what ways.

For instance, a parent may permit their student to text with adult leaders and volunteers, but not for their student to interact on social media with adults. In another example, a guardian may approve of Facebook and Instagram, but not want their child using Snapchat with others.

Each of these release forms is important to create a safer sanctuary for leaders, participants, and their families. For safe ministry to take place, there must be a level of transparency and trust that exists among all parties. The use of release forms ensures clear communication among parties regarding what is okay and what the participant is uncomfortable with.

8) Separate shower and bathroom facilities should be maintained for each gender and for adults and vulnerable people.

This rule often falls into what some might call common sense. However, it is best to be specific about what is expected in ministry spaces. Separate spaces for showering and using the restroom should be provided as appropriate to your context. When planning for ministry events, consider the space you will use and those participating when putting in place plans for the event.

9) Separate sleeping quarters should be provided for each gender.

As stated in the previous suggestion, this will rely heavily on the ministry context. Overnight events are common in ministry, specifically in youth ministry, and it is important that a plan is in place to have separate sleeping areas for those attending. This allows for everyone to be safe, comfortable, and to get the rest they need for the ministry in which they are participating.

> For safe ministry to take place, there must be a level of transparency and trust that exists among all parties.

10) Each person should have a personal space for rest. Beds should not be shared.

When overnight events are planned, it is important that all those attending, both participants and leaders, get good rest. For this to happen, each person should have his or her own sleeping space. In an ideal setting, beds should not be shared. Parents should not share an air mattress with their children, and friends or siblings should not be asked to share a sleeping space.

Once again, this is a policy that should be developed and adapted with consideration for the context of the event. For instance, it is often harder to maintain separate sleeping spaces in hotels, as the cost can dictate the need to put more people in a room. However, in a space that has bunk beds or floor space, individuals should maintain a healthy distance from those sleeping around them.

For example, when traveling with middle-school girls, I have often run into a situation where students want to push all their beds or sleeping bags together and make a big group sleeping pile. This leads to several issues. No one gets any rest; it is uncomfortable for all those involved; the students keep the rest of the room awake by talking; and often there is peer pressure to join this group even when a student would rather not. It is best to have a policy in place that can prevent these types of situations.

It is the intention of this book to give the readers the best information possible, but the length of this chapter, and this resource in general, may have you questioning how simple these rules actually are. As you read through the suggestions made, recognize that these are best practices and that each may need to be adapted to fit the ministry context of an event.

Following these rules as closely as possible can create a space that fosters trust, safety, and acceptance. As ministry leaders, we are called to create Christ-centered spaces. By following these suggestions, you are on your way to creating safer sanctuaries for all your ministry participants.

Notes

> As you read through the suggestions made, recognize that these are best practices and that each may need to be adapted to fit the ministry context of an event.

CHAPTER 9

Forms of Abuse and the Basics of Our Legal Obligations

Bonnie L. Bevers

It can be hard to discuss the specifics of abuse in a straightforward way, but it is necessary to precisely define the terms we are working with in order to unpack the basic facts about abuse, abuse prevention, and our legal obligations as those responsible for taking care of children, youth, and vulnerable adults.

Abuse is a general term that covers many different situations. For instance, The Federal Child Abuse Prevention and Treatment Act (CAPTA) (42 U.S.C.A. § 5106g) defines child abuse and neglect as "any recent act or failure to act on the part of a parent or caretaker which results in death, serious physical or emotional harm, sexual abuse, or exploitation; or an act or failure to act which presents an imminent risk of serious harm."[1]

As mentioned in that definition, abuse comes in many different forms from physical abuse to neglect to emotional abuse to sexual abuse. There are also forms of abuse that we don't think about as much, such as financial abuse and elder abuse. Each of these forms of abuse has specific definitions, but they all share one thing in common: they are all ways of hurting people, most often intentionally.

To provide you and your community with a shared vocabulary for the important work that you will be doing, here are several working definitions of different kinds of abuse that you may encounter in your work.

Forms of Abuse

Physical Abuse

According to the American Psychological Association, physical abuse is defined as "deliberately aggressive or violent behavior by one person toward another that results in bodily injury. Physical abuse may involve such actions as punching, kicking, biting, choking, burning, shaking, and beating, which may, at times, be severe enough to result in permanent damage or death."

While it is often assumed that physical abuse is obvious to the public due to physical signs, it is not always easily seen. Victims and abusers are often skilled at hiding signs of abuse from others to protect themselves and the person or people they love. It should be noted that physical abuse most often occurs in "relationships of trust, particularly between parents and children or between intimate partners; indeed, violence against women and children in these types of relationships is recognized as a major public health problem."[2]

Emotional Abuse

Emotional abuse is a form of nonphysical abuse. It is defined by a pattern of behavior in which one person deliberately and repeatedly subjects another to nonphysical acts that are detrimental to the individual's daily life and overall mental well-being. Researchers have yet to formulate a universally agreed upon definition of the concept, but they have identified a variety of forms that emotional abuse may take, including verbal abuse, intimidation and terrorization, humiliation and degradation, exploitation, harassment, rejection, withholding of affection, isolation, and excessive control. This is also known as psychological abuse.

Neglect

Neglect occurs when a person endangers a child's health, safety, or welfare through negligence. Neglect may include withholding food, clothing, medical care, education, and even affection and affirmation from someone who is under the abuser's care. This is perhaps the most common form of abuse. This is also an important form of abuse to note because it does not have to be an intentional act for it to be abusive. While a significant amount of abuse inflicts intentional harm, neglect inflicts harm without necessarily intending to. However, this is still abuse.

Sexual Abuse

Sexual abuse is defined as sexual contact inflicted upon a person by forcible compulsion. Additionally, sexual abuse refers to engaging in sexual contact with a person who is below a specified age or who is incapable of giving consent because of age or mental or physical incapacity. While the most commonly recognized forms of sexual abuse are sexual assault, rape, and molestation, these are not the only types of sexual assault prevalent in modern society. Sexual abuse can also include unwanted sexual attention, such as cat-calling or unprovoked comments about one's appearance or sexuality. Sexual abuse also includes unwanted or nonconsensual touching, such as pinching a person's buttocks or brushing one's hand against another's chest.

As a youth pastor, I have dealt with many sexual misconduct and abuse cases and have worked with families of sexual assault survivors. Each situation is unique and requires the adult to listen carefully and respectfully. As teachers, ministry leaders, and volunteers, it is not our primary role to investigate these allegations. Our first job is to listen to the victim, document the conversation, and report the abuse to the proper channels.

Notes

> While a significant amount of abuse inflicts intentional harm, neglect inflicts harm without necessarily intending to. However, this is still abuse.

69

_____

_____

_____

_____

_____

_____

_____

_____

_____

_____

_____

> **Spiritual abuse can happen within a religious organization or a personal relationship. It is not limited to one religion, denomination, or group of people.**

Spiritual Abuse

Spiritual abuse is any attempt to exert power and control over someone using religion, faith, or beliefs. Spiritual abuse can happen within a religious organization or a personal relationship. It is not limited to one religion, denomination, or group of people. It can occur in any religious group as an element of many forms of abuse, including child abuse, elder abuse, and domestic violence.

Financial Abuse

Financial or economic abuse occurs when a person controls another's ability to access, acquire, use, or maintain control of economic resources. This diminishes victims' capacity to support themselves, and it fosters forced dependence. Financial abuse is cited as the main reason many victims stay or return to abusive relationships.[3] While financial abuse can occur in any intimate relationship, it is most often seen in scenarios of domestic violence and elder abuse.

Elder/Caregiver Abuse

According to the Administration for Community Living, elder abuse is defined as "any knowing, intentional, or negligent act by a caregiver or any other person that causes harm or a serious risk of damage to a vulnerable adult.[4] We also refer to this as caregiver abuse, as it can happen to vulnerable adults who are not elderly. In this context, a vulnerable adult means an adult who has one or more mental, physical, or emotional impairments that render the person incapable of self-care or independent living without help. This type of abuse can occur within a home, medical facilities, care facilities, or other institutions.

Domestic Violence

Domestic violence is an umbrella term that can encapsulate a number of different relationships and different forms of abuse. However, it is also a useful term to define for the purposes of our work.

Domestic violence is defined as a pattern of abusive behavior in any relationship that one person uses to gain or maintain power and control over an intimate partner or family member. Domestic violence can be physical, sexual, emotional, or economic in nature. It can also include other patterns of coercive behavior that influence another person within an intimate relationship. This can include behavior that intimidates, manipulates, humiliates, isolates, frightens, terrorizes, coerces, threatens, blames, hurts, injures, or wounds someone.

What Does This Mean for Me?

If you are reading this resource, you have already have a vested interest in the safety and protection of vulnerable people. This protection comes in many forms. You may be a teacher, a ministry leader, a volunteer, a scout leader, a parent, or an adult who wants to have all the necessary information. Whatever the scenario, I applaud you for taking the time to read this text and grow your understanding of what it means to create safer sanctuaries for the vulnerable people in your life.

Each state requires certain adults to report any reasonable suspicion of abuse to the proper authorities. This is generally referred to as a mandated reporter or mandatory reporter. While we can generalize about the types of people who are included as mandated reporters, you need to become familiar with the laws in your particular state as these positions vary slightly. In some states, only those working directly with the vulnerable such as teachers, social workers, and doctors, are mandatory reporters. However, in some states, such as Texas, all adults over eighteen years old are mandated reporters. In most situations, the mandated reporter has 48 hours to report the suspected abuse to the proper channels.

If you are unfamiliar with how to make a report and your community currently has no formal policy, a simple online search of "report abuse in" your state should provide you the information needed to make a report. Each state I have worked with has had both online reporting and a phone number that can be called twenty-four hours a day.

However, it is also essential that each organization have its own standards about documenting abuse and neglect for internal purposes. For instance, as a youth pastor, I am tasked with documenting the reasoning behind my suspicions of abuse whether it be a conversation, visual marks, or other circumstances. Depending on the severity of the situation, I contact my senior pastors or the police. My first obligation is to notify law enforcement to ensure the victim's safety if there is an imminent threat of death or harm. After this call is made, I would report to my senior pastors, who will also be involved with documenting the incident within the organization. If the threat is not imminent, I can contact my pastors before I report to the state. The pastors may sit with me in moral support as I make the report, but it must be the person who has reason to suspect abuse or neglect who makes the report. Another person cannot call or report in that person's place.

Reporting abuse can be difficult, especially if a person disclosed the abuse or neglect to you in confidence. When I was a very young youth worker, a young man came to me and told me that his father had broken his nose during a fight the previous week. The boy was terrified and upset. He wanted to talk, but he also wanted me to assure him that I would not contact the police, as he was afraid of his father losing his job or being arrested. I told the boy that I had no choice. I was legally obligated to make a report.

Notes

Reporting abuse can be difficult, especially if a person disclosed the abuse or neglect to you in confidence.

_____

_____

_____

_____

_____

_____

_____

_____

_____

_____

The young man was irate. He felt hurt and betrayed. Nevertheless, after he left, I made the report and informed the pastors at the church where I was volunteering at the time. The young man did not speak to me for several months. I would see him at church, and he would turn and walk away. It was painful to see him, knowing how I had hurt him. However, I had to remind myself that I not only did what the law required but also what my faith required. I was protecting him from a dangerous situation.

About a year later, the young man came to see me and apologized for how he reacted. He told me that things were much better in his home due to the investigation that my report had initiated. While this healed our relationship, it is not necessarily common. I have made other reports that did not end this way. In some situations, a child was removed from the home, and both the child and the parent remained angry with me. While this was not what I wanted to happen, my responsibility was to keep those children safe.

Each time I sit down with a person, whether a child or adult, I remind that person that our conversation is always confidential unless it can't be. I explain that there are certain things that I must report either to parents, guardians, or the police. It helps remind both that person and me that I have a legal, moral, and ethical obligation as a ministry leader to keep those I work with safe. Each of you has the same responsibility. God has tasked us with protecting those we care for, and it is a responsibility that we should take very seriously.

Notes

1. "Definitions of Child Abuse and Neglect," Child Welfare Information Gateway, website, https://www.childwelfare.gov/topics/can/defining.

2. "APA Dictionary of Psychology," American Psychological Association website, https://dictionary.apa.org/physical-abuse.

3. "Financial Abuse," Pennsylvania Coalition Against Domestic Violence, https://www.pcadv.org/financial-abuse.

4. "What Is Elder Abuse," Administration for Community Living, https://acl.gov/programs/elder-justice/what-elder-abuse.

Each time I sit down with a person, whether a child or adult, I remind that person that our conversation is always confidential unless it can't be.

CHAPTER 10
Consent and Healthy Touch

Bonnie L. Bevers

Growing up as a young child in Texas, I was always surrounded by my elders. We were a close family, and I often spent time with my aunts, uncles, cousins, grandparents, and great-grandparents. Some of my earliest memories involve family events with more people present than I could reasonably comprehend as a tiny human.

These gatherings were also full of physical affection. My family loves to hug and give kisses on the cheek. I often sat in the lap of different adults or found myself being carried around by various cousins who regarded me as more of a doll than a person. I never felt threatened or unsafe in any of these situations. I was used to being touched, always appropriately, by my family, by the people I loved.

The situation was similar at the church we attended. The parents of my friends treated me as if I was one of their own. Older congregation members adopted me as a surrogate granddaughter and would hug and kiss me. They'd bring me gum to chew during the service. All of these things felt normal and comfortable in my world.

It wasn't until my teenage years that I first experienced the feeling of dread around a hug at church. When I was about sixteen, there was a man in our church who loved to hug everyone at the end of the service each week. He would stand at the back of the sanctuary and embrace people as they left. For some reason, this man made me uncomfortable. I couldn't verbalize my reasons, but I knew that I did not like it when he hugged me. I began searching for alternate exits after weekly services, anything that could help me avoid him. I would go out the front doors instead of the back and circle around the church, even in bad weather, to avoid his hugs.

My sanctuary, both literally and metaphorically, no longer felt like a safe space. When I was there, I harbored a sense of discomfort and danger. I had never been taught that I had the right to tell this man that I did not want a hug. I was never told that I did not owe him an explanation for this denial, that my comfort and safety were more important than his desire to hug each person in the congregation. I was lacking knowledge and understanding about consent and the importance of healthy touch.

At its core, consent is simple. It means that someone must provide affirmation or approval before something takes place. Historically, the church has not always had a good track record with this idea. The

_____

_____

_____

_____

_____

_____

_____

_____

_____

_____

When we ask for permission to touch others, to hug others, to show affection for others, we are empowering them.

reason for this oversight is not necessarily bad. As highlighted in my story, it was expected that children give adults hugs out of respect for their elders. Respect is a good thing! Showing love and affection for one another is good. Physical touch is an important way that we connect with one another.

However, when there are unspoken rules in place that force people to accept unwanted physical touch, it undercuts the healthy traits that we are trying to foster in our communities. One person's show of love and affection is another's violation. One person's source of connection is another's source of anxiety.

Consent is the tool we use to bridge this gap. When we ask for permission to touch others, to hug others, to show affection for others, we are empowering them. We are building community by honoring their boundaries and communicating openly. It is a sign of respect and love in a community to ask for consent rather than assuming that a person wishes to be hugged or touched. This goes for people of all ages as well, from children all the way to the most elderly members of our congregations.

Another concept related to consent is healthy touch. According to the Center for Disability Leadership, healthy touch is defined as two people trusting one another and giving permission to be touched and being in a location, whether public or private, where each is comfortable with the touch.[1]

In ministry, healthy touch is generally best displayed in handshakes, high fives, fist bumps, and side hugs. These forms of physical affection and acknowledgment allow each person in the group to greet others in non-sexual, non-threatening ways. Consent, however, is still necessary for these interactions.

Over the past few years, we have seen more and more examples of people being uncomfortable with any form of physical touch. For instance, one church I attended implemented the elbow bump during flu season. If a person did not want to touch hands or hug, that person would hold out an elbow to lessen the likelihood of spreading germs. This became even more common during the COVID-19 pandemic.

Accepted forms of healthy touch are also age dependent. If one is working in the nursery, there will be much more touch involved than when working with youth. It is necessary for a nursery volunteer to hold small children and babies, rock them, change diapers, and sometimes help with potty training. In contrast, it would be highly inappropriate for a teenager or even an older child to sit on an adult's lap.

Forms of healthy touch are also something that must be learned over time. Small children and toddlers, for instance, may not understand the concept of a side hug. They will often run to those they know and love and throw their arms around them with full force. Often, they will hug an adult's legs due to the height difference, but if the child and their guardian are comfortable with the situation, this is a consensual, healthy touch. This provides an opportunity for adults to begin teaching children about consent and healthy touch. As adults, we are responsible for modeling safe behavior and teaching those we mentor about appropriate interactions with others.

When talking about the concepts of consent and healthy touch, we must also factor in cultural differences. Some cultures place more emphasis on touch as a sign of respect. Others generally avoid physical touch. For instance, in Korean culture, the respectful greeting of another is a slight bow. This is how children greet elders, friends welcome one another, and leaders greet those to whom they speak. Yet, in some European countries, it is traditional to give small kisses on each cheek in greeting. We must pay attention to these cultural differences when creating policies and educating our communities about healthy touch and consent.

A colleague of mine described her experiences growing up in a large Mexican family. Her older relatives, particularly the women in her family, greeted everyone with a kiss on the lips. It was not until my friend was in her mid-twenties that she felt comfortable telling her aunts that she was not comfortable with this. Her family members were offended and hurt. They told her that she was being disrespectful to her elders. This was a cultural tradition with which my friend was not comfortable, and therefore she had to make the choice to stand up for what she needed for her own safety.

Similarly, a family member of mine is Jewish. In her family, children are expected to hug and kiss older family members. One young child is currently at a stage where she does not like to hug anyone but her parents. Her parents have told her that she does not have to hug anyone with whom she is not comfortable.

I have similar conversations with many people of different religious and cultural backgrounds. Whether Christian, Jewish, Muslim, or another religion, there is often a generational difference in interpretations about consent and healthy touch. Older generations, particularly in the United States, were often raised with an implicit understanding that a child did not have autonomy over his or her body. Children were expected to do as they were told and not question their elders. However, there has been a cultural shift around this idea. Today, we give children the freedom to say no, just as we do to adults. All people, regardless of age, sex, gender, sexuality, race, or other defining characteristics, have the right to decide whom they are comfortable touching or receiving touch from. We must model and teach this in our ministry spaces to create safer sanctuaries for all people.

Signs of Abuse

This conversation about consent and healthy touch is also a conversation about being aware. We must be aware of what people are comfortable with and how to approach them. We need to be aware of how we interact and touch other people. This awareness not only enables us to help others be more comfortable in our communities, it also helps us keep an eye out for indicators of abuse.

All people, regardless of age, sex, gender, sexuality, race, or other defining characteristics, have the right to decide whom they are comfortable touching or receiving touch from.

_____

_____

_____

_____

_____

_____

_____

_____

_____

_____

_____

_____

We must be aware of what people are comfortable with and how to approach them. We need to be aware of how we interact and touch other people.

In many situations, the way a person interacts with others can be an indicator of abuse. Some behavioral signs that might be signs of abuse can be:

- excessive crying or developmental delay in infants
- excessive fear, anxiety, and clinging behavior
- nightmares, sleeping problems, or bed wetting
- social withdrawal
- hyperactivity or poor concentration/distractibility
- decreased school performance and chronic school absenteeism
- speech disorders or regressive behavior for age
- eating issues
- depression, passivity
- increased verbal abuse or physically aggressive behavior with others
- destroying objects or injuring pets
- substance abuse
- self-harm such as cutting
- sexualized behavior
- avoiding undressing, withdrawal from touch, or fear of physical examination

Similarly, some physical signs of abuse can include:

- poor hygiene
- dressing inappropriately for the weather
- poor weight gain or malnutrition
- lack of care for medical needs, including wound care and forgetting medication
- fractured bones, dislocations, lacerations, bruising, or injuries on the forearms
- bite marks—human bites are more superficial than an animal and show up better two to three days later
- burns from a cigarette, rope, immersion, or shape of a hot object
- signs of restraints
- traumatic hair loss
- facial injuries without a reasonable explanation
- oral/dental injuries, such as torn or bruised frenulum, lips, teeth, palate, tongue, or oral mucosa
- diagnosed sexually-transmitted disease or pregnancy

This is not a complete list of possible signs of abuse, but it does provide a wide range of potential behavioral and physical signs that can represent that something is wrong. When operating in a respectful environment that encourages consent and healthy touch, this also teaches children and others to understand what unhealthy touch looks like and to be better able to express when someone is touching them or treating them in an unhealthy way.

It also important to remember that these signs do not always indicate abuse or neglect. People fall, get sick, and accidents happen. However, it is our responsibility to remain vigilant and be caretakers, watch over those for whose care we are charged, and look into any situations that raise red flags or suspicions.

Notes

1. "Session 3 Tip Sheet: Healthy Touch," Center for Disability Leadership at Virginia Commonwealth University, Richmond, VA (2019), https://cdl.partnership.vcu .edu/healthy-relationships-leap/leap-partner-guide---tip-sheets/session-3-tip-sheet -healthy-touch.

Notes

It is our responsibility to remain vigilant and be caretakers, watch over those for whose care we are charged, and look into any situations that raise red flags or suspicions.

CHAPTER 11

Common Concerns and Questions

Bonnie L. Bevers

This resource is filled with lots of information, guidelines, and best practices to follow as you work to build safer sanctuaries for your communities. It can seem daunting as you consider how to put it into practice. It can also feel like it's difficult or impossible to do ministry the way you have before while putting these new practices into place. There are always questions about what to do, what others are doing, and how to balance safety with the relational nature of ministry.

It's important to acknowledge these questions and discuss a few of the questions that you are probably asking yourself as you work through this resource. This chapter is designed to highlight some of those questions and provide the most helpful answers available.

1) How are we supposed to do ministry with all these rules?

This is a valid question, and it's one that comes up all the time when I am leading trainings about Safe Sanctuaries. First and foremost, I want to assure you that it is possible! Ministry might not look the way that it has in years and decades past, but you can still do good ministry and do that work in a safe, healthy, and thriving environment.

The most significant step you can take is to train your volunteers in these ideas, guidelines, and practices. In particular, train your volunteers about the principles behind the policies and procedures that you have put in place in your community. The three principles that support all of the recommendations you will see in this resource are honesty, communication, and accountability. Keeping to these three principles in any situation helps to build a healthy environment that not only keeps people safe, but also allows ministry to thrive.

Beyond this, most organizations have a training and screening protocol set in place. In a later chapter, we'll talk about how to build a policy if you don't have one, and this is a key aspect of that process. You will want each volunteer and staff member to undergo a background check through a reputable organization. In The United Methodist Church, most conferences have a group that they use when screening clergy candidates, and you can use the same process. If your organization does not currently have a group it uses, contact your denominational offices or other local churches to see who they recommend.

Second, ensure that your group always has at least two screened and trained adults in your ministry space, whether physical or virtual. For many organizations, this can be the hardest part. One tip is to keep a list of all your certified volunteers. If someone must cancel at the last minute, you can go to this list to find a replacement. This frees the ministry leader from the stress of canceling an event due to a lack of adults.

If your church struggles to have enough adults in each room, you can implement a roamer who bounces from room to room. This also allows for help if there is an incident in a room, such as someone needing a restroom break.

If necessary, you can also combine groups as your context allows to ensure there is enough adult supervision in each space. This option will depend on your space, the type of group you lead, and the ages of those involved. This will not always work but can be done if necessary. If your building has enough space, you can also place more than one group in an area, such as a gym, with enough space between them to dampen sound but allow an adult to be a part of both groups.

Sometimes it might feel impossible to create sacred spaces that are also safe. However, it is possible. It may require a little creative thinking, but we are called by God to protect the people in our care and must always strive to have spaces where everyone is safe and accepted.

2) How are other groups following all these rules?

The greatest resource we have is one another. I have visited many churches across the United States and spoken with many youth pastors, children's pastors, and other ministry leaders about how they are creating safer sanctuaries. Each church does it a little bit differently. None of us have spaces that are the same. None of us have the same participants, volunteers, and staff. None of us are doing everything identically in our programming. We must adapt to our contexts.

However, there are things we can learn from one another. The idea of roamers was one that I first heard of from a rural church in central Texas that wanted to do Sunday school for multiple age groups but didn't have enough adults to make it happen. They started using roamers and have had great success. Another church I worked with faced an issue where an adult got sick on the day that the youth group was supposed to leave for a retreat. No one in their church could take that adult's place. Instead of canceling, they got creative and contacted a neighboring church that also had certified adults and was able to enlist a volunteer to help. This allowed the retreat to happen safely and for the work of ministry to continue.

Notes

> It may require a little creative thinking, but we are called by God to protect the people in our care and must always strive to have spaces where everyone is safe and accepted.

Identifying certified adults is also a way to make parents and participants feel safe. This can be done in several ways. One church created name badges with photos on them for each certified adult. Staff members had one color lanyard and volunteers had another. The name badges for the certified volunteers in this example were printed on card stock and laminated in the office. This was a relatively easy and inexpensive way to denote certified adults in the space. Creating photo badges can be time-consuming, but it can also be useful. This is something you would want to review with your ministry staff and leaders at your congregation.

3) I know it's important, but isn't this hurting relational ministry?

This is another question I get asked in almost every session I lead. It's usually framed as something like, "How are we supposed to love students if we can't touch them?" or "How do we show we care if we're facing the hug police?" To be clear, no one is saying you cannot hug your participants or others in your community. However, there are better ways of doing this that can make others more comfortable.

The side hug is a great go-to. It allows for space between bodies while still showing affection. I also offer fist bumps, high fives, and elbow bumps. However, we must gain consent before we do any of these. We should always ask permission before touching another person.

Years ago, there were two sisters in my youth ministry who could not have been more different. One of the girls ran to me every time she saw me and wanted to hug me and would hang on for a long time if I let her. However, her sister did not like to be touched. I knew if she wanted a hug, something was either really good or really bad. I learned how to read her body language to see if I should even put a hand on her shoulder, which I did not do unless she invited that comforting touch. By acknowledging her resistance to touch, I made the space more comfortable for her and it became the safe sanctuary that a youth space is intended to be.

It is important to remember this, even when dealing with small children or older adults. They are often the most resistant to being touched. As discussed in the previous chapter, consent and bodily autonomy are imperative for building safer sanctuaries. Regardless of age, race, gender, sexuality, or other identifying characteristics, a person always has the right not to be touched.

Beyond this, it is important that we not make a direct connection between physical contact and the relational connections at the core of ministry. While some people find connection, others see kind words, thoughtful actions, and even our mere presence as foundational ways of connecting with others. Instead of thinking about the policies and procedures of Safe Sanctuaries as a limitation, it can help if we view them as an opportunity to consider all the wonderful ways that we can connect with others beyond physical touch and affection.

It can help if we view them as an opportunity to consider all the wonderful ways that we can connect with others beyond physical touch and affection.

4) How do we implement this in unique situations?

Each ministry in your congregation will need to find a way to implement these policies and procedures in a unique way that fits their the context. For instance, I once served at a church that had an agricultural ministry that met in the barns at a local farm. To create safe spaces in this context, each adult who helped with the program was certified in their church's Safe Sanctuaries program. These adults made sure that there were always at least two of them in each barn. Since the animal stalls were built with half walls, those in the barn were in an open space where everyone could be seen and heard. The barn was also open to the pasture so participants working outside could also be supervised by certified adults.

Another unique situation are outside groups that use our church facilities, like scouting organizations. While these groups should have their own policies regarding safe spaces and protection, it is essential that these policies line up with your congregation's policies and that those involved in this work be trained on all the policies in place. If your congregation charters the group, then that group will need to follow the guidelines of your church's policy. This would include adult background checks, training, the two-adult rule, and all other policies put in place to keep everyone safe.

As mentioned earlier, when dealing with unique situations and new ministry contexts, always keep in mind the fundamental principles of honesty, communication, and accountability. Be honest about what you are doing, the risks involved, the possible issues that might arise, and what you will need to provide a safe environment. Communicate the policies, procedures, and expectations you have in place to everyone involved including staff, volunteers, participants, and the parents of participants. Finally, put in place policies and processes that keep you accountable to do the things that you have said you will do and how you will respond to any issues that arise.

5) Who is responsible for making sure all of this actually gets done and these rules are followed?

While each organization will have its own hierarchy and structure, the simple answer is that you are responsible for putting this into practice. There may be specific people who are assigned to oversee certification and training and a defined structure for reporting abuse or the suspicion of abuse, but ultimately each of us is responsible for our actions and oversight. If you know that your certificate is about to expire, take the initiative to schedule a new training. Don't wait for someone else to tell you it needs to be done.

Notes

> Communicate the policies, procedures, and expectations you have in place to everyone involved including staff, volunteers, participants, and the parents of participants.

Notes

_____

_____

_____

_____

_____

_____

_____

_____

_____

_____

_____

Volunteers and staff members, hold your leaders accountable! Ask to see copies of the policies you are being asked to follow. Do not assume you know what they say. You may get asked questions, and you will want to be able to answer them honestly and correctly.

Create covenants with your leadership team that commit to upholding the standards your ministry organization and ministry program have set. Remind yourselves regularly what those covenants say. This not only allows everyone to be on the same page, but it also holds each person responsible for his or her actions. If an adult acts inappropriately, you have a signed document saying the adult would not act that way. This takes pressure off the leadership. Each person decides to sign the covenant, and it is each person's responsibility to uphold the policy.

Final Thoughts

These are only a few of the questions that have probably come to your mind as you read through this resource. An exhaustive list would be impossible to create in such a limited space. However, if you are still questioning how to implement your Safe Sanctuaries policy or wondering where to begin, reach out to someone in a nearby church who has a policy or a similar program to yours. Get together with them and brainstorm ideas. If you are in a United Methodist church, most conference offices have a person who oversees these policies. Reach out to that person for examples of forms, policies, and ideas on implementation.

Remember, as you work to create safer sanctuaries, that sacred spaces should be safe for all people. If implementing a few safety standards can make more people comfortable and everyone safe, what reason could we have for not doing so?

Ask to see copies of the policies you are being asked to follow. Do not assume you know what they say. You may get asked questions, and you will want to be able to answer them honestly and correctly.

PART IV
THE SPECIFICS

CHAPTER 12

Safer Sanctuaries for Nursery and Preschool Children

Leanne Hadley

I have worked with children my entire life. I started babysitting at the age of twelve; I helped raise my niece who was born when I was sixteen, and I worked in the nursery at church as soon as I was old enough for them to allow it. During my seminary training, I even spent time working in the neonatal intensive care unit at a children's hospital holding the tiny newborns.

I thought that babies, and children in general, were the most precious gift God had ever created! Caring for children has long been a source of joy for me.

Then I had children of my own. I realized that, as much as I loved children before, I had never felt love like this! Holding my own baby in my arms, looking into his tiny face, I was overwhelmed with emotion. It was the deepest feeling I have ever had. This child, my child, was the most precious gift God had ever given me. I felt an incredible need to protect, love, and care for this little one.

Trusting anyone else with my baby was almost more than I could handle. Fear was the first feeling I experienced when I let someone else care for my baby. I worried that they would drop him. I worried that he would need me and I would not be there. I worried that the caregiver would forget to feed him. My fear that they might hurt him, either intentionally or unintentionally, made it almost impossible for me to ever leave my baby.

When I think back on this time, I realize that the caregivers at our church did more for me than simply care for my baby. They also taught me that I could trust others to love my child and to help me raise him. I look back and give thanks to God for each person who listened, who had sympathy and patience for an anxious mother, and who, time after time, lovingly cared for my son. They demonstrated the love of God to him and to me. They laid the foundation for him that church was a place where you would be loved and cared for.

My son cannot remember those days spent in nursery and preschool classrooms, but still they shaped him. He learned about the love of God as caregivers held him, spoke tenderly to him, and taught him. He learned to see church as a place where you are held, loved, and comforted. He heard his first Bible stories in those rooms and listened to the first songs of his faith.

_____

_____

_____

_____

_____

_____

_____

_____

_____

_____

_____

When we care for these young children, we are living out our calling to care for the least. And, according to Jesus, when we care for the least, we are caring for him!

Caring for the infants and the preschool children in our congregations is more important than we often realize. Long before these tiny little ones can even speak or truly make sense of the world around them, they are learning, they are *absorbing* church. Our behavior towards them and our care for them lays the foundation for the way they will feel about church later in life. This same behavior also demonstrates to parents that they can trust the church to help them raise their child and gives them the support they need as they continue their own faith journey.

Caring for these children also allows us, the caregivers, to live out our faith. I think often of the parable about the sheep and the goats found in Matthew 25:31-46, where we are reminded that we are called to care for the least of God's people. Young children, especially babies, are so vulnerable, truly they are some of the *least of these*. They are dependent on the people around them to fulfill their most basic needs. They rely on these caregivers for their very survival.

In verse 40, Jesus says, "Truly I tell you, just as you did it to one of the least of these who are members of my family, you did it to me." When we care for these young children, we are living out our calling to care for the least. And, according to Jesus, when we care for the least, we are caring for him!

What an amazing calling we have been given! By caring for the young children in our congregation, we get to shape their lives, set the foundation for their lifelong relationship to the church, introduce scripture and songs that they will remember for a lifetime, care for their parents, and, most of all, through all of this, we will show our care for Jesus.

Perhaps there will come a day when we, like the people in the parable, are told that we have lived a good life and have cared for Jesus. Perhaps, like them, we will ask, "When did we care for you?" and Jesus will respond, "When you rocked the babies to sleep and changed their diapers, when you sang songs with the preschoolers and made them snacks, when you wiped away the tears as a young child anxiously waited for mommy or daddy to return, you did it for me. Well done!"

Five Steps for Safety

You understand the work that you are called to do. You understand the importance of the role you have in the lives of the children you care for and in the lives of their parents. However, underlying all of this is the task of keeping these children safe. This is the most important thing you can do for the children in your care. This is why the guidance of Safe Sanctuaries policies and guidelines is so important. As we consider this aspect of your calling, let's focus on five areas that will help you make sure that the children in your care are safe so that the love of Christ can be experienced by everyone.

Finding Loving, Caring Staff and Volunteers

Training volunteers and staff is essential whenever working with children. For infants and young children, it is even more important because the demands on the caregivers is heightened. In a nursery setting, for instance, diapers need to changed often and unexpectedly, babies need to be soothed and fed when they need it, not on a pre-arranged schedule. It is difficult for a caregiver to schedule a time to rest or to plan. This all creates stress.

Because of the demands placed on the caregivers of children at these age levels, it is imperative that you find people who not only enjoy children, but who also have a heart for their work. We can train someone about how to do all the tasks involved with caring for a baby or a young child, but we simply cannot teach someone to love and appreciate children if that person don't like being around them. This will make the work and ministry easier for all involved.

While this is certainly true for those working with preschoolers, it goes double for those working in the nursery. These volunteers and staff members must be able to extend empathy for the anxious parents and guardians who are entrusting the care of their little ones to these caregivers. It is easy to mistake this anxiety as dislike from a parent or guardian, and caregivers need the emotional maturity to recognize this. When accidents happen, and they will happen, caregivers of young children must have the ability to focus on the well-being of the child in their care.

Screening Volunteers and Staff

There are many reasons that people offer to volunteer or apply for employment at a church. It is our sacred responsibility to make sure that the people we recruit and hire to work with infants and preschoolers are people who:

- Understand the sacred worth of infants and children and treat them with deep respect and care.
- Enjoy working with children in these age groups.
- Can relate to adults and build relationships with parents and guardians.
- Are open to being trained and who enthusiastically fulfill the expectations of their role.

Here are six suggestions for screening a person you are considering to work with the infants or preschoolers in your church.

1. **Provide a clear and thorough job description for all volunteers and staff.** In the job description, include requirements for both caring for children and also requirements for building and maintaining relationships with parents. There is no age group where relationships with parents is

When accidents happen, and they will happen, caregivers of young children must have the ability to focus on the well-being of the child in their care.

_____

_____

_____

_____

_____

_____

_____

_____

_____

_____

_____

Finally, when making a decision, trust your gut. If anything on the application or in the reference checks gives you reason to pause, listen to the inner voice and follow up.

more critical. Remember, young children, particularly infants, cannot care for themselves. Caregivers will need to be relaxed with parents to ask about schedules and other individual considerations for children.

2. **Recruit a pool of people to interview.** You can approach people you have noticed have a heart for children of this age, but this is also an opportunity to enlist the help of others on your ministry team and ask for their recommendations. I also suggest that you talk to parents to get suggestions and to talk to them about whom they would feel most comfortable leaving their child with.

   After you identify a person you think would be a great fit, confidentially check with others on your staff before approaching that person. It's important to make sure that no one on your staff has any information about the person that would prevent that individual from meeting the basic qualifications for this position. For example, being a known sex offender, having a criminal record, or ongoing addiction issues would eliminate a person from consideration. While it is difficult to learn these things, it is better to know earlier rather than later.

3. **Meet with the candidate and go over the job description.** After the meeting, provide the candidate with an application (either in print or digital) and ask the candidate to return it within 48 hours. Handling this application is the first step to test if the candidate is dependable and open to taking direction. If the candidate loses it, forgets to bring it back, or brings it back five days late, then this might be a red flag that this person is not dependable or open to following procedures.

4. **Look over the application and double check that the candidate meets your congregation's Safe Sanctuaries guidelines.** This means that the person is at least eighteen years old and has been part of the church for at least six months in addition to passing the necessary background check that your church will perform. The application should also include the following information:

   - Name and contact information
   - How long the person has been attending your church
   - Why the person is interested in ministry with children and families
   - What ages of children the applicant prefers to work with
   - Why the applicant feels called to serve in this position
   - Any relevant experience (You can choose someone without experience, but experience is a definite plus)
   - At least three references. You need to check these references and note anything you should ask more about during an interview. It is tempting to skip this step, especially when you think you know a person, but it is a requirement of the process.

Finally, when making a decision, trust your gut. If anything on the application or in the reference checks gives you reason to pause, listen to the inner voice and follow up. When you meet with the person, you can clarify any red flags you have discovered. A feeling of discomfort does not necessarily mean that you should not move on to the next step, but it does mean that you need to follow up and listen carefully.

5. **If you think a candidate is the one you have been looking for, meet with that person for a second interview.** It is a good idea to have more than one person in this interview, possibly even a team of people. I always like decisions about childcare to be done with a team, and I strongly believe in group wisdom. Together you can talk through any of the answers you receive and make sure you have the right person. Some sample questions you might ask include:

- Why do you want this role?
- What is your experience working with infants/preschool children?
- Is there an age you like working with better? Why? (This will help discover if the candidate really wants to work with older children and finds infants or young children stressful.)
- Tell us about a time a baby or young child really stressed you out. How did you handle it? What did you learn about yourself?
- Tell us about a time you had too much do all at once and the actions you took to make the situation more manageable.

There are also a few particular questions and activities you may want to walk candidates through if you're interviewing for nursery roles in particular.

- Invite candidates to share their views about the role of parents in the nursery. Do they think parents should be allowed to walk in and out whenever they want? What questions do they feel would be appropriate for parents to ask them about the care of their child? (The answers to these questions are "yes" and "whatever they want to know about the care of their child." Allowing parents full access to the nursery helps parents know that there is nothing being done to their child that they should not see. It also reminds the caregivers that they need to be professional and engaged with the infants the entire time they are working with them.)
- After listening to the candidates' answers, use a baby doll and roleplay a parent coming to the nursery to drop off their baby. Observe how the person being interviewed responds to this scenario. The candidate will not yet be familiar with your procedures, but you will get a glimpse into the candidate's people skills. Remember that many people who love working with infants and children are not as comfortable with adults, but in order to build the necessary relationships with parents, they will need some basic comfort with these situations.

Notes

Allowing parents full access to the nursery helps parents know that there is nothing being done to their child that they should not see.

To conclude the interview, walk through the Safe Sanctuaries guidelines for your church and inform the candidate that you will be running a background check after this interview. If the candidate refuses the background check, that person should not be considered for the job. If the candidate gives permission to run the check, remember that even if the person is an ideal candidate, you cannot hire that person or ask him or her to volunteer until the background check is completed and raises no significant concerns. Thankfully, most people have no problem with a background check, and these checks rarely return red flags.

Note: By law, the background check results must be kept in a confidential locked file cabinet. Make sure you know where it is and who has access to it. Children's ministries are not the only area on the church that is required to run background checks, so there is likely already a file cabinet used for confidential information. Your church or annual conference should also have clearly stated policies and procedures. Make sure that you are familiar with these policies and follow them.

6.   If everything checks out and you feel good with your choice, offer the candidate the role and begin the process of training this person on relevant Safe Sanctuaries policies and procedures.

Training and Procedures

Physical Safety of the Room and Environment

The physical safety of any classrooms or nursery facilities is essential to the work of creating a safer sanctuary. As you begin to work on this important step, take advantage of the resources in your congregation. It is likely that there are people in your congregation who have experience as medical professionals, police, fire fighters, and teachers. Put together a team of volunteers to compile a room safety checklist that ensures that furniture is up-to-date, that outlets are covered, toxic materials are safely stored, and that you have procedures for cleaning and sanitizing toys. Staff and volunteers should go over this checklist whenever they come into the room and begin their work to make sure that everything is safe for the infants and young children that they are caring for.

Physical Safety of the Child

Churches should also put in procedures for parents to safely drop-off and pick-up their children. These must be followed without exception. This is essential to keep the child safe. While we would like to believe the church is always a safe place, situations can arise that make these safe drop-off and pick-up procedures essential. In one of my past experiences, a set of grandparents attempted to pick up their grandchildren on behalf of their son who had been served with a restraining order the night before. Thankfully, our staff followed the pick-up procedure we had in place

> The physical safety of any classrooms or nursery facilities is essential to the work of creating a safer sanctuary.

and the grandparents left without incident. While scenarios like this are rare, they do happen, and following the policies in place allows them to be resolved in a safe way.

Beyond keeping the child safe, drop-off and pick-up procedures build confidence and trust between parents and caregivers. These procedures reassure parents that we have practices in place to protect their child and that caregivers are trained to follow them. If check-in and drop-off go smoothly, parents feel confident that their children are safe and well-cared for.

Policies and guidelines for children's safety must also be written and followed closely. Personally, I suggest working with a nurse or credentialed preschool director in your congregation to educate your volunteers and staff on the best ways to care for infants and young children in a safe way. To reinforce these practices, consider putting up posters around the room as a reminder. This will help remind regular caregivers and serve as a handy guide in the case of a substitute caregiver working in the room.

The following areas should be covered in your written policies and guidelines:

- Procedures for changing diapers.
- Procedures for feeding children (this includes storing bottles for infants and snacks for preschool children).
- Procedures for cleaning toys.
- Procedures for when a parent should be called. This should include situations such as when an infant has cried hard for longer than fifteen minutes, or if a child has hurt himself/herself, been hurt by another child, or accidentally injured by a caregiver.
- Procedures for two unrelated adults to be present at all times, especially when changing diapers or helping young children use the bathroom.

In addition to the procedures above, the following must also be stressed:

- There must always be two unrelated adults caring for children in the room.
- Parents must leave a cell phone number (or use a church-provided pager) each time they leave their child for care.
- Babies must never be lifted while the caregiver is angry and must never be shaken . . . never!!!
- Children should never be left unattended. This is especially true for infants when they are on a changing table or on the floor, as this could expose them to severe injury.
- There must be a clearly marked fire and emergency exit plan as well as a phone or other method to seek immediate help in case of an emergency.
- If an accident happens, no matter how small, it should be reported to a staff member of the church and to the parents in written form. A follow-up

Notes

_____

_____

_____

_____

_____

_____

_____

_____

_____

_____

If an accident happens, no matter how small, it should be reported to a staff member of the church and to the parents in written form.

_____

_____

_____

_____

_____

_____

_____

_____

_____

_____

_____

Since toddlers and infants are among the most vulnerable group in our congregations, we want to make sure that we have done everything in our ability to ensure that they are safe in our care.

call to parents must be made within two hours and a second follow-up call should be made the next day.

- There should be a clear procedure in place for identifying and reporting suspected abuse. All people working with children in the church are mandatory reporters and all suspected abuse must be reported. This policy applies to a suspected parent, caregiver, or any other adult. All suspected child abuse must be reported, even if you trust the people or feel certain that they would never hurt an infant. This is the law, and it must be reported. No exceptions.

Spiritual Safety of the Infant

While we've talked extensively about protecting children and infants from harm, we must remember that all of these safety efforts are in place to provide young children and infants with a safe space in which they can grow, develop, and thrive within the church. In keeping with this goal, let me take this opportunity to encourage caregivers to also address the spiritual needs of young children and infants. Do not think that an infant or toddler is not yet capable of learning or being shaped in spiritual way. These early years are the times when brains grow and change the most. They are a critical time for neuropathways to develop.

I suggest using an age-appropriate curriculum or Bible story books and songs that are designed for easy repetition. This creates a stimulating experience for children and helps them develop. Additionally, it sets a foundation that your church is one where children will be spiritually safe as well as physically safe. This helps parents and caregivers understand the importance of exposing their children to stories and songs of our faith at the earliest ages and throughout their childhood.

Training Reinforcement Throughout the Year

While yearly training is important for all volunteers and staff, I also recommend that staff and volunteers refresh themselves on these policies every three months. We tend to get relaxed with policies as we ease into our roles. Since toddlers and infants are among the most vulnerable group in our congregations, we want to make sure that we have done everything in our ability to ensure that they are safe in our care.

These quarterly reminder trainings do not need to be long, especially if the caregivers are following the procedures, but they are good reminders, for everyone, of the importance of the task they have accepted.

Please note that these brief trainings should not take the place of any one-on-one meetings that might need to happen now and again. If you see someone doing something that is wrong, you must address it as soon as possible. There is no need to wait and no need to get upset about having to provide a reminder. Simply pull the person aside, explain what you observed, and then demonstrate the proper procedure. People often feel ashamed when corrected, so I suggest following up after a few days and telling them how much you appreciated them listening and working to care for the children of the church in the best way possible. This follow-up helps the caregivers know that you still respect them and believe in them.

In keeping with this theme, I also suggest writing lots and lots of thank-you notes that include specific times where you noticed something a caregiver did well. Perhaps you walked by and saw the caregiver doing fingerplays or singing to a baby; write a note! Perhaps you went into a room after the children left and noticed that the toys had been cleaned and were ready for whoever came in next; write a note! Positive reinforcement is inspiring, and working with infants and young children is a demanding job. Affirming thank-you notes will help reinforce the behavior you hope to observe and will remind you of how blessed you are to have the caregivers you have.

The Importance of an Open-Door Policy

While we cannot allow strangers or people who are not approved to come in and play with or interact with the children in our care, we must maintain an open-door policy to other staff members and parents. There are many reasons for this. First of all, it communicates that our facility is a safe place with qualified caregivers who have nothing to hide. There is no reason that people who have the authority to be in these rooms cannot come and go as they like.

The second reason is that it reassures parents. Parents often see and hear news reports of child abuse. Remember that their anxiety is not personal, even if it feels that way. However, if parents are able to check on their child whenever they would like, it can calm any anxiety they might feel. This can make the job of caregivers harder because babies may cry out for a parent, and young children may run to see them. But this is just part of the job and should be accepted. In the long run, an open-door policy will make your job easier and less stressful.

The third reason I suggest an open-door policy is that staff should be checking in on one another on a regular basis. This helps build trust and connection among caregivers. You should also be checking in on your staff as often as you can so that you know them and can sense if they are stressed or acting strange. Stopping in regularly also builds trust with staff and volunteers. If the only time you show up is when there has been an issue, then your team will start dreading your arrival and will start to avoid you. Show up often just to say hello, build relationships, and see if caregivers need anything. Mistakes and accidents happen. Even the most caring and qualified people slip up sometimes. It is important that you know when an accident or mistake happens. Maintaining good relationships and

Notes

Maintaining good relationships and trust with your volunteers and staff is the best way to ensure that, if something happens, they will tell you.

93

_____

_____

_____

_____

_____

_____

_____

_____

_____

_____

_____

_____

trust with your volunteers and staff is the best way to ensure that, if something happens, they will tell you.

You Can Do This!

When we start listing all of the procedures and steps required to make sure that our infants, toddlers, and young children are physically, emotionally and spiritually healthy, it can start to feel overwhelming. But remember, the work you do on the front end will save you headaches, confusion, and possible harm to a child as time unfolds. You have been entrusted with caring for a child, one of God's precious gifts! The joy of the children you care for will outweigh all of the work and elbow grease it takes to prepare well to receive them. It takes a very special person to work with children. God chose you! Congratulations!

Finally, I'd like to end with a prayer for you:

God, thank you for all those reading this book and bless them with a loving heart, patience, forgiveness, and self-care so that they might be the hands and feet of your son, Jesus, to the little ones entrusted to their care. In the name of Christ, who deeply valued and loved children, I pray. Amen.

The joy of the children you care for will outweigh all of the work and elbow grease it takes to prepare well to receive them.

CHAPTER 13

Safer Sanctuaries for Elementary-Age Children

Brittany Sky

I started attending East End United Methodist Church in 2016. I had taken a break from volunteering at church for awhile and spent those years hiding in the pews of an Episcopal church, but I was married now, and my husband and I wanted to find a faith community where we could raise our future family. When we got married, we agreed that our child would take my partner's last name, but that the child would be raised as a United Methodist, as I was. I started looking for our church, and East End was on the shortlist.

I remember sitting in the pew that first Sunday watching the people greet one another in the sanctuary. There were kids everywhere, and that really excited me. Children are a vital part of Christ's body, and seeing a congregation that embraces that truth and takes it seriously is rare.

The pastor stood up, invited everyone to find a seat, and service began. A few minutes into the service, a child got up and started walking toward the exit alone. I watched as two ushers headed down the aisle behind him. It caught my attention, and I wondered what was happening. A few minutes later, the three of them came back into the sanctuary together.

After the service, I was introduced to the pastor for children and youth. I asked her about what I saw with the child and the two adults who had followed him out of the sanctuary. I was curious about the situation. She responded matter-of-factly, "It's part of our Safe Sanctuary policy. Our ushers are background checked, and part of their job is to make sure kids are safe in our church. If a child gets up to go to the bathroom, two safe adults go to make sure the child makes it safely to the restroom. That's what you saw."

I didn't try out another church. I knew that this was where I wanted to be. I knew that this was where my child would be safe.

This lesson has stuck with me in the years since. Safe Sanctuaries is less a set of policies and procedures and more a culture based in healthy theology and practice. The church I visited, and ultimately began attending, had that culture, and I believe that this foundation of safety and security is something that many families gravitate toward when searching for a community of faith. When we encounter a culture like this, one that cares about children, that supports them and protects them to the point where even users are part of the culture of safety, then there is no question that this church truly values children.

Ten Simple Rules (for Safety)

As a pastor to kids and families, it has often fallen on my shoulders to create and implement the practices that help create a culture of safety for everyone, including children. Sure, my annual conference has a policy that I can use to glean some general principles; I've even worked in conferences that would pay for all the background checks that we need to run, but at times, it has felt like Safe Sanctuaries had become just one more thing to check off on a list of things before our end-of-year review. At times, it feels like the theological importance and the essential culture of Safe Sanctuaries has been lost in the day-to-day work of executing the plan.

Many of you may relate to this description. It can be hard working with kids. It's the kind of work that is often undervalued and underpaid in our society and in our churches. Since the work of Safe Sanctuaries is often handed to the person working with kids, it can end up feeling like it is isolated from other ministries in the church. This is why it's essential to approach the work of Safe Sanctuaries with the right spirit. We must approach this ministry as an opportunity to show our communities how important physical, mental, and spiritual health is to us.

As we focus on this task, the task of placing safety, security, and healthy flourishing at the foundation of our ministry, I've put together a list of ten things every church should implement to keep our kids physically, mentally, and spiritually safe because when we keep our children safe, we give them the ability to thrive.

We must approach this ministry as an opportunity to show our communities how important physical, mental, and spiritual health is to us.

1. Listen to Kids

Simply put, there is nothing more foundational to safety than listening to our kids. Unfortunately, it is also something that many congregations overlook. When I say that we should listen to kids, I am not simply referring to their words, but listening to everything they are saying, listening to their whole spirits, and taking them seriously. Listening to kids means respecting them. It means paying attention to who they are and noticing if something changes. A church that embraces a healthy culture and hopes to build safer sanctuaries will incorporate the voices of children into the life of the church. Children are not liabilities. When we talk about issues of abuse, they are not merely targets who must be protected. They are a part of Christ's body. They are part of our ministry, not simply the object of it. When we listen to children, we begin to truly act as if they are a necessary part of our congregations and we develop a more complete picture of who God is.

Our children are hardwired to survive. When faced with a difficult or scary situation, they will internalize conflict, critiques, or reprimands and assume responsibility, even if they are not responsible. This is a biological impulse because they need their caretakers to continue caring for them. If a child has a healthy, loving attachment to the caretaker, then this works out great, but when the child does not, problems can arise. Without safe relationships and a safe place where they feel like they belong, our children may not have the courage to tell us when something is wrong.

At their best, churches can offer healthy environments for our children where they can form supportive, loving attachments with others. However, this requires that we foster an atmosphere of mutual respect where the people of the community show up for every who that comes through the doors. This is what it looks like to build safer sanctuaries that help children thrive.

2. Recruiting and Screening Volunteers

Creating a safe and healthy culture requires that ministries find the right people to join the team. These volunteers should be inspired to support kids and their families. To attract the right people, start by creating a vision statement for your ministry area. The vision statement we have for my congregation is, "Thriving kids, thriving families." Every pastoral care interaction, every program, and every resource we create must help kids and families thrive. Once you've written your ministry vision statement, share it with your whole congregation. Our statement appears in our communications with both families and the wider church. Our hope is that this statement will resonate with those who are inspired to help children and families thrive and this will encourage them to join us in our ministry.

In my first job in a local church, I learned a lot about volunteer recruitment and retention. I was so new to all of this! All I knew for sure was that I felt God's presence the most when I was with kids, and I wanted to find others who felt this too. My senior pastor suggested that I write job descriptions for the roles I needed to fill, just as I would if I was hiring for a full-time role. The process of putting down these expectations for teachers, greeters, and special events teammates helped me hone my vision and set clear boundaries for myself and my team.

People are more likely to say yes to a tangible commitment than a general idea. "Teacher" can look like so many different things! Do teachers have to get their own supplies? Do they have to choose their own lesson? How often will they be expected to teach? Are they committing for a year or forever? Communicate what is expected clearly so those who are interested in helping you achieve a culture of mutual respect with kids can give a clear yes.

After you have written and shared your job descriptions, ask for applications. This doesn't need to be a resume, but you should find out the following information:

1. Name and contact information
2. How long they have been attending your church (Volunteers for children's ministry need to have been attending for at least six months.)
3. Why they are interested in ministry with kids and families
4. Why do they feel called to serve in this role

> At their best, churches can offer healthy environments for our children where they can form supportive, loving attachments with others.

5. Any relevant experience working with children

6. References (and yes, you should check these!)

If you are like the rest of us, you will also have to actively recruit and ask for volunteers. Before you begin recruiting folks to volunteer, ask your senior pastor if there is anyone who should not be asked. Your senior pastor is more likely to be aware of any people in your congregation who are not legally allowed to work with children or who it would be a good idea to keep from working with children. Once you've had this conversation, look over your job descriptions and imagine the people who you would like to see filling each role. Write down these names and reach out to them. Be sure to reference the job descriptions and tell people why you thought of them for this role. Beyond explaining the role, also be sure that you remind them of your vision statement and your commitment to creating a culture of Safe Sanctuaries. Remember to make safety a priority and not an afterthought once you've already brought new recruits on board.

Once your volunteers have signed on, run both a state and federal background check to make sure volunteers do not have a history of child abuse or violence. It is important to do both to have a thorough history. Depending on who your church or annual conference uses to complete these background checks, you may receive lots of information including things like traffic tickets and credit history, or you may receive a simple report that says whether a given person is eligible or ineligible to work with kids. Regardless of what the report looks like, it is a crucial piece of information! This simple check has the power to keep our kids safe, and it also eases some of the fears our parents have about leaving their children in our care.

After completing a background check on anyone who will work with or support kids, you must print the report and lock it in a special background check cabinet. Make a note to run another background check on this person in a couple of years, or use a background check service that stays on top of this for you. This time frame will be different depending on which service you use and the type of background check that service runs. If you do a state and federal check that includes fingerprinting, you will have five years before you need to run another check. These are the most expensive checks, and often churches will choose to do a check that doesn't include fingerprinting. These checks should be rerun every two years. If your church uses a database for member data, check to see if the database has a background check plug-in to help you keep track of this information.

All these background-checked adults are considered mandatory reporters. This means they must report any suspected or confirmed abuse of the children in their care. Many churches will ask that volunteers who suspect abuse tell the person overseeing ministry with children. This person will then make an official report to the police along with the pastor. If the person suspected of abuse is a staff member or pastor, then this should also be reported to a staff-parish relations committee.

> **This simple check has the power to keep our kids safe, and it also eases some of the fears our parents have about leaving their children in our care.**

3. Two background-checked non-related adults all the time (both in-person and online)

I have a dear friend who once told me that, of all the Safe Sanctuary rules, this one was the most important to her. She told me a story of a person she knew who passed every background check, yet had inappropriate conversations with kids whenever the person was alone with a youth. To her, the best way to keep everyone safe is to never let an adult be alone with any number of children.

I happen to agree with her assessment. It is essential that you have two non-related adults present wherever children are. You will need two adults present when gathering in the nursery, the sanctuary, classrooms, fellowships halls, the church gym, an office, or even outside. This also extends to digital spaces like Zoom rooms and other live online meetings. Best practices would also include those like the one I described at East End United Methodist Church, where two adults were available to usher children to the bathroom during the service.

Our central goal in all of this is for our kids to feel safe at church. It's important then to recognize that sometimes safety looks like privacy. Privacy can create bodily autonomy. Privacy can also allow space to share a traumatic experience with a safe adult. This is a gray area and must be considered when shaping your culture for safer sanctuaries.

The bathroom is one place where it's important to create a sense of safety and privacy. Here are a few tips for when kids need to go to the restroom:

- Have one adult open the bathroom door and leave it open so each adult can see the other. One adult will stand with the child, and the other adult will look to see if anyone else is in the bathroom. Never send a child into the restroom alone without checking the restroom first.
- If there is no one else in the bathroom and the child does not need help while going to the restroom, both adults can wait outside of the main bathroom door.
- If the child needs assistance in the bathroom, one adult should stand at the stall with the child while the other adult stands at the open bathroom door watching the interaction between the child and the adult at the stall.

One-on-one pastoral care is another scenario when safe privacy is essential. Here are a few tips for creating a sense of safe privacy in this situation:

- Invite a non-related adult to be present.
- Keep the door of the office or meeting room open, and have the other adult sit outside the office where that person can see the pastor and hear what is being said.

Notes

_____

_____

_____

_____

_____

_____

_____

_____

_____

_____

Our central goal in all of this is for our kids to feel safe at church.

_____

_____

_____

_____

_____

_____

_____

_____

_____

_____

_____

On occasion, you may not have enough adults for there to be two non-related adults in every situation where a child is present. While this should be avoided if at all possible, this is where a "roamer" can come in handy. A roamer is an adult who roams the premises and can show up at any time. This person is often the one overseeing ministry with kids and families and can ensure that policies and procedures are being followed in every space.

4. Traveling and Off-Site Ministry with Kids

If you are traveling or going off-site with kids, the general rules remain the same.

1. All adults must be background checked and eligible to work with kids.
2. There must always be two non-related adults with kids.

Whether you are in a car or van, at camp, visiting a museum, taking a day-trip, or anything else, the culture of safer sanctuaries must permeate through your ministry area regardless of location.

5. Healthy Touch

If you were meeting me for the first time, you probably wouldn't guess that I don't like hugs. I look like a person who would love a hug! Despite that appearance though, I have never really liked hugging. My touch quota gets filled quickly, and I have had some past experiences with unwanted and unhealthy touch that have discouraged me from freely giving or receiving hugs. That doesn't mean that I never want a hug, but instead that no one should assume that they know what sort of mood I am in, or whether I want to be touched from one moment to the next. The best thing you can do is ask me, "Can I give you a hug?" and then let me say either yes or no.

While this is only my personal experience with touch, everyone falls somewhere on the spectrum of how much they desire physical touch. This can change every day because of changes to our situation, our comfort level, or our mood. Our kids are on this spectrum, too. Sometimes they want a hug, sometimes they want someone to ruffle their hair, and sometimes they would rather not.

Just as importantly, our kids are also learning how to communicate when they do or don't want to be touched. One awesome opportunity in ministry with children and families is that we can offer our kids practice in communicating their consent for touch and asking for consent from others. In a culture of safer sanctuaries, everyone should be sensitive to the concept of healthy touch and consent. Similarly, we can keep our eyes open for these learning opportunities and navigate them based on the age and individual preferences of each child. Kids mirror the actions and words of their caregivers. To help kids practice healthy touch, ask for

One awesome opportunity in ministry with children and families is that we can offer our kids practice in communicating their consent for touch and asking for consent from others.

their consent. If you have a child you would like to pat on the shoulder, ask the child if you can before you do it.

Obviously, there are limits to this. You can't get verbal consent to hold a baby, and it is never appropriate for a tween to sit in your lap whether that tween wants to or not. It's important to use age-appropriate boundaries and logic when thinking through healthy touch scenarios. Nevertheless, it is helpful to let the child initiate and lead you. If you've set up a culture where children feel heard and respected, you can trust them to tell you what works for them.

6. Annual Training for All Volunteers and Ministry Leaders

Training is important, and not just the first time you go through it. Think about all the things that you've learned in your life, all the things you didn't know how to do that are now second nature. Think about how many times you needed to practice each behavior before it finally stuck. Think about how many times you needed a reminder about what to do and when. This is the exact same situation when it comes to building a culture of safer sanctuaries.

If possible, training should take place every year for everyone involved in ministry with children. There are many ways to train, whether meeting in-person, using online videos and quizzes, or listening to podcasts. Whatever way you choose, it's important to remind and refresh everyone on the guidelines that help our children feel safe at church. This should include Safe Sanctuaries policies, first-aid (and CPR for staff members), and the policies and procedures used for successful ministry at your church.

7. Safe Spaces

Our physical space communicates how we view our kids. If we want to communicate that they are important to us and that they are invited to be full members in our congregations, we need to create clean, decluttered, warm, and bright spaces for our kids. Before you tackle this step, go to the spaces where your children meet. What do you notice? Do you feel at ease, or do you feel anxious? How far away are these rooms from the rest of the action at your church? How easy would it be for a new person to find this space?

Once you have assessed your spaces, work toward creating physical spaces that create a sense of ease for your kids. Begin by cleaning and sanitizing each room. Throw out any broken toys or unsafe materials that have found their way into your classrooms. Make sure all shelves or bookcases are screwed into the walls. Install doors that either have a windowpane or are half-doors that allow for your roamer to easily see whatever is happening in each space.

Notes

If we want to communicate that they are important to us and that they are invited to be full members in our congregations, we need to create clean, decluttered, warm, and bright spaces for our kids.

A culture of safer sanctuaries also includes the way we manage our groups. This is often called "classroom management" and refers to the way we navigate the different needs of each participant. Many groups will create a shared covenant about how each person will engage with the group and the space. This includes adult leaders. For instance, an adult should never yell or hit anyone else, and an adult should never make a child sit outside of a gathering space alone.

Another way of creating safe spaces and managing group dynamics involves making sure that your adult-to-child ratio is in a good range. Here are the ratios we should be following based on the age-level of the children

- 0-12 months—2 adults, 8 kids max (1:4)
- 1-3 years—2 adults, 12 kids max (1:6)
- 3-5 years—2 adults, 20 kids max (1:10)
- School-age—2 adults, 24 kids max (1:12)

When you reach the maximum number of kids for a given age group, it is time to start another group in a different space. Ministry with children often requires groups of different age levels to mix together. In these situations, abide by the lowest ratios to ensure the safety of the youngest children who often need the most supervision.

8. Registration and Permission Forms for Kids

As a parent, I tend to dislike the number of registration and permission forms I have to fill out for my child. It can be time-consuming and meticulous. I can only imagine what it was like for my mom who had to fill them out for five children! As a pastor, I try to keep these forms as simple as possible while also keeping my database as accurate as possible, so that I am not asking for the same things from parents over and over.

Nevertheless, churches do need some vital pieces of information about the children in their care to keep them safe. When a new family begins attending, you will want to have them fill out a family form that asks for the following information:

1. The names and pronouns of each member of the family
2. Birthdates and grade level for each child
3. Allergies for each child
4. Any modifications or accommodations each child might need
5. Who is allowed to pick up each child (This is especially important for foster families.)
6. Photo and video release (Include check boxes that allow for different levels of photo and video release.) For example, I am okay my son's photo being

> As a pastor, I try to keep these forms as simple as possible while also keeping my database as accurate as possible, so that I am not asking for the same things from parents over and over.

taken at church. I am okay with that photo being used for print publications when I have been asked directly. I am not okay with that photo being posted online. If given a blanket release, I am one of the parents who will never give permission. However, I will sign a form that allows me to opt-out of photos and videos being posted to social media.

7. Best ways to contact the family (include various options like text message, social media, email, phone, or by mail)

Each year at our kickoff, I ask families to fill out a new registration form. This allows our team to check in, find out any new updates about the family, and keep our database up to date. This up-to-date data, like new allergies, new accommodations, or new phone numbers, will keep our kids safe.

9. A Check-in and Check-out Process

Setting up a check-in and check-out process can be as easy as a clipboard with a spreadsheet on it. At check-in, you need to know the name of the child, the name of the caretaker leaving the child in your care, a contact number if you need that person, any allergies the child might have, and, if the child is young, when the child needs to eat again. This list is essential if you have to leave or evacuate the classroom for any reason—fire, flood, or even a trip to the playground. This roster helps you keep track of everyone you are responsible for.

At pick-up time, you can check the identification of the caretakers if you do not know them personally to make sure they are who they say they are and release the child to them. On your list, mark the time when the child was picked up and ask the caretakers to initial the spreadsheet indicating they have picked up their child.

Some check-in/check-out technologies can do this work for you. I have used a few of these systems, but I always end up back with a clipboard and matching number stickers that go on the kids and the parents. I find the clipboard method offers me time to talk to the families at drop-off and pick-up times. The fancy systems make it more efficient but getting to have these conversations allows me to incorporate more warm and fuzzy feelings like I used to get when I was a child at church.

By the time I was about eight years old, I was allowed to walk myself to Sunday school. My parents trusted that I would get to the classroom without getting too distracted by the stained glass or some other curiosity, and they knew that the teacher would get me settled into the classroom without much fuss. Usually, that is exactly what happened. I was a responsible child, and everyone at the church knew who I was and who I belonged to. There was no formal check-in policy, no one asked if I could eat the goldfish crackers, and no one worried about whether they would be able to find my parents if I needed something.

It's easy to convince ourselves that this is what church is supposed to feel like, that this kind of casual familiarity is the ideal that we should treasure. When we

Notes

> The fancy systems make it more efficient but getting to have these conversations allows me to incorporate more warm and fuzzy feelings like I used to get when I was a child at church.

Perhaps the the love and intimacy found in our communities takes a slightly different shape than in generations past, but it is not lessened by these types of policies and procedures.

think about setting up formal processes, we may be afraid that we are removing this comforting familiarity and the warm feelings that come along with being in a place where everyone knows one another.

But it doesn't have to be this way. Safety protocols are not opposed to comfort and familiarity, they just serve as a backstop, a way to ease fear and anxiety so that everyone can love and know one another. Perhaps the love and intimacy found in our communities takes a slightly different shape than in generations past, but it is not lessened by these types of policies and procedures.

10. Communication with Kids

Unlike in youth ministry, most of my communication with kids happens in person during one of the many programs for which I am responsible. I don't text, email, call, or direct message them personally. I talk to them when I see them in person. When we do talk, we have some awesome conversations about school, pets, siblings, and all sorts of other things. I also make sure to have these conversations in front of other leaders or their parents. It's important to me that the kids feel comfortable talking about whatever is on their hearts and minds and that someone else is within earshot just in case.

Having someone else know the content of our conversations is rooted in pastoral care. I want other adults to know what our children love, feel, think, dislike, and simply what they are going through. It helps us create relationships with the kids in our care. It helps us all be present for them, and that is what being a children's pastor is all about!

If you do find yourself in a situation where you are going to use a method of communication that isn't an in-person conversation with a child, use a service that can be accessed by other volunteers and staff. This means setting up any social media accounts your ministry may have with an email address that any staff or volunteer can access. Accounts should not be created using a personal email address for several reasons, but particularly because of the need for transparency.

Some great platforms have been created to stay connected safely to groups of kids. Personally, I like texting services like REMIND and video messaging services like Flipgrid. When using these services, you can set up accounts for other background-checked adults that allow them to stay connected with the kids with whom they have relationships.

Signs of Abuse in Children

Signs of abuse have already been discussed earlier in this resource, but I want to highlight a few of these signs that you should pay specific attention to when working with children. If you notice any of these, first ask the children about whatever you have noticed, and note how they respond. Then, ask the caregiver about it at pick up and take note of their response as well. Try to avoid jumping to conclusions, but trust your gut, especially if you have implemented a culture where every child feels heard and respected.

1. Signs of Physical Abuse
   a. Bruises in places where a child wouldn't normally get bruises
   b. Frequent injuries
   c. Physically aggressive with self and others
   d. The child tells you he/she is being hurt by someone
2. Signs of Emotional or Verbal Abuse
   a. Shows low self-esteem
   b. Isolates from others
   c. Appears depressed
   d. Yells or curses at others excessively
   e. Seems overly nervous in unusual situations
3. Signs of Sexual Abuse
   a. Talks about sex and other related topics
   b. Initiates inappropriate physical touch from other kids and adults
   c. Has difficulty walking
   d. Demonstrates potty training regression
   e. Has bruises on private parts
   f. Tells you he/she is being sexually assaulted
4. Signs of Neglect
   a. Poor hygiene
   b. Persistent hunger or thirst
   c. Overly self-reliant

How to Respond When You Suspect a Child Is Being Abused

If you suspect one of the children in your care is being abused in any way, it is your moral responsibility to care for that child. Any discomfort you may feel pales in comparison to the pain the child is experiencing. All of God's children deserve to thrive, and they need trusted adults in their lives to do so.

If the suspected perpetrator is a church volunteer or staff person:

1. Believe the child. Care for the child.
2. Report your suspicions to the senior pastor, unless the senior pastor is the suspected perpetrator. In that case, report your suspicions to the staff-parish relations committee or a similar oversight board.

Notes

> Try to avoid jumping to conclusions, but trust your gut, especially if you have implemented a culture where every child feels heard and respected.

105

3. Remove volunteer or staff from contact with all kids.

4. Contact parents/caregivers.

5. Call your local Department of Social Services.

If the suspected perpetrator is a family member or friend of the child:

1. Believe the child. Care for the child.

2. Report your suspicions to the senior pastor.

3. Call your local Department of Social Services.

Conclusion

A while back, I helped lead a large research study on the present and future states of ministry with families. As part of this project, we got to interview kids about God, faith, and church. These sweet kids articulated a deep belief in a loving and forgiving God. They told us about how much they loved going to church—a safe place where they belonged. These kids went to their churches a couple of times a month, and they knew that when they were there, they were loved and safe.

That's what Safe Sanctuaries can provide for every child who walks into one of our spaces—a safe space to find a loving God. While it takes a lot of work and may feel overwhelming at times, this result, the kind of safe space where a child's faith can grow and thrive, is worth it. Our families are looking for faith communities that care for each person holistically, just as God does. Be the hands and feet of Jesus. Be the safe space where everyone belongs. That is my prayer for all of our ministries.

That's what Safe Sanctuaries can provide for every child who walks into one of our spaces—a safe space to find a loving God.

CHAPTER 14
Safer Sanctuaries for Youth

Kelly Peterson

Youth Ministry Is Different

Our world is constantly changing and nowhere is the pace of this change more evident than when it comes to young people. Over the past twenty years, social media and mobile phones have changed the way that everyone communicates, especially youth. Easy access to information has reshaped the world that young people live in today. In turn, the way we interact with youth has also changed.

While all ministry is based on relationships, youth ministry places an even greater emphasis on the relational. I have told many parents that they should view it as a blessing when their teenager finds a Christian role model who is not related to them; someone to guide them, minister to them, and help them in their faith journey.

Yet all of this leaves us with a fundamental challenge. How do we create youth ministries that are safe while also creating space for the relational ministry that young people are seeking?

Youth ministries present a complex set of dynamics as leaders work with young people who are exploring their own sense of identity, their new-found independence, and often, their first taste of an individual life of faith beyond what has been taught to them by their parents. I have worked with many churches as they struggle to find answers to this challenge. The solution is not simple, but guidance can be found in the best practices of Safe Sanctuaries ministry. Over the years, the lessons we have learned from Safe Sanctuaries have changed the way that youth ministry looks. The practices and guidelines of Safe Sanctuaries have encouraged us to change the dynamics of these vital relationships and re-evaluate the shape that they should take.

I do not simply mean that we must put down a policy on paper, but that we must intentionally embed the elements of healthy boundaries and Safe Sanctuaries into everything that we do. This requires weaving these practices into every element of the ministry program until everyone knows that this "the way we do things around here." This ultimately leads to a healthier ministry for everyone involved, both youth and the adults who serve in youth ministry.

When I first began with youth and camping ministries as a member of the conference staff, I was committed to conference-wide guidelines, education, training, and recordkeeping. There were challenges. I received pushback. I was told, "it couldn't be done." Nevertheless, I made a commitment that every conference event would demonstrate that it could be done. We would work with churches to find solutions that helped us overcome challenges, and we would provide training and resources so that everyone could create a safe youth ministry program. I hope the lessons I've learned on this journey of commitment and the best practices I've discovered will be helpful as you search for answers for your community and your ministry.

Healthy Relationships

What does a healthy relationship in youth ministry look like? It can be a challenge to be a youth's biggest ally and a mentoring adult while also maintaining a safe and healthy relationship for all involved. However, it is possible, and the key elements are transparency and maintaining best practices. I regularly tell my staff and volunteers that perception is 99% of what we do. The way youth, parents, pastors, and the public perceive your relationship with youth and your ministry can make or break your ministry. It is vital that everyone involved in ministry maintain an attitude of respect, patience, professionalism, courtesy, tact, and maturity to serve as a positive model for children, youth, and adults. As we proceed, let's take a look at a few areas where youth ministry leaders and volunteers often struggle or run into conflicts around maintaining healthy relationships, transparency, and best practices for creating safer sanctuaries.

The way youth, parents, pastors, and the public perceive your relationship with youth and your ministry can make or break your ministry.

Rule of Three

This is the most consistent challenge for many ministry programs. The "rule of three" means that no adult should ever be alone with a young person. It also requires that the two adults not be related and not be in a relationship. Churches often struggle to find one youth leader, let alone, two unrelated adults who are not in a relationship. However, there are ways to approach these challenges while also upholding the rule of three.

- **Ask for another adult volunteer, perhaps a parent who drops off youth for youth group, to be your second adult during drop-off and pick-up times.** This is the time when leaders are most at risk of being alone with a youth. If you only have one youth leader and it is not possible to have two adults present during the whole program time, other youth, who are not your child, can fill the role of this "third person." This not optimal and should be avoided if at all possible, but it can create an environment where you, as a leader, are not alone with a youth and where your actions and words can be witnessed by the entire group.

- **Find a volunteer to be a floater.** A floater is an adult who "floats" in and out of program spaces unannounced. Ideally, this person would also carry a radio allowing contact with other program leaders. It is often easier to fill this role with a volunteer because the floater is not required to be involved directly with either children or youth. This solution works well when multiple programs are happening in the building at one time (for example: Sunday school, midweek programs).

- **Be proactive in knowing your numbers.** Communicate regularly with your youth and their families about your events each week and find out if they will be able to attend. If you are at risk of having only one youth show up to a particular event and you are the sole leader, then move the event to a public place rather than risk being alone in a building with only one youth. In addition, let both the family and your supervisor know the situation, including where youth group will be held (for example: a coffee shop, ice cream parlor) and where they can drop off and pick up their child.

- **The rule of three applies to transportation too.** I always receive a lot of questions and pushback around this topic, and it always starts with the same concern: "If I don't pick them up, they won't attend youth group." This is frustrating, but the fact remains that you should never put yourself in a position of being alone with a youth. In the past, I have worked to help youth who live close to each other gather at one person's house to be picked up or dropped off as a group. I also recommend having parents help with transportation as much as possible to help alleviate this concern. In the worst-case scenario, when it is unavoidable and a youth leader finds himself/herself alone in a vehicle with a youth, then the youth leader should call someone, whether it is the youth's family, another staff member, or a supervisor, and keep an open phone line during the car trip.

- **Never seek out youth to spend one-on-one time.** Singling out youth for a special outing is highly discouraged and could easily be perceived as crossing a boundary, even if done with the best intentions. This is also a useful time to address the difficulties of maintaining boundaries as a mentor who is trying to connect with a youth. This can be a tricky dynamic. No one wants to be seen as uncool, but, as the adult leader, you must be aware of your language, your dress, and what personal information you disclose to your youth. Additionally, when discussing topics where your views might differ from those of their parents, it is important to keep these discussions at a higher level. Using phrases like "some people think" rather than "I think" as you explore a topic allows for a healthy discussion without the youth feeling torn between their family's values and those of a person they look up to.

- **Always follow protocol and best practices when involving other adults in your program.** At a minimum, any adults who will be in continual contact with youth should be trained in your policies and procedures. Additionally, any adult in this situation should undergo a background check. For one-off events, churches may not have the resources necessary to run background checks on the large groups of volunteers required. For these circumstances, I suggest running a check through the national sex offender registry, which is free, and holding a volunteer orientation that covers your policies and

Notes

_____

_____

_____

_____

_____

_____

_____

_____

_____

_____

> No one wants to be seen as uncool, but, as the adult leader, you must be aware of your language, your dress, and what personal information you disclose to your youth.

practices for the group. These volunteers should also be under the direct supervision of ministry staff who are fully vetted and trained.

Communication with Youth

Communication is another area that leaves both youth and youth leaders highly vulnerable, especially in our increasingly digital world. According to a survey done by Common Sense Media in 2018, three out of every five teens preferred using text or social media to communicate over in-person or "live" communication. This preference has only increased since the COVID-19 pandemic.[1] The general rule in youth ministry is that all conversations should be done in the open. This rule applies to electronic conversations as well. Do not isolate yourself to have a private conversation with a youth. Face-to-face conversations can take place away from the group but should always be held in the open in view of others. Electronic communications should always be transparent as well. Here are a few more tips on how to effectively, transparently, and safely communicate with youth as a part of your ministry work.

- **The vast majority of digital messages should be informational only.** These messages should include necessary information for events like the time, location, and any other pertinent information. Ideally, these messages should be sent as group texts or from a shared email address that multiple adults can access.

- **A quick check-in or word of encouragement can build relational connections.** Simple, straightforward, and limited messages like "Good luck on your test" or "Are you feeling better?" are acceptable and can help to build connection with youth. However, if a response goes beyond something simple like, "Thanks," you should tell the youth that you would be happy to continue the conversation in person and arrange to do so in clear view of others.

- **Any online profile used to communicate with youth should be open and accessible by other adults.** I often request that my staff create a separate online profile for their interactions with youth and that this log-in information be made available to youth ministry staff. Similarly, a profile can be created in the name of the youth ministry and shared by staff who can then communicate with youth while also maintaining transparency with other staff members. Furthermore, I ask that staff never be the person to "friend" or request to "follow" a youth, as this can be perceived as crossing a boundary. Finally, I regularly remind staff that anytime they engage with someone based on their employment or association with our ministry, they represent the ministry and need to abide by our digital communications policy. Every ministry program should have a policy like this. Ours is included in the appendix on page 245.

- **Never promise to keep secrets when a youth wants to confide in you about something that is going on.** I am always up front with youth when we talk and tell them that if they want to share something about someone harming them, them harming themselves, or them wanting to harm others,

> A quick check-in or word of encouragement can build relational connections.

110

then it is my responsibility as an adult who is responsible for keeping them safe to tell others who can give them the support they need to stop the harm.

- **Invite a local agency that specializes in online risks for youth to speak with parents and youth.** Invite parents and youth to participate together and let the group provide insight about how to enjoy safe online activities and maintain safe and healthy communication.

- **Be aware of how the relationships and interactions between your youth and other adults, interns, and youth.** According to the National Society for the Prevention of Cruelty to Children, there are seven distinctive steps in grooming a young person for abuse:

  - **Targeting the victim**—Abusers often choose someone that they feel is vulnerable and an easy target.

  - **Using their position**—In a ministry setting, the groomer often has power and prestige due to their age, seniority, expertise, connections, or by presenting themselves to the youth as the person "who gets them."

  - **Gaining Trust**—This often happens by providing the youth with extra attention, gifts, and in-person or online compliments and messages. This is where transparent avenues of communication become essential.

  - **Fulfilling a Need**—Groomers often provide a listening ear and persuade their victim to be alone with them to talk. They also emphasize the empathy or sympathy they have for their victim's situation whether it be lack of friends, parents who do not understand them, the absence of a romantic relationship, or other similar teenage frustrations.

  - **Isolating the Victim**—At this point, the groomer convinces their victim to cut themselves off from friends and family and persuades the youth to have an extended secret interaction with them.

  - **The End Goal**—The abusive and exploitative behavior begins.

  - **Maintaining Control**—Abusers will often use scare tactics, threats, and guilt to keep the abuse secret and maintain the status quo.

- **Educate youth and parents on all Safe Sanctuaries policies and practices.** As you shape and implement your Safe Sanctuaries policy for your ministry, hold informational meetings, publish your policy and practices publicly, and provide a space for open discussion so that the whole congregation is aware of expectations when interacting with young people. If your abuse prevention policy is only known to leaders, staff, and volunteers, then it will not become a part of the culture at your church. The most effective abuse prevention plans are ones that are so deeply woven within the ministry and life of a church that they become innate.

Special Events and Travel

Unique ministry settings often present some of the biggest challenges for youth ministry leaders and staff. As we've discussed, youth ministry comes with unique

Notes

> If your abuse prevention policy is only known to leaders, staff, and volunteers, then it will not become a part of the culture at your church.

complexities, and these only become harder to navigate when ministry moves beyond the confined area of the church building and into more public spaces. Let's spend some time looking at some of the special considerations and intentional adaptation that are essential for creating safe and healthy ministry in these more unique settings.

- **It is important that you set guidelines and expectations before lock-ins.** Lock-ins are a staple of youth ministry, and many view them as a rite of passage, but they also provide a unique set of challenges for maintaining safe and healthy practices. First and foremost, the rule of three should be applied to all areas of the building. Second, there needs to be a clear division of sleeping areas for each gender. Adults should also take shifts in pairs, staying awake and supervising the youth, at least until all youth are asleep. This essentially requires that more than two adults be present for lock-ins. It is also recommended to recruit volunteers for specific shifts so that fresh volunteers can relieve youth workers during the night. If this is not possible, set regular times to wake and check on youth after all youth are asleep. This check should be carried out by both of the two adults present.

- **When traveling with youth, establish guidelines about where youth should be at all times and where they can gather together to hang out.** In the absence of firm guidelines, it will be tempting for youth to gather in one another's rooms. This should be avoided if at all possible. As in every situation, the rule of three should be implemented as well. If there are multiple areas where youth are gathering, assign one youth worker to be a designated floater. If you are gathering in one area of a hotel, say by the pool, and someone needs to go back to the room for a forgotten item, two adults should accompany the youth to retrieve the item if at all possible. If maintaining supervision ratios is a challenge, then send three youth (preferably not youth who regularly hang out together or who are in a relationship), or one adult and two non-related youth.

- **Set expectations for youth and discuss boundaries when gathering in public.** While it is not likely, predators have sought out victims at publicized youth events. When gathering for public events, set times for check-ins and remind youth that they need to be at all scheduled events. Have a plan if your hotel is in a different location than the event, and set times when groups will return to the hotel. I have also found that a group text app is helpful during events to send information and updates to a large group at the same time.

- **Try to arrange in advance for rooms to be grouped together.** When staying somewhere overnight, supervision at night is important. Adults should be the last to bed and active in supervising all rooms until everyone is asleep. One trick of the trade is to put tape across the hotel door of youth as they go in for the night. If the tape is broken later in the night or in the morning, then you know if youth have left their room.

As we've discussed, youth ministry comes with unique complexities, and these only become harder to navigate when ministry moves beyond the confined area of the church building and into more public spaces.

Harm From Within

One out of every three sexual abuse cases involve peer-to-peer abuse by other children or young people who are still minors. Over the last five years, there has been a 300% increase in reported cases. According to Ministry Safe, adult male offenders typically begin abusing others when they are approximately thirteen or fourteen years of age.[2] This disturbing trend has made another layer of awareness necessary and reinforces that importance of best practices to prevent harm within your youth group. It is essential to know the signs of peer-to-peer bullying and abuse. These signs include:

- Withdrawing from or avoiding activities or people a youth previously enjoyed
- Trouble sleeping or excessive sleeping
- Being easily and uncharacteristically brought to an emotional response of anger, tears, or aggravation
- Change in school effort or attendance
- Obsessing over social media posts
- Substance abuse
- Self-doubt or lack of self-esteem
- Aggression toward others
- Physical injury

In addition to these signs, be aware that in dangerous dating and relationship situations, the abusive partner will often try to isolate the victim from friends, family, and regular activities. The abuser will also often display controlling behavior over the youth's phone and social media use. The youth who is being controlled will often show signs that they are afraid or worried about upsetting their partner.

Self-harm is another disturbing trend among youth. Self-harm is different from a suicide attempt. Instead, it is an extreme emotional reaction and unhealthy coping mechanism to deal with difficult emotions. Youth may see it as a release from their pain or current situation and a way to exert some control over their life. The most common form of self-harm is cutting, but there are other methods. Burning oneself, for instance, can often be a method of release. Reports indicate that 30% of teenage girls and 10% of teenage boys engage in some measure of self-harm. This trend has also rapidly increased in recent years. Discussions about self-harm on social media have created awareness, but have also unfortunately normalized this behavior for young people. Some signs of self-harm include:

- Wearing clothing that covers up injuries or scars, especially when the clothing is not temperature or seasonally appropriate
- Isolating oneself to spend alone time
- Negative self-talk
- Brushing off injuries as the result of being "clumsy"
- Changing interest levels about being with people or engaging in activities in which they previously enjoyed participating

One out of every three sexual abuse cases involve peer-to-peer abuse by other children or young people who are still minors.

_____

_____

_____

_____

_____

_____

_____

_____

_____

_____

_____

There is rarely a single solution that meets the needs of every situation. However, it is crucial that open and frank discussions take place for all participants involved to feel comfortable.

Inclusiveness in Youth Ministry

Questions of sexuality and gender have roiled within the church for years, but our task here is not to solve issues of polity, but to encourage safety, healthy boundaries, and building flourishing ministries for all involved. It is not a matter of if you will face questions about inclusivity in your youth ministry, but a matter of when. In light of this reality, here are a few considerations that I have found useful when making decisions and policies involving LGBTQIA youth:

- Make no assumptions about a young person's sexual orientation or identity.
- Educate yourself and train your staff on proper use of terminology.
- Be intentional about creating a safe environment and culture by inviting awareness and providing training around homophobic language and bullying.
- Create a policy or behavior covenant that everyone, including youth, volunteers, and leaders, are aware of and commit to uphold.
- Everyday actions like using the bathroom can become complicated for transgender and gender non-conforming youth because our world often offers only two options: male and female. Consider whether all of your facility's restrooms must be gender specific or whether one could be made available to everyone. This need not be complicated. Covering the "Men" or "Women" sign with "All-gender restroom" is sufficient. Remember to do this for temporary, shared, or rental facilities also. When possible, I also encourage using private restrooms as an option when youth need to change clothes.
- Ensuring comfortable housing for LGBTQIA youth is often a challenge for overnight camps that have traditional all-male and all-female bunks or cabins. There is rarely a single solution that meets the needs of every situation. However, it is crucial that open and frank discussions take place for all participants involved to feel comfortable. Here are a few suggestions based upon different situations you might encounter:
  - There is not a one-size-fits-all housing policy for transgender or gender non-conforming youth. It is vitally important to openly communicate with the youth and their parents about their needs and desires to create the best solution. Some transgender youth may feel more comfortable housing with the gender that correlates with their full-time presentation and identity, while others will be more comfortable bunking with those who share their biological sex. If given the option, some may want to room with a few select friends or may prefer their own room. Some accommodation choices can be made easier if hotel-type rooms are available and the youth can choose their roommate. Again, it is important to work with the youth to create a reasonable accommodation that best suits everyone.
  - There is absolutely no reason why an LGBTQIA youth should not be allowed to bunk with their straight or cis peers. The primary concern in this situation is the possibility for bullying and harassment. Counselors

and chaperones should be trained to identify and deal with bullying and harassment and should seek support from youth directors or other leaders if it persists.

- With all of your youth, a profile sheet can be helpful when you are communicating with families. Gather information on your youth including their preferred pronouns, the gender they identify with, their preferred name to be called, and other relevant information. It is important to know who in their family knows about their preferences. You don't want to "out" a youth by communicating with their family.

General Statements and Types of Abuse

There are several fundamental guidelines that everyone involved in your youth ministry should agree to and strive to follow in all situations. These statements are as follows:

- While working with children and youth I will . . .
  - Treat all children, youth, and adults with respect and consideration.
  - Respect the rights of children, youth, and adults to decline being touched in ways that make them feel uncomfortable
  - Maintain an attitude of respect, patience, professionalism, courtesy, tact, and maturity as a positive role model for children, youth, and adults.
- In situations in which I work with children and youth, I will seek to . . .
  - Use positive guidance techniques, such as redirection, positive reinforcement, and encouragement rather than competition, comparison, and criticism.
  - Refrain from any behavior that could be considered abusive to children, youth, or adults, including physical abuse, emotional abuse, neglect, and sexual abuse.

In addition to these statements, volunteers and youth leaders should be trained about what the defined types of abuse might look like in a youth ministry setting.

- **Physical Abuse**—This is abuse in which a person deliberately and intentionally causes bodily harm. In situations specific to youth programming, this can be the result of physical punishment (for example, spanking or grabbing), withholding food or water, or using excessive exercise as punishment. Physical intervention is allowed only in the case of youth hurting themselves or another person.
- **Emotional Abuse**—This is abuse in which a person exposes young people to either spoken or unspoken violence or emotional cruelty. Emotional abuse sends a message to the youth that they are worthless, bad, unloved, and undeserving of love and care. In the context of youth programming,

Counselors and chaperones should be trained to identify and deal with bullying and harassment and should seek support from youth directors or other leaders if it persists.

Notes

_____

_____

_____

_____

_____

_____

_____

_____

_____

_____

_____

_____

this can take the form of put downs, playing favorites, hurtful nicknames, ignoring signs of bullying, and not giving equal attention to all participants.

- **Neglect:** This is abuse in which a person endangers the health, welfare, and safety of youth through negligence. In the context of youth programming, this can look like providing inadequate hydration, not seeking medical attention when a participant is injured or ill, or not allowing youth to eat, shower, or change clothes.

- **Sexual Abuse:** This type of abuse occurs when there is sexual contact between a youth and an adult or between a younger youth and an older youth who is operating from a position of power or authority. Sexual abuse can also include comments of a physical or sexual nature, unwanted physical contact such as hugging, lap-sitting, and shoulder rubs, or a lack of privacy for participants when showering or changing in front of adults or other youth-group participants.

Conclusion

Ministry is always evolving, and that is never more obvious than in the world of youth ministry. While this chapter has explored current trends and best practices that can help you and your fellow ministry workers keep both youth and adults who work with youth safe, I also encourage you to never feel that abuse prevention, education, and training is something that you can master. This is not a one-time thing, and there are always new lessons to be learned. It is essential that those of us in ministry stay current and seek new information and resources in the ever-changing landscape of youth ministry. As I discussed earlier, building a safer sanctuary and a flourishing ministry is not about creating a written policy, but about embedding these practices into the life of our ministry until they become a natural part of our work. When that happens, our communities, our ministries, and our youth will not only be safe, they will also be healthy, vibrant, and welcoming spaces for everyone.

> Ministry is always evolving, and that is never more obvious than in the world of youth ministry.

Notes

1. "Social Media, Social Life: Teens Reveal Their Experiences, 2018," Common Sense, https://www.commonsensemedia.org/research/social-media-social-life-teens-reveal -their-experiences-2018.
2. "The Risk," Ministry Safe website, https://ministrysafe.com/the-risk.

CHAPTER 15

Safer Sanctuaries for People with Disabilities

Lynn Swedberg

with the Disability Ministries Committee of The United Methodist Church

Why a Chapter on Disability?

Children and adults with disabilities are a diverse group of individuals found in every form of ministry discussed in this book. Therefore, you may wonder why a separate chapter is necessary. The simple answer is that there are specific concerns involving those who have disabilities that are essential to address in order to provide a safe space for everyone.

People with disabilities are the largest minority group in the United States, with one in four people reporting a disability that affects life activities such as walking, concentrating, making decisions, hearing, seeing, or independent living.[1] Every congregation and many families include members with disabilities.

As we endeavor to create safer sanctuaries for people with disabilities, we must start by addressing attitudes toward disability. Many of us are steeped in the medical model of disability that strives to cure or eliminate disability and considers all disabilities to be unfortunate. In contrast, a diversity/social model of disability celebrates that God creates each of us as unique beings, all equally valued in the body of Christ. This model points out that barriers of attitude and inaccessibility limit participation far more than physical or cognitive impairment.

People with disabilities also face discrimination and stereotyping. This type of discrimination is referred to as ableism. Ableism is at play when we assume that everyone can use stairs, see, hear, communicate, and think the same way, when accommodations are not provided, or when events are not held in accessible spaces. Both conscious and unconscious ableism maintain an underlying bias that nondisabled bodies and minds are better than disabled ones. Ableism also fosters a paternalistic belief that anyone with a disability needs protection and assistance with decision-making and most other tasks. Many see disabled adults as perpetual children who are asexual and are not reliable reporters.[2]

However, some disabled individuals do have increased medical needs and require physical assistance that often leaves them alone with their caregivers. They may lack access to transportation and be shut out of quality education and employment. These factors provide limited opportunities to develop protective relationships. Additionally, some disabled people have difficulty communicating or are unable to remove

_____

_____

_____

_____

_____

_____

_____

_____

_____

_____

themselves from harm's way. Some will trust all adults and take what they are told very literally. Others have not been taught to question authority or about personal boundaries. Together, all of these factors add up to an increased risk of abuse.[3]

Statistics vary widely but generally show that children with disabilities are between two to four times as likely as non-disabled children to experience physical abuse, sexual abuse, and neglect.[4] An inability to communicate, a lack of credibility, and the fear of losing their home and caregiver can all create barriers that cause many cases to remain unreported or uninvestigated.[5]

Around ninety-five percent of abuse is carried out by people known to disabled individuals, usually family members or outside care providers.[6] Adults with disabilities frequently experience domestic partner violence that may include withholding needed personal assistance and medication or destroying their medical equipment.[7] People with disabilities also experience financial exploitation at a higher frequency.[8] Additionally, many who live through abuse never receive follow-up support after the fact.[9]

Defining Vulnerable Adults

Everyone in our church community, both with or without disabilities, is covered by the Safe Sanctuaries policies that we put in place. Adults with disabilities, however, should not automatically be considered vulnerable in the legal sense. Most importantly, adults should never be lumped into policies written for the protection of children and youth. Historically, far too many policies have defined a vulnerable adult as someone with a mental, sensory, or physical disability. It is ableist when we patronizingly assume that someone with a disability should be treated as less competent than other adults in our ministries.

Your pastor and church leaders may have disabilities, and many congregational members have hidden disabilities. For safety policies to be meaningful, the definition of what constitutes a vulnerable adult must be nuanced and focus on individuals who are unable to

- recognize risk of or actual abuse
- communicate choices and consent, and
- remove themselves from potential or actual harm.

For clarity, vulnerable adults are people eighteen years of age or older who are unable to protect themselves from abuse, neglect, or exploitation. Even when individuals do meet the criteria to be considered vulnerable adults, our safety measures must not treat disabled adults as children.

Adults with disabilities who can understand risks, can express consent or nonconsent, and who can make informed decisions regarding risk should determine

For clarity, vulnerable adults are people eighteen years of age or older who are unable to protect themselves from abuse, neglect, or exploitation.

how these policies apply to them. In fact, these adults, along with parents of children with disabilities, should be consulted throughout the policy development process for their valuable expertise when shaping safety standards. Policies need to be crafted with flexibility so they do not become yet another barrier to full participation for people living with disabilities.

Here is an example of how policies can get in the way of ministry that was shared with our team recently:

> *Consider the case of a friend who lives alone but requires some supports to do so. She has a lovely voice, and she joined her church choir. She uses transportation shared by several other adults with disabilities, which sometimes causes her ride to be late in picking her up after choir practice. If my friend has to wait at the church for her ride, two unrelated adults, plus their spouses, must wait with her. She often skips choir practice if she knows her driver has to juggle several people's ride schedules and won't be able to pick her up exactly when choir practice ends. She is embarrassed to have so many people wait with her simply because she has a disability. Fortunately, her church values her and the choir members want a meaningful relationship with her, so they are working on a reasonable solution.*[10]

The rules in place at this congregation kept this woman from being a full, active member of the congregation and made her feel like an outsider because no one else in the choir had to follow the same rules.

Ultimately, all of us are vulnerable in some way and may experience abuse and exploitation. However, when we arbitrarily use a diagnosis to determine that some us require special treatment, we are discriminating and removing agency from adults with disabilities. As you develop policies, carefully consider the full implications of placing adults in a category that means they can never have personal conversations and must be always accompanied and under surveillance, even when using the restroom. We must use discernment if we want faith communities to be places where everyone is welcome and where everyone can flourish.

Vision and Need for Safe Ministries

What does a safe, nurturing place look and feel like for children and adults with disabilities? Safety can take on many forms, with prevention of abuse and neglect being one aspect of a wider conversation.

Many families and individuals who search for a disability-friendly church have encountered frequent rejection. Their defenses are on high alert from the moment they come through your doors. Families may be told that a congregation cannot meet their needs and they should look elsewhere because their children cannot sit still and behave in typical ways. Both in the church and the community, strangers

Notes

We must use discernment if we want faith communities to be places where everyone is welcome and where everyone can flourish.

119

Notes

may approach them and offer a prayer that their disability be taken away. People jump in and help without asking and become aggressively hostile when their unneeded and unsafe assistance is declined.

Parents and guardians of children with disabilities are protective because they have had to be fierce advocates and don't want to see their children hurt. They need reassurance and evidence that their child will be protected from abuse of any kind including exclusion, bullying, and unwanted touch or sexual attention. They also need to know that their loved ones will be safe from food and chemical allergies, contagious illnesses, and injury from inaccessible environments. Having congregational safety policies that address the needs and experiences of people with disabilities is a prerequisite for establishing trust.

These families and individuals are looking for the unconditional love and fellowship that churches can offer when at their best. To become a place where everyone belongs, congregations must see the whole person and recognize the gifts and strengths that individuals with disabilities bring. Change starts by asking disabled people already in our midst about how their needs can be better met. Ministry must always be done with, not for or to, disabled people. People with disabilities should be deeply involved in helping design procedures and programs that help everyone participate fully as disciples of Christ.

Protective Factors: Laying the Groundwork

Communications

Communication is key for any program, but is particularly important for ministries involving children, youth, or adults with disabilities. The following areas require attention to disability-related aspects of your policies and procedures:

- Does your enrollment form ask for both contact information and the best method to reach the participant and caregivers via email, video relay, text, or phone? You may need to contact someone if there is a delay or problem. Do not assume that everyone has internet or voice message access or that messages will always be relayed to someone in a residential setting.

- How can you collect information on strengths, interests, and needs in an inclusive manner? Consider creating a form to be completed by all parents of children and youth in your program. The form should ask about situations that might trigger a meltdown or other adverse responses from any participant and how that person can be best supported during this situation.

- What medical information do you need to know? How will you reassure those involved that the information will be kept confidential?

To become a place where everyone belongs, congregations must see the whole person and recognize the gifts and strengths that individuals with disabilities bring.

- Are all volunteers working with vulnerable populations considered mandated reporters, and what is the procedure to follow for making a report? Is state reporting information posted and easy to find? There may be different phone numbers for children and adults.
- How will you gather information from people who cannot speak and/or have intellectual disabilities that limit their ability to remember and explain?
- What are the procedures for handling money for an outing or fundraiser?
- For each participant, who is authorized to give permission to go on an off-campus activity, to sign a photo release, or to go to the emergency room?

Environmental Safety

Program spaces must also meet safety standards before a ministry is initiated. When putting together policies and working to make your ministries welcoming places for everyone, consider each of the following factors.

- **Undergo an accessibility audit.** Trustees and others should complete a building review to determine safety hazards and follow through with needed modifications to remove barriers to accessibility. The parking lot, church entrance, and restrooms are key spaces to check. Use the "Annual Accessibility Audit for Churches" to guide and record your process.[11]
- **Make a safety assessment.** Ensure that toxic substances such as cleaning supplies, sharp instruments, and items that could be swallowed are kept in locked storage when not in use. Safety also includes ways to prevent impulsive individuals from running away.
- **Implement a fragrance-free policy.** Since many people with disabilities have allergies and fragrance sensitivities, select unscented, environmentally friendly cleaning products. Remind volunteers and participants to avoid cologne and scented personal products.
- **Conduct a sensory assessment.** Replace flickering fluorescent light bulbs, or the whole fixture if possible, and eliminate any annoying noises in rooms used for ministry. Remove flashing lights that could trigger migraines or seizures.

Support Systems

A frequent question that arises when congregations set up programs that include children, youth, and adults with significant support needs is how to maintain and manage the levels of volunteer staff that are needed. The following are several ways to provide support, while also maintaining safety.

- **Roamers:** Assigned volunteers who are equipped with a system for immediate contact move throughout the building or wing and keep an eye on the groups. If they have received disability-specific training, they become the second adult when a volunteer needs to leave the room or can be on-call to help.

Notes

> Program spaces must also meet safety standards before a ministry is initiated.

_____

_____

_____

_____

_____

_____

_____

_____

_____

_____

_____

Your congregation needs to determine what level of support you can feasibly provide to people with disabilities.

- **Buddy System**: A trained adult volunteer (at least 4 years older than the person supported) is paired one-on-one with a participant. If the pair need to leave the common space for any reason, a second pair can accompany them or a roamer can be contacted.

- **Typical Peers**: In this set up, a same-aged youth works alongside a peer with support needs. They do not count toward the supervision ratio or two-adult rule but, when given training and feedback, can contribute significantly toward meaningful, engaged participation.

- **Family Members**: A family member may choose to stay during initial sessions until assured that volunteers know how to best support their loved one. Once they leave, inform them they are welcome to check in at any time and that they are expected to return and offer support during a behavior crisis. Unless they have met safety standards, they should not assist other participants and are not included in the two-adult count.

- **Personal Caregiver**: A group home staff member or other personal caregiver may accompany a participant. Unless they have met safety standards, these assistants should not assist with other group members and are not included in the two-adult count.

- **Program or Care Staff:** A larger program with many individuals needing extra support may hire a nursing or activity assistant. Such staff members would need to meet all program safety standards and complete all training.

- **Service Animals:** Some people use qualified service dogs to assist them with mobility, orientation, and other tasks. Trained dogs are barely noticeable and should be met with open hearts, a bowl of water, a designated outdoor relief area, and no attention from others while they work. We do not recommend that programs allow emotional support animals.

Medical Care and Caregiving

Your congregation needs to determine what level of support you can feasibly provide to people with disabilities and how to obtain additional assistance if individuals with higher support needs want to participate. Requiring all participants to be fully independent excludes many and is not in line with our calling and mandate as Christians. At the same time, accepting responsibility for a person's care before trained volunteers are available creates a high risk of injury for participants and volunteers alike.

- **Infection control and universal precautions.** COVID-19 has taught us all to develop strict cleaning protocols. These are particularly important for individuals with disabilities and chronic illness who may have compromised immune systems. Select items for program use that can be easily sanitized.

- **Dietary differences.** For an inclusive but safe experience, consider how you will meet the needs of individuals who may have food allergies or food intolerances, individuals who are unable to chew all textures, and individuals who will require some physical assistance. One church our team worked with had a basket with a variety of snack choices and invited parents to select the snacks that were safe for their children.

- **Restroom use.** Providing dignity and safety while assisting people in the bathroom is a major challenge. Procedures used for children are not appropriate for the privacy needs of adults. Unisex restrooms, family restrooms, and restrooms with at least one ADA-compliant stall work well for individuals who only need to be accompanied. When someone needs physical assistance with clothing or continence management, the person assisting needs to be trained, and a second adult should be just outside the stall or door. Ideally, at least one restroom should have a bench-style changing surface with a curtain or other privacy measure.

- **Transfers and mobility assistance.** Procedures should specify whether trained volunteers may assist individuals to move from one surface, such as a wheelchair, to another such as a car seat or toilet. Volunteers will need training to do this safely.

- **Medical events and first aid.** Policies should require leaders to be trained in first aid, including how to respond to seizures, choking, cardiac arrest, and allergic reactions. It is also important to outline your procedure for calling emergency medical personnel, notifying parents or caregivers, and documenting incidents where there is an injury or medical attention needed.

In Case of Emergency

All congregations should have written emergency policies and procedures that include disability-specific responses and interventions. These plans should be incorporated into training, kept readily available, and updated frequently as new information is available. Procedures will include what to do in case of accident or injury, elopement, fire, power outage, intruders intent on harm, and storms that are typical for the region. Questions to address include:

- How will someone who cannot hear know what is happening and what to do?
- How will someone who cannot see find the way out of the building or unsafe area?
- How will you reduce anxiety in a person who is triggered by sudden, loud noises and by changes in routine?
- How will you evacuate a wheelchair user if the elevator is not operational?
- Who needs to be contacted and where is that information kept?
- Are medical and sanitary supplies available in case of the need to shelter in place?
- Is appropriate emergency food available if needed for someone who is diabetic, has celiac disease, or is unable to chew typical food?

Notes

All congregations should have written emergency policies and procedures that include disability-specific responses and interventions.

123

Notes

_____

_____

_____

_____

_____

_____

_____

_____

_____

_____

_____

_____

Thoughtfully developed, regularly scheduled disability-related training for pastors, other church staff, and volunteers sets the stage for ministries in which everyone grows in faith and discipleship.

Transportation

Many people with disabilities have no independent way to get to church if it is not in their immediate neighborhood. Every congregation needs safe ways to provide access to transportation. Requiring people to find their own way to worship services or other events is a barrier to ministry.

- **Valet parking.** Drivers with difficulty walking appreciate being able to drive to a covered entrance and avoid struggling through rain or snow to enter the church. Liability and logistics should be carefully considered before implementing this type of plan.

- **Caravan.** Church leaders can organize for several cars to travel together and remain visible to one another as they pick up participants and take them home. This works best in a rural area with few other options.

- **Rule of three.** Some congregations allow volunteers to drive participants who reside together to a final drop-off point so that the driver is never alone with one person.

- **Church van.** Ideally, a church van with ramp or lift would be staffed with a designated driver and an unrelated assistant. The second volunteer helps participants board and engages them during the drive, makes needed phone calls, and assists with the wheelchair lift.

- **Ride-sharing services.** In larger communities, some churches use commercial drivers as a source of rides. This is safest for multiple participants who live at the same location, and it requires training for the person using the service.

- **Community transportation.** Many towns offer inexpensive door-to-door paratransit services to individuals with a qualifying disability. There may be limitations such as no service on Sundays, a requirement of 24-hour advance notice, or long rider wait times with little tolerance for the participant not being ready for a flexible pick-up time.

Training

Thoughtfully developed, regularly scheduled disability-related training for pastors, other church staff, and volunteers sets the stage for ministries in which everyone grows in faith and discipleship. Many youth and adults with intellectual disabilities also lack education in safety, self-advocacy, boundaries, and decision-making. The training introduced below is a necessary gift that congregations can provide their community. Training is a protective measure that can help make communities welcoming spaces where everyone thrives.

Training in Disability Awareness and Etiquette

Pastors, staff, and volunteers should all receive training in disability etiquette, the formal term for how one interacts appropriately with people with disabilities.[12] It is vital that people with disabilities are not made to feel that they are in the way or are only objects of ministry.

The language we use in our liturgies and sermons often harmfully equates disability with sin. For instance, consider the phrases "deaf to the cries of the poor" or "blind to what God is calling us to do." This type of language should be avoided. Similarly, it is best to avoid using mental illnesses, like schizophrenia and bipolar disorder, as metaphors. Whenever we set aside a group such as "the disabled," we are excluding people. Instead, language should reflect that all of us belong within the diverse body of individuals who make up the church.

Beyond the language used, individuals encounter spiritual abuse when well-meaning people insist on praying for a disability to be healed rather than asking people if, or for what, they want prayer. Relatedly, it is important to avoid assuming that someone cannot grasp faith concepts or to neglect offering religious education to individuals with significant intellectual disabilities.

Disability etiquette also includes learning how to guide a person who is blind—offer your elbow and have that person walk slightly behind you—and basic methods of communication with a deaf person. Training can also include learning how to assist with medical devices.

Respect for privacy and confidentiality also contributes to safety. Requesting or revealing a person's medical diagnoses or treatment information is never acceptable except to qualified first responders in an emergency.

Training in Support of Mental Health and Behavior

Since every congregation has individuals with mental health needs, training should include appropriate ways to safely support people in crisis. Mental Health First Aid is a curriculum offered by some annual conferences and readily available in many communities.[13] Organizations like the National Alliance on Mental Illness may be able to provide speakers or resources to help the congregation prepare to appropriately engage and assist someone experiencing symptoms of mental illness.[14] Understanding the impact of past trauma, which includes abuse, can make an important difference as we find ways to incorporate trauma-informed practices into our ministries.[15]

Our children and youth also have mental health and behavioral needs. Teachers can learn to avoid triggering behaviors by providing advance warning of transitions

Notes

> It is vital that people with disabilities are not made to feel that they are in the way or are only objects of ministry.

125

Notes
_____
_____
_____
_____
_____
_____
_____
_____
_____
_____
_____

Appropriate touch is an important topic for all of us.

between activities. Students may also need grounding and touch, but not from people. A sensory space to retreat to provides appropriate sensory inputs to help students experiencing sensory overload to manage their responses and avoid meltdowns. There are also easy-to-implement systems to help children recognize their emotional state (green = just right, yellow = starting to experience distress, red = angry or agitated) and find ways to regain their equilibrium and avoid out-of-control behavior.[16]

Training in Boundaries and Informed Decision-Making

Staff and volunteers should constantly be on the lookout for signs of abuse in all participants and how this might be communicated, especially by people who do not express themselves verbally.[17]

Training in personal boundaries, appropriate touch, and sexuality is seldom offered to young adults with developmental, intellectual, physical, or sensory disabilities, yet can protect against abuse.[18] Churches can offer these workshops by adapting secular curriculum and including a faith-based component.[19] Some programs help individuals develop a personalized self-care safety plan, a tool to remind them of ways to avoid risks and what to do in case their safety is violated.[20] When antisocial participant behavior is noted, modeling and instruction are needed, not punishment or rejection.

Appropriate touch is an important topic for all of us. Some of us are sensory sensitive and dislike being hugged or otherwise touched. Others love to hug, but avoid contact in one situation or another for personal reasons. One ministry leader and mother of an adult with a disability shared:

> I like the affirmative message one of our Special Olympics coaches started, when he greets athletes or if one starts to give a hug (they can get long and hard), he says, "Good friends shake hands," and he models that. The majority of athletes in our group are now hand shakers, fist bumpers, and/or air huggers (last one since the pandemic).[21]

Other greetings include using the American Sign Language sign for "peace," a high five, or elbow bumps. Groups might even use a poster with pictures of the greetings so individuals can point to their choice as they greet the leader and enter the room.

Training and support in decision-making are also key to promoting safety.[22] First, we need to provide information at a level the individual understands. Second, practice making small decisions builds the skills needed to make larger decisions. Individuals need to learn what options are available and be exposed to different viewpoints. Self-advocacy skills can be nurtured to help individuals feel comfortable expressing their viewpoint and saying no.

When Abuse Happens

While we focus most of our efforts on preventing abuse of any kind, abuse to vulnerable participants with disabilities may still happen. Later chapters in this resource cover procedures to follow for typical participants, but there are additional needs to consider when the person abused has a disability. In many situations, people with disabilities are not taken seriously when they report abuse. Communication differences play a big role, as a participant may not have the vocabulary to explain what occurred or may use an augmentative communication device.[23]

Even if your church follows best practices and offers disability-related accommodations through every step in your response, there may still be challenges once authorities get involved. A person with an intellectual disability is generally not familiar with the criminal justice system, and the interview process will likely be traumatizing. Make every effort to provide them with a support person during this process and advocate on their behalf with authorities. Be aware that many cases are not prosecuted and that lawyers work hard to discredit intellectually disabled people who make an accusation. The church will need to provide support at every level, especially after the case is closed and the effects of trauma remain. Support will usually involve referral to a safe outside counseling service skilled in helping people with disabilities.

Moving Forward to Create a Safe and Inclusive Community Where All Belong

Support within the Community

Environments that allow for abuse are never created in isolation, but rather come from several factors that leave individuals without a safety net. Our responsibility for safety does not end once participants leave the church building. In line with the Social Principles, we "call the Church and society to be sensitive to, and advocate for, programs of rehabilitation, services, employment, education, appropriate housing, and transportation."[24] We must work to ensure that our communities provide accessible and disability-friendly crisis care, safe and accessible housing, and access to in-home or residential respite services.

With the current lack of resources, we must help create employment and meaningful day and recreational programs that get individuals out into the community. We must advocate for funding for safe transportation and assistive devices that facilitate independence. Such services help develop the kinds of support circles that decrease the risk of abuse. We can go further and join coalitions to end abuse of disabled people and support people who have experienced it. We must not just talk and pray, we must act!

> **Our responsibility for safety does not end once participants leave the church building.**

_____

_____

_____

_____

_____

_____

_____

_____

_____

_____

_____

> **Together, we can help eradicate the ableism that causes society to tolerate ongoing abuse of people with disabilities.**

Hope for the Future

The awareness you have gained by reading this chapter gives you some of the tools necessary to help your congregation and community participate in breaking the cycle of abuse and becoming a space where all are valued and respected. Together, we can help eradicate the ableism that causes society to tolerate ongoing abuse of people with disabilities. We can join God's celebration of diversity in creation and overcome barriers to belonging and participation as we become safe places for all.

Notes

1. "CDC: 1 in 4 US Adults Live with a Disability," Centers for Disease Control and Prevention August 16, 2018, https://www.cdc.gov/media/releases/2018/p0816-disability.html.

2. Lynn Swedberg, "Understanding Ableism," Disability Ministries Committee of The United Methodist Church, https://umcdmc.org/resources/christian-education/theology/understanding-ableism/.

3. "Abuse and Exploitation of People with Developmental Disabilities," Disability Justice, https://disabilityjustice.org/justice-denied/abuse-and-exploitation/.

4. Leigh Ann Davis, "Abuse of Children with Intellectual Disabilities,", *The Arc*, March 1, 2011, http://www.thearc.org/wp-content/uploads/forchapters/Child%20Abuse.pdf.

5. Bernadette West and Sampada Gandhi, "Reporting Abuse: A Study of the Perceptions of People with Disabilities (PWD) Regarding Abuse Directed at PWD," *Disability Studies Quarterly*, Vol. 26. No. 1, 2006, https://dsq-sds.org/article/view/650/827.

6. "Crimes Against People with Disabilities," Office for Victims of Violence, 2018, https://ovc.ojp.gov/sites/g/files/xyckuh226/files/ncvrw2018/info_flyers/fact_sheets/2018NCVRW_VictimsWithDisabilities_508_QC.pdf.

7. "Survivors with Disabilities Facts," YWCA, September 2017, https://www.ywca.org/wp-content/uploads/Survivors-w-Disabilities-Fact-Sheet.pdf.

8. Elizabeth L. Gray, "Financial Abuse of Individuals with Disabilities, *The Voice,* April 2019, https://www.specialneedsalliance.org/the-voice/financial-abuse-of-individuals-with-disabilities/.

9. Nancy Smith, Sandra Harrell, and Amy Judy, "How Safe are Americans with Disabilities?" Center on Victimization and Safety, April 2017, https://www.vera.org/downloads/publications/How-safe-are-americans-with-disabilities-web.pdf.

10. Lida Merrill, email message to author, June 6, 2022.

11. "Annual Accessibility Audit for United Methodist Churches," Disability Ministries Committee of The United Methodist Church, 2019, https://umcdmc.org/resources/accessibility-and-united-methodist-churches/accessibility-audit/.

12. "Etiquette and Communication," Disability Ministries of The United Methodist Church, https://umcdmc.org/resources/ways-to-welcome-all/etiquette-and-communication.

13. "Research Summary," Mental Health First Aid, https://www.mentalhealthfirstaid.org/cs/wp-content/uploads/2013/10/2018-MHFA-Research-Summary.pdf.

14. Ivory Smith Causey, "Coping with Bipolar Disorder within My Faith Community," *NAMI Blog*, July 15, 2019, https://www.nami.org/Blogs/NAMI-Blog/July-2019/Coping-with-Bipolar-Disorder-within-My-Faith-Community.

15. "Trauma Informed Churches," TraumaInformedMD.com, https://www.traumainformedmd.com/churches.html.

16. Elizabeth Mulvahill, "What are the Zones of Regulation, and How Can I Use Them to Help Kids Manage Their Emotions?" We Are Teachers, March 25, 2021, https://www.weareteachers.com/zones-of-regulation-activities/.

17. "Childhood Maltreatment among Children with Disabilities, Centers for Disease Control and Prevention, September 18. 2019, https://www.cdc.gov/ncbddd/disabilityandsafety/abuse.html.

18. "Access, Autonomy, and Dignity: Comprehensive Sexuality Education for People with Disabilities, National Partnership for Women and Families, September 2021, 11-15, https://www.nationalpartnership.org/our-work/resources/health-care/repro/repro-disability-sexed.pdf.

19. "Guidebooks," NoraBaladerian.com, https://norabaladerian.com/guidebooks/.

20. "Safety Planning for Persons with Disabilities: Advocate Guide," Safety First Initiative, http://www.calcasa.org/wp-content/uploads/files/angie-blumel-advocate-guide-safety-planning-final-printer.pdf.

21. Debby Newman, email message to author, April 1, 2022.

22. "About Supported Decision-Making," Center for Public Representation, https://supporteddecisions.org/about-supported-decision-making/.

23. A Blueprint for Change: Toward a National Strategy to End Sexual Abuse of Children with Disabilities," Sandra Harrell, Center on Victimization and Safety, 2018, 13–14, http://www.nrcac.org/wp-content/uploads/2019/04/blueprint-for-change_kids-with-disabilities_2019.pdf

24. "Social principles, 162.I," *The Book of Discipline of The United Methodist Church*, (United Methodist Publishing House, 2016), 123.

Notes

_____

_____

_____

_____

_____

_____

_____

_____

_____

_____

We can join God's celebration of diversity in creation and overcome barriers to belonging and participation as we become safe places for all.

CHAPTER 16
Safer Sanctuaries for Older Adults

Robyn Arab

In the 1950s, fewer than one in every ten people in the United States were over the age of 65. Today, the ratio of people in the United States over the age of 65 is more like one in six.[1] As the country has aged, the church has aged as well. According to a 2020 study from Faith Communities Today, one out of every three church attendees is over the age of 65.[2] As the church ages, it becomes increasingly important for congregations to pay attention to the health and safety of older adults.

To be clear, most older adults live lives without much fear of abuse, neglect, or mistreatment from their loved ones or caregivers. Defining older adults as "people who are over the age of 65" is a broad brush that includes people with a wide range of physical and mental capabilities. With this in mind, we will focus most of our attention on older adults who are vulnerable due to social isolation, physical disabilities, or mental impairments such as dementia or Alzheimer's disease.

For many older adults, the church is a focal point of life, and this leaves many congregations well-positioned to provide support, education, and other resources to older adults and their caregivers to make sure that older adults are safe and well-cared for.

Raising Awareness

According to the National Council on Elder Abuse, approximately one in ten older adults have suffered from some form of elder abuse.[3] Elder abuse comes in many different forms including:

- Physical abuse—the use of force to threaten or physically injure a vulnerable elder.
- Emotional abuse—verbal attacks, threats, rejection, isolation, or belittling acts that cause or could cause mental anguish, pain, or distress to an older adult.
- Sexual abuse—sexual contact that is forced, tricked, threatened, or otherwise coerced upon a vulnerable elder, including anyone who is unable to grant consent.
- Financial abuse—theft, fraud, misuse or neglect of authority, and use of undue influence as a lever to gain control over an older person's money or property.

- Neglect—a caregiver's failure or refusal to provide for a vulnerable elder's safety, physical, or emotional needs.
- Abandonment—desertion of a frail or vulnerable elder by anyone with duty of care.
- Self-neglect—an inability to understand the consequences of one's own actions or inaction, which leads to, or may lead to, harm or endangerment.

The most common forms of elder abuse fall under the categories of financial abuse, both from family members and from strangers, neglect, and emotional abuse.

As highlighted earlier, Americans are living healthier and longer lives. While this is undoubtedly a good thing, it also increases the potential for age-related illness and disability to arise. This also means that there is a rise in the need for long-term care and help for older adults to carry out the usual activities of daily life. At the same time, the number of adult children serving as the primary caregiver for their aging parents is decreasing. The adult children who do take on this responsibility also face the pressures of their own family, work, and financial obligations. This mix of pressures and shifting needs increases the potential for elder abuse, whether in a private home or in a residential care setting. Sadly, the most common perpetrators of abuse are the caregivers of older adults, including adult children and spouses. This is the challenge facing the church and those responsible for protecting older adults.

Providing Support

There are a number of ways for congregations to provide support to their older-adult members. The first and most important is to encourage open communication about the needs of older-adult members and work to destigmatize the aging process.

Elder abuse victims often do not report their mistreatment because of fear. They may fear public exposure, embarrassment, or humiliation. They may be afraid that if they report the abuse of an adult child or spouse who takes care of them, then they will be left alone without any support. Many older adults may fear being forced to leave their homes and relocate to a nursing home if abuse is reported.

Aging is difficult, and it can be scary. When the church openly talks about the process of aging, the changes that people experience, the fears that they face, and the vulnerabilities that they may be navigating, it can encourage those who are experiencing abuse to come forward and talk about their experience openly. Many older people fear losing their limited independence; if the church can remind those suffering from abuse that they are not alone and that the church will help them find solutions to the struggles that they are facing, this can go a long way to keep older adults safe.

It should also be highlighted at this point that reporting possible elder abuse is a legal requirement in most states. However, the definitions of elder abuse are

Notes

_____

_____

_____

_____

_____

_____

_____

_____

_____

_____

> The first and most important is to encourage open communication about the needs of older-adult members and work to destigmatize the aging process.

131

Social isolation can be a serious problem among older adults. This leaves older adults more vulnerable to abuse and exploitation.

inconsistent since there is no federal law defining the exact nature of elder abuse. Today, all states have enacted laws to protect older adults.

Destigmatizing the aging process and talking openly about the needs of older adults also helps overcome dominant societal attitudes about elderly people. Older adults are widely depicted as being frail, impaired, and dependent individuals. These depictions contribute to the way society perceives and treats older people. A negative view of the elderly may thus result in a climate that is favorable to elder abuse.

Second, churches can work to actively include older adults in ministry and involve them in the day-to-day work of the church. In many churches, it is already the case that many older adults are actively involved in ministry. However, what we recommend here is for the church to actively pursue those older adults who attend church but are not involved in ministry. Social isolation can be a serious problem among older adults. This leaves older adults more vulnerable to abuse and exploitation. This can be countered by actively working to make older adults involved members of the community.

Third, churches can work to connect with the families of older adults who attend their congregations. When connected with the family, it is easier to notice signs of abuse and discover what may or may not be normal behavior for someone. Have they lost weight? Have they stopped coming to social events? Create a team that works to keep up with family members and caregivers who can report any concerns they might have to the church. This team can consist of trusted individuals in the congregation to help keep these matters confidential. Social workers, nurses, caregivers, and other members with older family can be a good start for such a group. This team also helps build trust with families. Families need to know that coming to someone in the church will be the right step. They want their loved one to receive direction and comfort from their church family.

Finally, education on issues surrounding abuse and neglect is essential. Helping older adults understand their rights in the hospital or in their long-term care facility is useful. Have classes to teach members to recognize the signs of abuse, neglect, and exploitation. When we educate, we create an atmosphere of protection and love.

This education also includes talking about frauds that specifically target the elderly. While this is often presented in a way that generates fear, it can be conducted in a matter-of-fact manner that informs without raising anxiety. Inform older adults in your congregation that they may be targeted by scams. Remind them that if or when this happens, it is okay to report it. It is not a reason for shame, and by reporting it, they are helping others. Education takes away the fear of the unknown and the embarrassment that can come with reporting abuse.

Churches can also create classes for older adults. Bring in different professionals to discuss the needs and resources available to the seniors in the congregation. Equip them with the power of knowledge regarding various issues they may be facing in the future. Examples could include legal information, caregiving situations, Medicare and Medicaid information, and a session on family dynamics. The professionals do not need to be from the congregation. They can be trusted community resources.

Signs of Abuse

Churches should also be on the look out for signs of abuse in the older-adult members of the congregation. Warning signs of abuse include the following:

- Physical abuse—slap marks; unexplained and repeated injuries and bruises; welts, lacerations, or bite marks; and certain types of burns or blisters, such as cigarette burns.
- Neglect—poor personal hygiene; untreated bed sores; unsafe or unsanitary living conditions; lack of medical care; and malnutrition or dehydration.
- Emotional abuse—withdrawal from normal activities; lack of communication; unexplained changes in alertness; and other unusual behavioral changes, such as depression or talk of suicide.
- Sexual abuse—bruises around the breasts or genital area; pain or itching in the genital area; and depressed, withdrawn behavior;
- Financial abuse and exploitation—sudden change in finances and accounts; altered wills and trusts; unusual bank withdrawals; checks written as "loans" or "gifts"; mail redirected to new locations; loss of property; unexplained disappearance of funds or valuable possessions; and "new best friends."
- Abuse in care facilities—inappropriate restraints, over- or under-medication; severe weight loss; disappearance of personal items such as dentures, hearing aids, money, and mementos; and long periods of time during which residents are left alone.

Church members can play a vital role in identifying and helping victims of elder abuse. The following questions can provide a helpful guide for leaders who are concerned about possible abuse in an older adult member:

- How is your social life? When was the last time you went out with family and friends?
- Who makes the decisions at your house? Who decides how your money is spent?
- How are things going with your spouse or partner, caregiver, or adult child?
- Is there someone in your family who has emotional, drug, or financial problems?
- Are there strangers coming in and out of your home without your permission?
- Are you afraid? Has someone made you feel uncomfortable?

Notes

Church members can play a vital role in identifying and helping victims of elder abuse.

133

Notes

- Have you ever been hit, kicked, or hurt in any way?
- Does anyone threaten you or force you to do things you do not want to do?

As mentioned earlier, known or suspected cases of abuse should be reported to the appropriate agencies. When in doubt, err on the side of caution and report. Intervention can save a life!

Providing Safe Environments

Congregations should also seek to provide safe environments for older adults when they are at the church building or attending church-sponsored events. The ability to provide appropriate medical care for older adults is one important factor in providing a safe environment. First-aid training, Automated External Defibrillator (AED) training, and CPR training classes are all useful tools for ministry leaders working with older adults. Staff and volunteers should be aware of where first-aid kits and any AEDs are located in the church building for easy and quick access. Additionally, the local Red Cross and YMCA are often good sources of qualified trainers who may be available to provide classes for your church.

Churches can also provide safe environments by supporting the caregivers of older adults. Many caregivers cannot attend services or events because they are caring for their loved ones. Putting together a trained team of people who can assist loved ones while the caregivers attend services would be a welcome relief. This both supports the family member and also provides additional social interaction and connection with someone involved in the church's ministry.

Beyond these recommendations, many of the standard Safe Sanctuaries practices used in other ministries are also suggested for working with older adults. For instance, the two-adult rule should still be in place. When working with older adults, this not only reduces the likelihood of abuse, but it also ensures that assistance can be quickly delivered in the event of an accident or emergency. It also raises the likelihood that one of the volunteers will be trained in first-aid or CPR.

Similarly, all leaders within older-adult ministries should be over the age of eighteen. Youth are, of course, highly encouraged to participate in ministering to older adults. Teenagers may visit older adults in assisted-living and nursing facilities. Teenagers may work with older adults on mission trips and service projects. The possibilities are endless, but the leaders of these ministries should always be adults, and youth should be assistants only.

Finally, pastoral counseling for older adults is a vitally important ministry in every congregation. The value of a window in the door is every bit as important in the context of counseling as it is in any other type of meeting and ministry. The pastor and the older adult both want to ensure confidentiality in the counseling session. However, ensuring confidentiality regarding the substance of the conversation does not require that the session be held in isolation or secrecy. Assuring confidentiality

The ability to provide appropriate medical care for older adults is one important factor in providing a safe environment.

regarding the substance of the conversation also does not require that the identity of the older adult be kept secret. Accountability and transparency always help to promote a safe environment.

Final Thoughts

One final way that congregations can work to provide a support for older adults is by partnering with local agencies, nursing homes, assisted living facilities, veterans affairs offices, and other groups that provide support for older adults. Churches do not have to provide all assistance on their own, and these organizations are designed to provide older adults with the kind of help that many need to live active, healthy, and fulfilling lives. Churches can, however, be a focal point in the community that helps to connect older adults with the services and resources that they need.

When working with older adults, churches should always be seeking to maintain a balance between the agency and independence of people and helping them get the support and protection they need. We should not treat older adults like children, but we should provide them with the support and care they need as they age.

Our seniors are true gems in our congregations. The wisdom and direction they provide can teach our younger parishioners much. When we provide welcoming, supporting communities for older adults, the whole congregation benefits.

Notes

1. Erin Duffin, "Share of Old Age Population (65 years and older) in the Total U.S. Population from 1950 to 2050," Statista, September 30, 2022, https://www.statista .com/statistics/457822/share-of-old-age-population-in-the-total-us-population.

2. Scott Thumma, "Twenty Years of Congregational Change: The 2020 Faith Communities Today Overview," Hartford Institute for Religion Research, (Hartford, CT: Hartford Seminary, 2021), https://faithcommunitiestoday.org/wp-content/uploads/2021/10/Faith -Communities-Today-2020-Summary-Report.pdf.

3. "Get the Facts on Elder Abuse," National Council on Aging, February 3, 2021, https:// www.ncoa.org/article/get-the-facts-on-elder-abuse.

Notes

> Churches can, however, be a focal point in the community that helps to connect older adults with the services and resources that they need.

CHAPTER 17
Safer Sanctuaries for College Ministries

Derrick Scott III

My journey to ministry began at the age of twenty-two. I was working in a moderately-sized United Methodist congregation that was only minutes away from a large public university. I was what can be euphemistically called a "seasoned sophomore," whose academic history was as colorful as it was regretful. When I was offered the opportunity to serve as a minister to other college-aged young adults, it became a lifeline of sorts and shaped my career and area of expertise for the next two decades.

At the time, I did not realize that I was able to thrive in collegiate ministry because of the foundations that had been laid before me in the church where I served. This church, which served as the umbrella for my work, had already established a culture of safety that permeated its ministry. Many of the policies that they had already put in place, such as background checks for those with access to our large church building, made it possible to create an environment that was safe for college-aged young adults.

Nearly a decade later, when I left my position at this local church to start a new Wesley Foundation for our area, many of the new ministry's policies were based on the Safe Sanctuary protocols I learned from the church where I first served. This new ministry was a regional one, serving multiple campuses, and did not have a central location or building on any campus. As a mobile ministry, it was even more important that we have protocols and policies in place. Clear communication about carpools, who would be on campus for the set up and breakdown of events, and the day to day life of ministry all came with an understanding that it was just as important to keep college students and young-adult volunteers safe as it was to accomplish the tasks laid out for us.

All of this to say, the technical aspects of Safe Sanctuaries are extremely relevant to collegiate ministries, whether on or off campus. College ministry leaders should require background checks for volunteers. Care should be taken when coordinating rides for students, planning retreats, and endorsing activities that go late into the night. The same general guidelines used for children, youth, and vulnerable adults can and should be adapted for collegiate ministries of any size and in any context. These protocols should be put in place in consultation with other leaders as well, including, but not limited to, college and university administration and local church leaders.

The Challenges and Opportunities of Collegiate Ministry

Collegiate ministries, including Wesley Foundations, local church college ministries, fresh expressions, and new church starts geared toward younger generations, all have the chance to shape the spiritual trajectory of college-aged young adults in a profound way. The next generation of clergy and lay leadership will likely have their calls nurtured in the context of one of these ministries. As we consider the future of the church, it is clear that our continued witness and service to transform the world as disciples of Jesus Christ will be shaped by a new generation of spiritual leaders who are being shaped and inspired within a collegiate ministry environment.

Collegiate ministry spaces often serve individuals from many different backgrounds. No collegiate community is truly homogenous, and serving this community well means taking into account different backgrounds, perspectives, aims, and expectations that students bring with them. One challenge is that we cannot always to point to our United Methodist baptismal vows or a shared theological heritage, as our students may not be familiar with these concepts. However, we can emphasize the values and commitments highlighted by these vows and beliefs in a way that can be received by students from any religious or philosophical background.

When it comes to Safe Sanctuaries policies, this means framing these protocols less as an institutional mandate, and more as a practical way of loving our neighbor and proclaiming the gospel. This framing shapes the way that young adults will engage with one another both in this ministry and in community space for years to come. I invite you to pay close attention to the other sections of this resource for practical guidelines and protocols to include in the ministry you lead.

As you consider these guidelines, reflect on the unique needs of emerging adults and the kind of leadership, support, and boundaries that would assist in their flourishing. As leaders of a collegiate ministry, faithfulness means thinking through the dynamics of nurturing individuals who are learning to live in the tension between autonomy and accountability. This tension shapes many of the unique challenges and opportunities of collegiate ministry and informs our work in building a safe community for everyone. We must look closely at the health and capacity of our own leadership. We must also pay attention to our commitments to confidentiality as we seek to provide gospel-inspired ministry that is safe for all college-aged young adults.

Autonomy and Accountability

While there are some similarities between youth ministry and ministry to college-aged young adults, and therefore things we can learn regarding best practices for creating safe environments, the differences between the two contexts are

Notes

> As leaders of a collegiate ministry, faithfulness means thinking through the dynamics of nurturing individuals who are learning to live in the tension between autonomy and accountability.

_____

_____

_____

_____

_____

_____

_____

_____

_____

_____

_____

_____

> **Often, our students' desire for new experiences and self-exploration can lead to new, and at times, difficult choices.**

enough to place them in different categories. For one, young adults who attend collegiate ministry events are more likely to come because they have chosen to participate. Unlike youth ministry, college ministry is almost always a ministry to legal adults. The way we respect the autonomy of a fourteen-year-old looks quite different from the way we treat a nineteen-year-old.

Yet, we also recognize that the nineteen-year-old is learning how to handle the balance between autonomy and accountability. The nineteen-year-old is responsible for everything from getting to class or work on time to managing a meal plan to paying his/her own bills. College-aged young adults are learning that while they may legally be adults, the responsibility of being an adult comes with challenges and consequences that are connected to their freedom of choice. We must always keep this dynamic in mind as we develop our own Safe Sanctuaries guidelines for these ministries.

The need for risk management efforts is high when individuals are exploring their own decision-making and its impact on others for the first time. Often, our students' desire for new experiences and self-exploration can lead to new, and at times, difficult choices. Bringing these moments into the light on a regular basis through conversation can help to create a safe environment for everyone. It also allows students to learn from their peers about how to make good choices and avoid unfortunate outcomes.

For instance, first-year students often experiment with alcohol, non-prescription medications, and other substances.[1] This creates a dynamic where harm to oneself and others is an unforeseen, but highly likely outcome. While most collegiate ministries are alcohol free, it is important that there are regular conversations and education about these choices within the ministry context. Leadership teams should also establish protocols in advance about how to handle a situation when a student comes to a ministry event under the influence of a substance. Similarly, broad guidance should be in place to mitigate the chances that ministry participants will find themselves together in unsafe scenarios due to alcohol or substance use.

Beyond these guidelines, students should know that their campus or collegiate ministry leader is a safe person to talk to about these choices and their consequences. In this way, creating safer sanctuaries also means building braver sanctuaries where the consequences of our choices and the impact of these choices for ourselves and others is openly and regularly discussed. We will talk more about confidentiality and disclosure later in this chapter, but students should know that collegiate ministry spaces are a place where individuals are learning to take responsibility for their actions. Setting this standard will both support the continued development of emerging adults and help maintain a safe environment for them.

Another feature of the autonomy gained by college-aged young adults is the ability to independently define aspects of their identity and personal experience. Some students will be doing this for the first time, and this process may involve acknowledging past trauma as they explore new ways of seeing themselves. This stage of life is often a time when emerging adults begin to recognize their vulnerabilities. The late teens and early twenties are also a time when many students first reckon with a world that marginalizes those society deems weak, divergent, or different in some way.

In response, collegiate ministries that aim to be places of safety and refuge for young adults must not only be physically safe, but also psychologically, intellectually, and spiritually safe. The way that collegiate leaders respond to a student's journey of self-discovery and disclosure is important. Emerging adults should be encouraged to consider the ways that they are uniquely created, gifted, and called during this stage of life. College-aged young adults should know that as they come to terms with their identity, whether that is a question of gender and sexuality or theological and political identity, their collegiate ministry leaders are available to support them on their journey.

Again, this is an area where creating safer sanctuaries also means creating brave and courageous sanctuaries. College-aged young adults should be regarded with tolerance, appreciative inquiry, and gracious disagreement. Young adults must have a deep sense that they are being listened to and respected for who they are. Ministry leaders and leadership teams can cause harm when they respond poorly to a student who is, for example, exploring personal pronouns or questioning long-held religious convictions held by the family of origin. Leaders can short-circuit this process of development by ignoring or diminishing the experiences of young adults. Creating a culture of safety in the collegiate context means that students are safe to try on new ways of seeing themselves as they learn to personally own their faith in Christ and their calling as Christians.

Safety as Commitment to Gospel Community

Many aspects of collegiate ministry are focused on the individual. Discipleship, mentoring, and pastoral counseling are all tailored to the individual needs of college students. Yet, there is also a clear and obvious connection between the way we serve individual students and the ways that we serve the larger college or university campus.

For many collegiate ministries, community takes on primary importance. Focusing on community as a key facet of their ministry means that collegiate ministry leaders must also integrate a commitment to safety, healthy boundaries, and appropriate means of relating to ministry participants into their ministry. In this way, Safe Sanctuaries policies are deeply connected to how we proclaim the gospel on campus. Safety is both a theological mandate and a practical application of our witness to the love of Christ on campus.

Notes

> Creating a culture of safety in the collegiate context means that students are safe to try on new ways of seeing themselves as they learn to personally own their faith in Christ and their calling as Christians.

139

_____

_____

_____

_____

_____

_____

_____

_____

_____

_____

_____

Community is messy, and a commitment to safety includes access to confidential spaces when necessary.

Creating and maintaining a culture of safety and protection enhances our evangelism, shows our hospitality toward those outside our ministry, and helps us foster meaningful connections for those who are part of our ministries. For example, using personal pronouns and chosen names for those exploring their gender identity is both an act of gospel-inspired welcome and a practice in emotional safety for trans and gender non-conforming students. Similarly, when we address issues of ableism within our ministry contexts, it is both a sign of gospel-inspired inclusion and a way of ensuring the safety of those who are disabled and differently-abled on campus. The way of Jesus requires a deep commitment to meeting individuals on their own terms and providing safe and brave spaces for their personal and spiritual flourishing. Faithful, gospel-driven collegiate ministry communities are safer sanctuaries for all students.

When we think about what it means to make safety a key commitment within our gospel communities, the role of leadership is extremely important. The image of a shepherd is often used in scripture when describing the work of spiritual leaders. Like shepherds, we are encouraged to "Tend the flock of God among you. Watch over it" (1 Peter 5:2a). The words _tend_ and _watch_ point to a specific way of leading. This kind of leadership is not about the leader, but about the health and growth of those within the leader's sphere of influence.

On the other hand, the health and development of ministry leaders is directly correlated with the health and safety of the ministry space. Collegiate ministry is often an exhausting, frustrating, and, at times, lonely extension ministry. Leaders in the collegiate context should also be on their own journeys of spiritual discipleship, mental health, and wellness. Clergy and lay leaders, as well as student and graduate volunteers, need to tend to their own souls as they live in the tension between autonomy and accountability.

Ministry leaders should consider the ways that certain models of ministry, seasons of success, and periods of decline can cause unhealthy patterns of behavior when left unchecked. Even the most humble and experienced leaders are prone to narcissism, passive-aggression, manipulation, and other problems. In many ways, the policies of Safe Sanctuaries provide a support system that forces leaders to assess their behavior. Similarly, making sure that participants know about these policies is an important act of accountability for ministry leaders. Ultimately, the ministry leaders are responsible for maintaining their own health, maintaining their own boundaries, and encouraging healthy, thriving communities that allow the work of the gospel to thrive on campus.

As we think about leadership within the context of Safe Sanctuaries, we must also consider the commitments we make to confidentiality. As college-aged young adults navigate this experimental and exploratory stage of life, it is critical to provide safe spaces where they can share openly and honestly without fear of judgment. Community is messy, and a commitment to safety includes access to confidential spaces when necessary. The importance of confidentiality is not new to our ministry. The examination for potential clergy within The United Methodist Church even includes the question, "Will you regard all pastoral conversations of a confessional nature as a trust between the person concerned and God?"[2] Young adults need assurance that there are leaders and spaces where their honest statements are both sacred and private.

However, this is a skill that requires discernment for all leaders, particularly the leaders of collegiate ministries. A commitment to confidentiality must be paired with an understanding of when appropriate and timely disclosures are necessary. At times, a ministry leader is obligated to report information that they have learned, including instances of self-harm and potential harm to others. Depending on state regulations, university policies, and even congregational guidelines, employees and volunteers associated with a collegiate ministry can be legally obligated to report certain incidents, especially when the safety of vulnerable individuals is at stake.

It is, therefore, essential that leaders talk regularly about the commitment to confidentiality within the ministry. They should be clear with ministry participants about when confessions can and cannot remain secret and why it is in everyone's best interest to trust those who have been charged with the care of the collegiate community. Leaders must also cultivate trust with college-aged young adults as some may have already experienced a failure within the system. Once again, faithfulness to the gospel community means that building safer sanctuaries where privacy is honored, healing is possible, and safety is paramount.

A Team Approach

The work of cultivating a safe, healthy, and thriving community of gospel-inspired welcome and inclusion for all students can be daunting. Collegiate leaders cannot do this work alone. While some ministries have the capacity for additional staff, others are led by part-time and bivocational ministers. Fundamentally, building a culture of safety and protection requires a team approach. When possible, align your policies and procedures with other ministries that are adjacent to the collegiate environment and involve other leaders in developing these policies.

Similarly, it can be useful for your ministry and your efforts at promoting safety to become acquainted with campus employees in housing, student affairs, and other offices. These relationships can be both life-giving and life-saving loops of communication that ensure students do not fall through the cracks. It may also be helpful to invite mental health counselors, spiritual directors, and others in similar work to serve as advisors or board members for the ministry.

Parents also have a role to play in collegiate ministry, even if it is a somewhat more distant role than in children's and youth ministry. Their emotional support and experience can provide a necessary aid to college-aged young adults, while still prioritizing their autonomy.

Leaders must also cultivate trust with college-aged young adults as some may have already experienced a failure within the system.

_____

_____

_____

_____

_____

_____

_____

_____

_____

_____

_____

_____

Tending the collegiate community means creating a circle of leaders and experienced volunteers who share the commitment to safety and understand it as an essential part of proclaiming the gospel to college-aged young adults. As stated above, the hard work of cultivating safer sanctuaries within a collegiate ministry has the ability to shape the way emerging adults think about leadership, community, and ministry in the church and in the world.

Notes

1. "How Does Your Campus Create a Supportive, Safe Environment for First-Year Students?" National Center on Safe Supportive Learning Environments (NCSSLE), https://safesupportivelearning.ed.gov/voices-field/how-does-your-campus-create -supportive-safe-environment-first-year-students.

2. *The Book of Discipline of The United Methodist Church*, 2016. (Nashville, Tennessee: United Methodist Publishing House, 2016), ¶335. c.5.

> **When possible, align your policies and procedures with other ministries that are adjacent to the collegiate environment and involve other leaders in developing these policies.**

CHAPTER 18

Safer Sanctuaries for Camping and Retreat Ministries

Jessica Gamaché

Camp and retreat ministries are often vital to an individual's faith journey. This is especially true for children and youth. A church camp or retreat experience offers young people a safe space to fully disconnect from the expectations and pressures of society, while being uplifted by strong Christian mentors. In this environment, surrounded by creation, campers can hear the quiet voice of God and practice living as a disciple in every moment of the day. The adult leaders who guide these experiences carry a heavy responsibility, both to facilitate this faith development and provide a safe environment. While risk cannot be entirely eliminated from the camp experience, adult leaders can create the safest possible situation by following best practices. It is the responsibility of all caregivers in both camp and retreat settings to implement the standards of Safe Sanctuaries to decrease the risk of harm from abuse.

Responsible caregivers in camp and retreat settings include all those who provide oversight or are in direct contact with children, youth, and young adults. This includes, but is not limited to, year-round staff, seasonal and summer staff, retreat leaders, and all volunteers. These individuals are crucial to every camp and retreat experience. By following the agreed upon policies and procedures, caregivers intentionally and effectively reduce the possibility of abuse to the children, youth, and vulnerable adults in their care. Additionally, by following these same standards, caregivers also protect themselves from false claims of wrongdoing.

That said, implementing the basic principles of Safe Sanctuaries at camp can be more complex than in other types of ministry. The unique setting of both camps and retreats brings along with it some situations that aren't found in other types of ministry. Questions about sleeping arrangements, bathing facilities, and onsite healthcare are essential elements of camping and retreat ministries. Similarly, activities like swimming and remote hikes in nature present unique challenges for implementing aspects of Safe Sanctuaries for camp and retreat ministry leaders. Adequate training and adherence to the camp or retreat center's rules are crucial in helping caregivers create safe environments for campers and retreat attendees. As we consider the work of creating safe environments for camping and retreat ministries, let's take a closer look at best practices and explore strategies for implementing them in a camp setting.

_____

_____

_____

_____

_____

_____

_____

_____

_____

_____

_____

_____

Best Practices for Camping and Retreat Ministry

The Two-Adult Rule

Like every other type of ministry that works with children or youth, two unrelated adults must always be present when in contact with children and youth when camping or on a retreat. There are two prominent situations when this becomes a struggle during camp and retreat events. The first occurs when camp directors struggle to find enough volunteers or staff. Staff and volunteer shortages are, of course, a challenge for many ministries across our connection. The second common situation happens when church retreat leaders have volunteers back out unexpectedly. There are, however, strategies that can be used to ensure that the two-adult rule is always operating, even when it seems impossible.

First, approach camp and retreat planning with the Safe Sanctuaries standards in mind. Keeping these at the forefront of planning will help mitigate challenges. During the registration process, limit the number of campers or retreat attendees based on the number of staff or volunteers that are already secured. It is easier to move campers from a waitlist into a program as counselors and chaperones confirm their participation than it is to cancel registrations because of issues finding the number of adults you were hoping for. This may be frustrating at first since we want to serve as many people as we can. However, if the setting isn't safe because of a lack of supervision, then the whole event may need to be canceled. Plan for the two-adult rule from the beginning. This will reduce the number of challenges faced later.

> **A roamer is an adult who moves between multiple activities or groups.**

Now, consider a situation where the event has already begun and a staff member or volunteer needs to leave the group unexpectedly to retrieve supplies. The group is unexpectedly short an adult. In a situation like this, it is acceptable to utilize a roamer until the first group leader returns. A roamer is an adult who moves between multiple activities or groups. The roamer drifts from group to group at unannounced intervals to serve as a constant presence, ensuring adequate oversight. When utilizing a roamer, it is best to keep activities or groups close together and in an open space.

Unexpected trips to the nurse can also make this a difficult standard to implement. When a camper or retreat attendee needs to leave a group in order to visit the nurse, one adult and at least one additional camper or retreat attendee should accompany the sick young person. The extra youth will then need to stay with the nurse to help avoid any one-on-one situations. The adult can then transition back to the group.

Five Year Age Difference

This rule states that no person should supervise a group unless that person is at least five years older than the oldest group member. This standard is most challenging for events serving campers and retreat attendees who are older youth. However, there are ways to plan ahead and make sure this standard is in practice.

Whether at summer camp or on retreat with a youth group, organizers can successfully use junior counselors, who are within the five-year age range, alongside senior counselors, who are beyond the five-year age range. When both junior and senior counselors are adults, then the two-adult rule is satisfied. While both junior and senior counselors are responsible for providing supervision, the senior counselor is the primary caregiver in this situation.

Training is also needed to clarify what responsibilities can fall to a junior counselor. For example, during group activities, a senior counselor needs to be in place to oversee the campers, but the activity can be led a junior counselor. Similarly, junior counselors can fill the roamer role while a senior counselor provides the primary supervision for a group or during an activity. However, it is important to remember that two junior counselors working together would not fulfill the two-adult role. A senior counselor must also be present.

Open Space Rule

This rule states that when working with youth and children indoors, interior doors should be left open when possible. Alternatively, all doors should be equipped with windows that provide open sight lines at all times. Outdoor spaces should also be considered when considering this principle. The rule of thumb is that clear lines of sight and sound should be available at all times.

However, there are times during camps and retreats when adhering to this rule would be inappropriate. For instance, leaving doors open during changing times would actually increase the chances of abuse. When campers and retreat attendees are sleeping and changing, the correct practice is to close all doors and curtains. Outside of those times, cabin and room doors should remain open and window curtains pushed aside.

Relatedly, situations often arise at camp when a camper would like to speak to a counselor in confidence. The same is true during retreats. These private conversations should be allowed to take place in a way that honors the camper's wish, while at the same time complying with appropriate safety standards. For these situations, designate an area in plain view where staff can be in conversation with campers. This could be an outdoor bench or a grassy area. The location needs to be in an open space, preferably outdoors, with clear lines of sight and sound for another adult to witness.

Special Considerations

While some unique aspects of camp and retreat ministries may make compliance with best practices seem daunting, over time leaders can develop an approach to

Notes

The rule of thumb is that clear lines of sight and sound should be available at all times.

thinking about these questions that places safety at the forefront of the planning process. The previous section gave suggestions for implementing some of the basic principles of Safe Sanctuaries in the challenging situations of camping and retreat ministries. However, there are also a number of areas of special consideration that apply primarily to camping and retreat scenarios, but are not present in other ministries.

Staffing

Whether you are trying to hire sixty young adults as summer staff or find six volunteer chaperones for a church retreat, ensuring the presence of enough onsite staff should always be a priority. As you are building a staff, be aware of the ages and familial relationships of all staff members and volunteers. This knowledge will be essential in ensuring that there are appropriate staff with each group of young people.

It is also important to remember that adequate training will be required for all caregivers who are in contact with children, youth, and vulnerable adults. Do your part to make sure that regular Safe Sanctuaries training is available for all of your volunteers, year-round staff, and summer staff. This training should be so regular that it becomes a part of your ministry's culture. In addition to regular training, background checks for all staff, volunteers, and even program guests should be standard practice.

Twenty-Four-Hour Live-in Environment of Camp

Camp and retreat experiences often require staff and volunteers to step into roles that a parent would normally fill. In order to responsibly care for each young person, some information needs to be regularly collected and reviewed through the use of various permission forms. The parents or guardians for each event participant should complete all health forms, media release forms, and any other necessary permissions or forms before they arrive at the event. Event leaders must be sure to regularly review and update these permission forms as well.

Summer camps and retreats are also an opportunity for many young people to practice their newfound independence. The twenty-four-hour setting, often without their parents present, gives individual campers and retreat attendees the chance to experiment with this freedom. To help young people gracefully live into this new independence, consider having older campers develop and sign behavior agreements or participation covenants. This both encourages them to behave appropriately and to model good behavior for younger participants.

A live-in environment also means that everyone will require time for changing and bathing. Privacy is essential for changing and bathing at all camp and retreat

> Summer camps and retreats are also an opportunity for many young people to practice their newfound independence.

facilities. However, while privacy is required during these times, adult supervision must always be within listening distance of those in their charge. It is also useful to arrange for separate bathing and changing times for leaders outside of the normal times when campers or retreat participants will be using these facilities.

Facilities

The facilities at camp and retreat sites vary greatly from venue to venue. When planning an event, it is essential that event leaders gain a proper understanding of the facilities that leaders and participants will be using before the event. This will help leaders better prepare for a safe event.

When looking at the facilities of a camp and retreat center, always consider the need for privacy. Open showers and communal changing spaces are no longer appropriate for any camp or retreat event. Always provide for private changing spaces within all lodgings. If these spaces are not provided at the site in question, simple privacy curtains can be hung inside cabins as a way to provide private changing space.

Secondly, be aware of what space is available for indoor programming. Because of the heightened need for privacy, sleeping spaces should not be used for program activities such as Bible study, crafts, or any other similar activities. These should take place in separate event spaces.

During Camp Interactions

Even when all the standard practices of Safe Sanctuaries are in place, inappropriate or abusive actions can still take place. With that in mind, all leaders, whether full-time staff or volunteers, should keep an eye on interactions between staff and campers during events.

Sometimes these concerns are a matter of perception. For instance, there may be words that leaders use that could be perceived negatively by campers and parents. If this is the case, it is best to discuss the issue with those involved to address any concerns before they become serious issues. Additionally, leaders should be aware of the level of attention given to each young person who attends a camp or retreat. Giving more attention to one camper over another could be perceived as favoritism. Similarly, giving participants nicknames may seem like a fun way for the group to bound, but may actually cause a young person to feel uncomfortable or boxed in to a particular stereotype or social role.

Camp also has a reputation for being "touchy-feely." When in camp or retreat settings, remind staff what appropriate physical interactions with campers look like. High-fives and side hugs, for example, allow adults to show affection while also maintaining healthy boundaries in most situations.

Notes

All leaders, whether full-time staff or volunteers, should keep an eye on interactions between staff and campers during events.

Notes

_____

_____

_____

_____

_____

_____

_____

_____

_____

_____

_____

_____

_____

Relatedly, be aware of conversations and actions that may break down healthy boundaries. For instance, complimenting a young person on his or her physical appearance can create uncomfortable situations and should be avoided. In the same manner, adult leaders should be cautious about discussing their personal life with those in their care and should express similar caution asking about the dating lives or romantic interactions of youth.

After-Camp Connections

In the modern world, it is easy to stay in contact with campers and youth beyond the camp and retreat setting. Therefore, social media and other forms of online communication need to be approached in an intentional way.

Leaders should consider their own online presence and should encourage both staff and volunteers to create separate social media profiles that will solely be used for ministry purposes. It can also be a good practice for another staff member or the event leader to have access to the credentials for this social media profile as a way to practice accountability.

Additionally, photos posted to social media should not be tagged with camper names or any location information. Always be aware of any campers or retreat attendees whose parents or legal guardians have opted out of sharing their images online or in print materials. Never post any photos of campers if their guardian has opted out.

Finally, after a camp or retreat event is over, campers may ask staff members or adult volunteers for additional mentoring. Similarly, parents may reach out for babysitting help. By general rule, these types of one-on-one relationships after the end of a camp or retreat event are highly discouraged as they put both the young person and the adult in a vulnerable situation.

LGBTQIA Inclusion

Protecting all children and youth who come to camp and attend retreats includes protecting any young people who identify as LGBTQIA+. When preparing for any camp or retreat event, try to avoid making assumptions about the sexual orientation or gender identity of the participants. It can be helpful to keep in regular dialogue with the parents of LGBTQIA+ campers and retreat attendees and follow their lead. Parents want their child to be safe and to feel safe. They are your best resource when considering questions about housing, resources, and providing the best environment for their child.

You can also take simple steps before an event to make sure all young people feel welcomed. For example, consider whether all bathrooms must be gender specific. A simple change of signage designating a restroom as a "family restroom" will ensure all campers have a place they feel comfortable using.

> **Parents want their child to be safe and to feel safe. They are your best resource when considering questions about housing, resources, and providing the best environment for their child.**

In a similar vein, work with parents and other leaders to develop reasonable flexibility in housing. There is absolutely no reason why LGBTQIA+ youth should not be housed with their straight-identifying peers. The primary concern in this situation should be the possibility of bullying or harassment toward the LGBTQIA+ youth. Counselors and volunteers should be trained to identify and deal with bullying and harassment and should seek support from other leaders if the problem continues.

With this in mind, it is also vital that all staff be intentional about creating a culture free from all homophobic language and bullying. Educate staff and volunteers on the proper use of terminology related to gender and sexuality before the event and encourage them to gently correct campers when they say something that could be considered offensive.

Finally, leaders, staff, and volunteers must ensure that the privacy of all campers and retreat attendees is protected at all times. There is no reason for any leaders, staff, or volunteers to divulge the sexual orientation or gender identity of any campers or retreat attendees.

Final Thoughts

The goals and aspirations of United Methodist camp and retreat ministries are expressed in the "Seven Foundations" that serve as the bedrock for our work. In this ministry, we are called to provide sacred places apart, to nurture Christian faith and discipleship, to extend Christian hospitality and community, to develop principled spiritual leaders, to partner with United Methodist churches and agencies, to teach creation care and appreciation, and to inspire and equip lives for love and justice.

These foundations cannot be truly lived out unless the environments we welcome young people into are safe for everyone and that all participating children, youth, and adults are protected from potential harm. By approaching each camp or retreat event through the lens of Safe Sanctuaries, camp and retreat leaders can responsibly provide life-changing experiences in God's creation.

Notes

A simple change of signage designating a restroom as a "family restroom" will ensure all campers have a place they feel comfortable using.

CHAPTER 19

Building and Maintaining Safer Sanctuaries

Lynn Caterson

While this resource has paid a significant amount of attention to the roles of ministry leaders, staff, volunteers, and participants in fostering safer sanctuaries, the physical environment in which we conduct ministry is also an important factor in creating safe, healthy, and thriving environments. A safer community is not only one filled with thoughtful, well-trained, and dedicated people, it is also a physically safer space.

The suggestions and guidelines covered in this chapter are designed to shape physical spaces that support the work of Safe Sanctuaries ministry. While some of these recommendations may be more easily applied during the construction of new facilities, all of these suggestions should be seriously considered for use, even in our beloved older houses of worship.

Inside The Building

Lighting

Lighting is essential for providing safer spaces within a congregation. All hallways and rooms should be well-lit when people are present for ministry activities. Motion sensor lights are a useful tool, especially in hallways and lobby areas. If lighting is appropriately placed, it will not only light the main area, the hallway for instance, but will also allow for some visibility inside every room that adjoins the main area. This allows visibility into each room from the main area.

Windows

Visibility and clear sight lines are essential for maintaining safe spaces. Every door in the church should have a window, including doors to supply closets. The window should be large enough so that any activity in the room will be visible through the window. Ideally, the window will also be large enough for light from a hall or lobby to shine into the room when the lights in the room are off.

Restrooms

Restrooms are also an important consideration when building safer sanctuaries. While there obviously should not be windows in restroom doors, there should be adequate lighting that turns on when the door is opened and allows for vision in all areas of the restroom.

If possible, churches should consider the use of family restrooms or non-gendered restrooms. This allows for increased privacy while also making facilities more welcoming. Additionally, as mentioned in an earlier chapter, it would be ideal for at least one restroom to have a bench-style changing surface with a curtain or other privacy measure for use by those who may require such an accommodation.

Keys

Access to church facilities outside of traditional worship hours should be carefully restricted. Ministry leaders and church staff should know exactly who has keys, to what entrance they have access, and when this access will be used. As much as possible, people should be prevented from having access to the facility other than in accordance with established protocols and planned events.

Similarly, if a room has a door, it should also have a lock. Rooms not open for regular use should be locked when not in use.

Signage

Signage directing people to specific locations in the facility (restrooms, offices, prayer locations, and so forth) is crucial. This helps prevent people from getting lost and also helps everyone know where they are in the building.

Cameras

The most successful way to prevent abuse and harassment inside the facility is to have cameras that are clearly visible in all areas of the facility. These cameras should be set to record any motion in the covered area. This is obviously expensive and involved. However, even careful placement of a few cameras alerts people in the facility to the fact that they are being watched and protected.

Creating Safe Spaces

A house of worship, even one with older facilities, can create warm, decluttered, and bright spaces that are set aside for special activities for children, youth, and vulnerable adults. Creating these special areas is possible in all houses of worship.

Notes

A house of worship, even one with older facilities, can create warm, decluttered, and bright spaces that are set aside for special activities for children, youth, and vulnerable adults.

_____

_____

_____

_____

_____

_____

_____

_____

_____

_____

_____

It is in the best interest of a community to always know who is present inside the church facilities.

Outside the Building

Parking and Lighting

Parking should be as close as possible to the main entry of the facility, and all parking areas should be well-lit. All entrances accessible from the parking area should also be well-lit. This allows protection for those walking to and from their cars and peace of mind for all involved in ministry activities that take place after dark.

Other Outside Structures

Houses of worship often use outside buildings (garages, sheds, and so forth) for groundskeeping or storage. These areas lend themselves to inappropriate use. These structures should be kept locked at all times unless in use, and a careful record should be kept of who has keys to such facilities.

Signage

There should be ample and visible signage outside the facilities to direct people to the correct entrance or entrances. People entering through the wrong doors or wandering around outside is not conducive to safety.

Fencing and Landscaping

While fences are used by facilities to enclose and, in a sense, protect the outside areas, they may also lend themselves to hiding or concealing inappropriate activities. Good lighting can deter this behavior. Similarly, shrubs should not cover windows nor be situated so that it is possible to easily hide among the landscaping.

Access to the Facilities by Emergency Groups

All emergency response personnel in a community should be provided with a diagram of the church facilities that includes specific notes describing what activities occur at the facility and in what locations. This allows first responders to have proper and timely access to such areas in the case of an emergency.

Know Who Is in the Building

It is in the best interest of a community to always know who is present inside the church facilities. This is particularly important outside of regular worship times. The simplest approach to maintaining this information is to keep a record of who has keys to the facility and what doors they have access to. It is also imperative to know when events are scheduled, when people are expected to arrive, and what their purpose is in the building.

Generally, it is useful for the person responsible for unlocking and locking the facility for an event to maintain the knowledge of who is in the building at any given time. For example, if Sally has a key to open the door near the women's Bible study room, she should also be responsible for seeing who comes in for the event and for locking the door once the attendees have all arrived. Even with big events, only certain doors should be open, and someone should be responsible for seeing who comes in and ensuring that doors are locked when the event is over and that no one remains in the facilities.

Responsibility for Maintaining Sanctuary Safety

The board of trustees of each congregation should be responsible for making the physical improvements noted above and for seeing to it that lighting works, keys are distributed to the correct personnel, that doors lock and unlock safely and easily, and that all elements of a safe sanctuary are continually and carefully maintained by the staff of the facility.

Beyond using church facilities for regular ministry events, churches often rent out their facilities or allow outside groups to gather in their spaces for community events. First and foremost, all outside groups that use church facilities should be instructed on the Safe Sanctuaries policy that is in place and sign documentation agreeing to follow these policies and procedures.

Additionally, outside groups should sign a lease agreement. Note these important items that should be included in a lease agreement:

- Tenant is a 501(c)(3); this is important for maintaining property-tax exempt status in some locations
- The exact location being rented and time when the facility will be in use
- Who will be given access to keys or who will lock and unlock the facility for use by an outside group
- Agreement to follow Safe Sanctuaries policy

To do this work of shaping safe spaces and healthy, safe, and thriving communities, the board of trustees must also enlist the congregation's support. All members of the community should be advised on the details of the Safe Sanctuaries policies in place. They should be aware of which doors are unlocked and which should not be. Visitors should be easily able to find the correct entrances and should be welcomed into the community. Some congregations may find it helpful to have a

Notes

> To do this work of shaping safe spaces and healthy, safe, and thriving communities, the board of trustees must also enlist the congregation's support.

_____

_____

_____

_____

_____

_____

_____

_____

_____

_____

volunteer walk around both inside and outside the facility to simply keep an eye on things and provide guidance for anyone who may be lost.

Ultimately, we do this work to ensure that people can meet God in our communities. We seek to remove obstacles and concerns that might cause people to feel unsafe. In response, we hope to encourage them to engage in the thriving, inspiring work of ministry and to live into the life that we are all called to lead.

> **We seek to remove obstacles and concerns that might cause people to feel unsafe.**

PART V

THE PLAN

CHAPTER 20

Laying the Groundwork

Kevin Johnson *and* **Chris Wilterdink**

A Safe Sanctuaries Story

It all happened on a hot Kentucky day in July 2012. There were more than 350 kids involved in our vacation Bible school that week. It was our big summer children's and youth event, and it offered ministry opportunities for children ranging in age from babies all the way to high school students.

One of the boys in attendance, Elias, was a foster child who had experienced more than his share of brokenness in the world. He was born with a crack addiction that had also damaged his brain. He often felt that he wasn't a good fit for the church because he was a little different from others. He struggled with the whole concept of following Jesus and discipleship. He claimed to constantly hear the voice of evil speaking and tugging at him.

Perhaps it shouldn't have surprised me when I heard his leader that day shout as he took off running away from her. We were outside, and he was heading directly for the street. I immediately had a flashback to my life before ministry when I worked as a safe physical management trainer in a psychiatric residential treatment facility. I instinctively took off after Elias. He was yelling, "Just leave me alone. Jesus doesn't love me. Nobody cares. I am going to run into the street and be with the devil."

As he neared the busy two-lane highway, I had to make a decision. I either had to physically restrain him or we were going into the street. I grabbed him about three feet from the highway and, physically holding his arm, we headed back to the safety of the church building. I knew from my years of working in group homes that he was going to need to be physically restrained until he released all the anger and rage. As we got into a hallway, we went to the ground together, and I held him as he decompressed.

Along with another leader, who I am certain did not expect that volunteering for vacation Bible school would put him in this situation, we held Elias to prevent injury to either himself or others; another adult contacted his mom to come to the church. His mother arrived a few minutes later, and the three of us sat on the floor, leaning against the wall, emotionally and physically exhausted, not saying anything. As mother and son left the church, the other leaders and I looked on, unsure whether another visit to the hospital or a medication tweak was on the horizon.

The next day, I got a phone call. On the other end of the line, a young boy asked, "Um, Rev. Kev, can I come back to VBS tonight?"

I know that he was waiting for me to lay down the law. I know that he was waiting for me to tell him all the guidelines and new rules that he would need to follow if I allowed him to return that night. But all I said was, "You better!" before adding, "Can I sit next to you at dinner? Hey Elias, remember that Jesus loves you and so do I."

Fast forward a few years, and I was serving at another church. I was planning to preach from Matthew 25:31-36 one Sunday, the parable of the sheep and the goats, and I wanted to use the story of Elias and myself as an illustration. I reached out to Elias and his mother, asked for permission to tell the story, and then invited him to visit my church that Sunday to read the scripture. I told Elias to introduce himself by saying, "My name is Elias, and this morning's scripture is Matthew 25:31-46," then proceed to read the text.

During the sermon, when I got to the point in the story where I told Elias that Jesus loved him and so did I, the entire congregation immediately made the connection that the young person sitting in the first row, who had read the scripture moments ago, was the same child from the story. At the conclusion of the service, Elias was church-famous. Everyone wanted to shake his hand, give him a hug, and even get a photo with him.

A few years later, I was dropping off my sixth-grade son at an overnight youth event with other area churches. My son was a little nervous about spending the night away from home, and I was trying to reassure him when I saw a very familiar face who was serving as a high school counselor for the weekend. It was Elias! Seeing that my son was nervous, Elias told me, "Don't worry Rev. Kev, your son will be fine. I got this." My son had a great night.

At the time I'm writing this, Elias is a senior in high school and graduating in a few months. He is still active in the life of the church and participating fully in worship and in the youth group. I don't know if that would have happened without Safe Sanctuaries. I don't know if it that would have happened if he had not had adults in his life who cared for him, showed him love, and took the time to protect him, sometimes even from himself. Somewhere in the back of my mind, I hear the Holy Spirit telling me that when I demonstrated Christ's love for Elias, I did more than just tell him; I showed him.

> **Safe Sanctuaries is a calling, and it is a mandate to ensure that there are places of safety and protection for God's people.**

This my Safe Sanctuaries story. Safe Sanctuaries is a calling, and it is a mandate to ensure that there are places of safety and protection for God's people. On their surface, the policies and procedures of Safe Sanctuaries are about protection, but they are much more. When viewed through a theological and pastoral lens, building safe sanctuaries is about building a culture of safety, a culture where people are cared for, a culture where people can thrive and be free to experience the embrace of a loving God.

For the church to show the love of God to others, then the entire congregation, not just the volunteers and staff, but everyone, needs to embrace the policies of Safe Sanctuaries. These policies and procedures are not about a lack of trust in clergy, laity, staff, or volunteers, but about a culture of protection for our children, youth, vulnerable adults, employees, volunteers, and the whole church body. This is the reason we do this work, so that the whole church might thrive.

The Level of Need

It feels like we find out about another story of abuse in the news every day. Sometimes it's a story about past incidents of abuse that had been going on for years; sometimes it's a story about a cover-up or people willfully looking away; and sometimes it's simply a story of pain, of people hurting someone that they should have been protecting. Each one of these stories is heartbreaking. The statistics surrounding abuse today are alarming. In fact, these statistics change so frequently that we have decided not to include specific numbers in this section for fear that they would be out of date by the time you read this resource. (For current abuse statistics in the United States, check out https://www.rainn.org/statistics.)

Churches are a place that we look to for sanctuary; they are supposed to be a places of safety and refuge. For that reason, reports about abuse in churches can be even more devastating. Not only is there the pain of the abuse itself, but there is also the violation of trust and the destruction of this sense of safety. This is one of several reasons that make it vital that local churches put in place Safe Sanctuaries policies and adhere to these policies without fail.

Churches tend to operate on the basis of trust, relying upon their members and their leaders to conduct themselves appropriately. For the most part, this is a healthy situation. Unfortunately, this trusting attitude can persist in times when it shouldn't, like in the face of questions about safety or reports of misconduct. The truth is that approximately ninety percent of reported incidents of abuse are perpetrated by an individual that the child already knows and trusts. Sadly, this mean that children and other vulnerable people may be targeted by people they know and trust, including the people they trust at church.

For a long time, churches were notoriously inattentive when it came to screening volunteers and employees who work with children and youth. Too often, no application was used and no references were checked before a total stranger was welcomed aboard. Thankfully, this has gotten better over the years as many churches have implemented Safe Sanctuaries policies or other similar programs, but there is still significant room for improvement.

Churches routinely provide opportunities for close contact between adults and children and provide an environment for close personal relationships between adults and youth. Indeed, these relationships and connections are essential to the way we live out the gospel message and should be encouraged, but this trust and

> Churches are a place that we look to for sanctuary; they are supposed to be a places of safety and refuge.

Notes

_____

_____

_____

_____

_____

_____

_____

_____

_____

_____

_____

_____

_____

connection is also why we must remain vigilant about screening who works with the most vulnerable in our communities.

In addition, a Safe Sanctuaries policy is not simply about preventing abuse, it is also about responding to abuse when it happens. Let me repeat, not *if* it happens, but *when*. It is tempting to believe that your church, your community, your family is immune from the dangers of abuse, but abuse takes place even in situations where we would never expect it. Keeping this in mind helps all of those invested and involved in the life of the church focus on the importance of putting in place policies and following those to the letter. It helps us move from thinking "It will never happen here" to being prepared to respond appropriately when it does.

A Team of Champions

Creating and following a Safe Sanctuaries policy is essential for the life of the church. While it may be daunting to consider at first, we want to assure you that it is also something achievable. In this chapter, we will outline practical steps to help jump start the process of developing and implementing abuse prevention policies. Furthermore, we will also look at putting in processes for responding to abuse or allegations of abuse.

Recruiting a team of people who will champion your policies and procedures is the first step in creating your church's policy. When recruiting these "champions," look for people who are passionate about creating safe spaces, people who have time to dedicate to the work of this ministry, and people who have relationships and connections across a variety of ministries and social groups in the church. Once you've recruited a handful of champions, they can help you identify others who would be well-suited to the work of building safer sanctuaries. These champions will also share in the work of researching and developing policies and procedures and will partner with you to generate energy and buy-in to make cultural changes as the whole church works to embrace this ministry of protecting the vulnerable.

If you're having trouble thinking of who you can recruit to form this team, take a look at the "Safe Sanctuaries Task Force for the Local Church" form found in the appendix on page 229. This form lists a number of key stakeholders in the typical congregation, including the pastor, youth minister, children's minister, and members of various relevant committees. Remember, however, that these roles are starters and that your team of champions can be made of anyone in your congregation who is passionate about this ministry.

The United Methodist Church is a connected denomination. To embrace this core aspect of the church, we recommend that leadership develop a connection between each ministry area and the expression of Safe Sanctuaries in your local church. Even if a church member does not directly volunteer to work with children, youth, or vulnerable adults, having a basic knowledge of Safe Sanctuaries policies and

When recruiting these "champions," look for people who are passionate about creating safe spaces.

procedures, and background about why they are important for the health of the church is incredibly important.

The champions on your Safe Sanctuaries team can help you coordinate and consult with every ministry area in your church as you go about creating and implementing your church's policy. Even in areas where church members may be more difficult to engage, there are connections to be made. For instance, they can help the finance team learn about the importance of paying for the cost of background checks or they can help the trustees committee examine building issues related to Safe Sanctuaries policies, like the need for windows in doors and access to bathroom facilities. Additionally, the entire church staff, regardless of their role, should receive annual training and keep up current background checks to remain in compliance with Safe Sanctuaries guidelines. Your team can be essential in keeping all these moving pieces organized and on track.

This initial team of champions is also useful for implementing your Safe Sanctuaries policy. The final policy should include designated leaders who are responsible for the implementation of the policy, including trainings, documentation, responding, and reporting. These designated leaders should then report to a single point person who will serve as the church's Safe Sanctuaries coordinator. This person will be responsible for keeping records of trainings and background checks, maintaining accountability with the congregation, and most importantly will be the first person to notify when reporting concerns about violations of Safe Sanctuaries policies.

Typically, these leaders naturally come from children's and youth ministries, but ideally they can come from any area of the church. Your initial team of champions can be a great resource for those who are passionate about safety, but are not directly involved with these other ministries.

Like in any area of ministry, the first and most important resource we have available are the people in our communities and their passion for the work we do. When you can recruit a team of people passionate about safety, healthy communities, and thriving ministries, you are well on your way to creating a safer sanctuary.

Creating a Plan

Now that you've identified your champions, it is time to organize, plan, and implement Safe Sanctuaries strategies in your congregation. Using the language that you've developed for your group of champions (squad, task force, committee, council, admin board, etc.), communicate with your champions as you create and launch your holistic plan. Remember, *begin with the end in mind!*

- Know **why** you and your champions are putting energy into this effort.
- Remember that **what** you create reflects the values of your church.
- Finally, focus on **how** the whole congregation engages in abuse prevention and risk reduction to effectively protect your community and work together across every ministry area.

> **Like in any area of ministry, the first and most important resource we have available are the people in our communities and their passion for the work we do.**

_____

_____

_____

_____

_____

_____

_____

_____

_____

_____

_____

_____

For a plan to truly succeed, everyone needs to be on board from the pastors to the volunteers to the parents to the people in the pews who might not initially think this has anything to do with them.

There are many ways to organize this work. What follows here is one example of a roadmap followed by congregations that have successfully developed buy-in for Safe Sanctuaries in their communities.

1. **Organize and identify your champions.** We've covered this in the section above, but it bears repeating that the most important resource you have are the people in your community who are passionate about safety, healthy community, and thriving ministry.

2. **Invite your champions and other relevant staff members and lay leaders to join the Safe Sanctuaries team/committee/squad for your congregation.** Ideally, this group will represent a diversity of groups who each have unique needs regarding abuse prevention and risk reduction. Refer to the groups identified in the earlier chapters of this resource as a starting place for potential representation on this team.

3. **Ask champions to commit to a series of four to six meetings.** These meetings, which will also require some light work between meetings, will be used to identify congregational needs, create and refine policies and procedures, and determine how to roll out this plan and organize trainings. Use the following eight steps to outline the scope of your meetings (these will be covered in more detail in the next chapter):

   - **Step One**—Research issues related to abuse in your community, ministry context, and congregation.

   - **Step Two**—Determine the level of need for policies and procedures and the immediacy of this need.

   - **Step Three**—Evaluate current church practices about engaging with and caring for vulnerable groups.

   - **Step Four**—Develop new or updated policies and procedures.

   - **Step Five**—Develop and refine a plan for responding to recognized abuse and abuse allegations.

   - **Step Six**—Present policies and procedures to your church council (or other responsible party) for formal adoption.

   - **Step Seven**—Create an education plan for the whole congregation.

   - **Step Eight**—Review the plan creation process, evaluate future training needs, and create timeframes for future revisions.

4. **Challenge champions to be in regular communication with pastors and church leadership.** As this group works through each of the eight needs that we will outline below, invite them to keep up an ongoing dialogue with everyone in leadership at the church. For a plan to truly succeed, everyone needs to be on board from the pastors to the volunteers to the parents to the people in the pews who might not initially think this has anything to do with them.

CHAPTER 21

The Eight Steps for Creating a Policy

Kevin Johnson *and* Chris Wilterdink

When you first consider creating a new set of Safe Sanctuaries policies and procedures, the sheer scale of the project can seem daunting. It is natural to feel nervous at the scale of this work, but this is also a project that can be taken one step at a time. With your team at your side, you can boldly embark on the work of creating a fresh or updated Safe Sanctuaries policy by taking this process one step at a time.

Step One—Research Issues Related to Abuse

- Inviting your champions to research and share what they have learned about abuse will set the foundation for much of the work that your Safe Sanctuaries team will undertake. This is also a moment to recognize that some who are serving on your team may have personal experiences with abuse. What and how they share about their own experiences (if anything) can be determined during this stage as well.

- As a team, review the sections on recognizing abuse, signs of abuse, and definitions from Chapter 23. Discuss these sections to ensure that all team members are on the same page when talking about abuse. This is also a good opportunity to review section two of this resource ("The Reality"), with a particular emphasis on the discussion of adverse childhood experiences in chapter four ("Awareness of Reality").

- Review statistics on the frequency of abuse. The website for the Rape, Abuse, and Incest National Network, more commonly known as RAINN, is an excellent resource for general information. Your team should also do additional research using county-level or conference resources to learn about issues of abuse specific to your context, including sex offender registry information pertinent to your area. This research can also include congregational history with abuse and alleged abuse, particularly any incidents involving church staff, congregants, or outside groups using church facilities.

- Familiarize the team with people outside the congregation who can serve as useful resources, for instance the church's attorney, local child-protective services, or local psychologists who work with trauma survivors. Reach out to these resources for information about abusive behaviors, how to recognize abuse, how to handle reports of abuse, and the negative impacts of abuse on the victims and the community where the abuse takes place. Learn about the range of potential consequences including emotional harm, psychological harm, trauma, and distress for both the individuals involved and their families, as well as possible legal damages or verdicts that could be rendered against the church.

Step Two—Determine the Areas of Need in Your Context

- As you and your team work through this second conversation, allow space to prioritize needs. A helpful tool as you identify the different needs in your context is a simple risk evaluation matrix. As you identify risks, topics, and tasks, determine which things to focus on first based upon two factors:

  1. How probable is it that this issue will arise or that it will become a problem in the near future?

  2. How much of an impact would this issue have on our ability to do effective ministry?

  Any issues that are both high probability and high impact issues are critical issues and should be the first you address with your policies and procedures. Issues that have low probability and low impact are non-critical issues and can be among the last things that your team addresses.

- Have all team members complete a ministry activity survey where they list all of the ministries connected to your congregation, when and where those ministries meet, the responsible leaders for each ministry, the participants for each ministry, and the potential risks of abuse related to that ministry. To ensure broad input, consult with other ministry teams, church staff, and specific ministry groups to get a holistic picture of ministry activities and programming. This can help the process of engaging the entire congregation in the efforts of your team and create a safe space for future conversations about changes in policy or practice that may affect the manner in which different ministry groups operate.

- As a team, work together to answer why your church feels the need to implement Safe Sanctuaries policies and procedures in your ministry context. Consider how to answer this question in two to three sentences for anyone who asks. As you think about this question, consider the potential victims of abuse in your congregation who this work is designed to protect. Work through how your church is using this resource to define the word "vulnerable" and how this label applies to everyone in your congregation from children to adult congregants to ministry leaders, staff, and volunteers. This is also a good opportunity to reflect on the words of Bishop Peggy Johnson in the first three chapters of this resource.

- Research state and county reporting laws. As a team, discuss how your work will meet and exceed legal minimums and requirements put into place by

> To ensure broad input, consult with other ministry teams, church staff, and specific ministry groups to get a holistic picture of ministry activities and programming.

our government. As you work through this section, remember that your work in creating safe, healthy, thriving communities is a ministry, not simply a requirement. Think about both what you must do from a legal standpoint, but also what you ought to do from a moral, ethical, and pastoral point of view.

- Gather input and existing resources from conference staff or church insurance providers regarding current effective policies in use in your area. Consider whether everyone in your region is working with a shared understanding of terminology regarding abuse and a shared view about how to recognize abuse. If not, think about how can you gain that understanding.

- Remember that you are not alone when putting together the policies and procedures for your congregation. Research whether your local church, or whether your district, conference, or denomination either do or can contract with providers like Safe Gatherings, Ministry Safe, and others for support on abuse prevention and risk reduction. Providers like these offer online administration, background checks, administration, and training tools.

Step Three—Evaluate Current Practices

- It may sound simplistic, but one of the first steps to creating a new Safe Sanctuaries policy is to investigate whether there is an existing Safe Sanctuaries policy in place. If there is no existing policy, then it's time to start developing one! If there is an existing policy, this is the time for meaningful review and recommitting your team to what your church has already said that it will do to protect everyone in the community. Look at when this policy was created and adopted and consider how your context and your ministry has changed since it was first written. Look to see if there are any gaps in implementation, procedures, response protocols, or new ministry areas that did not exist when the policies were first created.

- As you work through any previous policies, consider how many people in your church know what your current policy says and whether there is already existing knowledge about how to report incidents of abuse. Investigate how the congregation has already been equipped to support one another and reduce vulnerability. Do not assume that work has not been done simply because you are not aware of it, but also do not assume it has been done simply because a written policy exists.

- Look back at the ministry activity survey you completed in the prior section. Spend some time with your team looking at any circumstances or gaps in policies or procedures that could make it easier for abuse to take place. Pay particular attention to newer ministries or ministries where cultural considerations and best practices have changed since the earlier policy was written, particularly in regard to youth ministry, camping and retreat ministries, and college ministries.

Notes

Do not assume that work has not been done simply because you are not aware of it, but also do not assume it has been done simply because a written policy exists.

165

_____

_____

_____

_____

_____

_____

_____

_____

_____

_____

_____

Throughout this resource, we have talked often about the importance of the whole community being involved in creating safe, healthy, thriving environments, and this all flows from the policy itself.

- Examine the existing policy to see if there are robust volunteer recruiting and screening policies. Also look to see if there is adequate supervision of volunteers or staff. A lack of policy guidance in these areas can lead to a lack of support for those leading ministries that rely heavily on volunteers.

- Investigate whether there are any areas of concern or topics where the policy is out-of-date or fails to accomplish the goals that you have outlined in your earlier work. Highlight these trouble spots so that your team can focus on shoring them up when putting together your new policy.

- Look carefully at the procedures around congregational education and the training of all staff and volunteers. Pay close attention to how the current policy discusses training, how often training should take place, how trainings should be organized, and who needs to undergo training. Furthermore, consider how the policy discusses educating the entire congregation on matters of Safe Sanctuaries. Throughout this resource, we have talked often about the importance of the whole community being involved in creating safe, healthy, thriving environments, and this all flows from the policy itself.

- Consider whether there are any unwritten rules, loopholes, or expectations that complicate the current written policy. For instance, how does the policy regard teenagers who volunteer in children's ministry, how long does someone need to be a member before volunteering in ministry? How does the policy regard volunteers who have undergone some form of Safe Sanctuaries training at another congregation before joining yours? While it may not be possible to make firm rules involving every case, try to write down any unwritten rules so that there is a standard to use going forward.

- Finally, review current abuse reporting processes for volunteers, paid staff, and clergy. Analyze the process of how victims of abuse might report abuse to the church. Consider whether abuse response procedures meet legal minimums for reporting in your area, and, more importantly, whether abuse response procedures are crafted in a way that they will prevent further harm. Again, while it is always essential to fulfill our legal mandates, it is equally important to exceed these legal minimums to fulfill our ethical, moral, and pastoral duties to the community.

Step Four—Develop New or Updated Policies and Procedures

- As you prepare to develop new or updated Safe Sanctuaries policies and procedures for your congregation, begin by reviewing the findings from the ministry activity survey and the risk evaluation matrix to determine the areas of greatest need and start by addressing these areas first. This part of your team's work will involve integrating all that has been learned in the first three steps so that you can close gaps in your policies and procedures that make space for abuse.

- If you are creating a new Safe Sanctuaries policy and are looking for a starting point, consider the "Core Four" of Safe Sanctuaries. These four fundamental aspects of a Safe Sanctuaries policy are screening, supervision, reporting, and response plan.

- Screening includes all policies related to background checks, references, and even the length of time that a volunteer must be active in the church. This should also include policies about how often background checks should be renewed, how they will be maintained, and who will be responsible for ensuring that these policies are followed.

- Supervision is the most involved of these four foundational aspects of a Safe Sanctuaries policy and includes most of the items that you likely think about when considering a Safe Sanctuaries policy. This is where you will cover everything from how volunteers and staff will be trained, how many adults must be in a room, how roamers will operate in your congregation, and how facilities must be used (for instance, keeping doors open at all times). This is also the area where you will want to get into the most specific detail about each individual area of your ministry and should include everything from procedures for medical release forms, liability release forms, social media behavior, and facility use standards for church ministries and third parties who are using the building for non-church functions.

- Reporting is required from any staff or volunteer 1) when that person personally witnesses an incident of abuse or exploitation, 2) when an allegation of an incident of abuse or exploitation is made to the staff member or volunteer by a third party, or 3) when a child or adult discloses an experience of abuse or exploitation. It is important to spell out not only these times when it is required for staff and volunteers to report abuse, but also to lay out how they should report abuse, whom they should contact, and when they should raise concerns about suspected abuse that they have not directly witnessed or been given information about.

- Finally, be sure to include guidelines in your Safe Sanctuaries policy about how staff members, volunteers, and the church as a whole should respond to those who suffer from abuse, those who report abuse, and those who perpetrate abuse. First and foremost, the victim's safety is the primary concern! Beyond that, the response should be quick, compassionate, unified, and no information should be concealed or disregarded. Furthermore, the accused should be treated with dignity, but immediately and discreetly removed from further involvement with children and youth until an investigation has been completed. Pastoral support should also be available to all involved.

Step Five—Develop and Refine a Response Plan

- The final aspect for the Core Four deserves its own individual area of focus. Much of what we have covered so far in this resource has focused

Notes

These four fundamental aspects of a Safe Sanctuaries policy are screening, supervision, reporting, and response plan.

_____

_____

_____

_____

_____

_____

_____

_____

_____

_____

_____

_____

_____

A complete Safe Sanctuaries policy must also include a clear playbook for responding to both allegations and proven incidents of abuse.

on preparation and practices to reduce the risk of abuse in the community. These preventative measures make all the difference in the world. But a complete Safe Sanctuaries policy must also include a clear playbook for responding to both allegations and proven incidents of abuse.

- The safety of the victim is always the primary concern when responding to an incident of abuse. Therefore, the most important part of your policy is laying out how staff members, volunteers, and the church as a whole will respond to both the victim and the person who first reported the abuse (in the event that these are different people). The response in these situations should be quick, compassionate, unified, and no information should be concealed or disregarded. Furthermore, the accused should be treated with dignity, but should also be immediately and discreetly removed from further involvement with ministry until an investigation has been completed. Pastoral support should also be available for all involved.

- Second, think about who should be contacted and informed when an incident of abuse is reported or when there is suspicion of abuse. A good rule is that staff members and volunteers should always report first to the person in charge of the ministry where they are involved and then this person should inform the pastor and contact the appropriate local authorities (for instance, the police, Child Protective Services). When dealing with incidents of abuse, there should also be a clear policy about who will inform the parents or caregiver of the victim if that person is not already aware of the abuse. All lines of reporting should be clear and well-understood by everyone involved in ministry.

- This is also an important moment to consider how information will be recorded and stored. It is good practice for the person responsible for reporting the abuse to authorities to also complete an incident report form. Consider how these forms will be updated, accessed, and stored and who on your team will be responsible for maintaining these documents. It is critical that those receiving reports understand the vital nature of confidentiality, reporting requirements, and limiting knowledge of the report to only those who need to know. When assigning someone to this role, whether it is the pastor or another trusted individual, consider how you will train this person (or group of people) on receiving reports, following legal requirements, and keeping the process confidential.

- Furthermore, consider whether these forms provide critical information necessary for further investigation both from outside authorities and within the congregation. Also, make a decision about how the completion of this form will trigger action in your response plan. When a form is filed, there should be a clear sequence of actions that follow up on the report.

- As discussed in several of these steps, the team should investigate how the response plan complies with local laws and denominational policies.

Consider talking with legal counsel, social services, insurance providers, or counselors regarding reporting responsibilities and requirements to make sure that your team, staff members, and volunteers are all clear about their legal responsibilities in your specific state and local context.

- Incidents of abuse can also generate outside attention. As part of your policy, designate someone who will be tasked with communicating with the media or handling any requests for comment. Generally, this should be one person, and if your church is part of a larger denomination, someone who can relate with and be in communication with denominational representatives as well.

- While we have largely focused on incidents of abuse that are proven to be true, it is also necessary to have a policy in place on how to handle both allegations that are found to be false, allegations that cannot be conclusively proven true, and allegations that do not meet the definition of abuse. These can be difficult scenarios and may often involve matters of discernment. This is why it is essential for your team to put in place guidelines and policies that your congregation will follow ahead of time.

- Finally, you will need to have a policy in place for when allegations of abuse are confirmed, We have covered certain aspects of this policy already, but it bears repeating them here as well. The components of this policy include, but are not limited to the following:

  - Providing emergency care for the victim. Also consider how to provide pastoral care and support for the victim when appropriate and desired.

  - Having a plan for notifying legal authorities, relevant church members, and parents or other legal guardians of the victim.

  - Determining how to protect or preserve evidence.

  - Determining how to communicate with the media, if necessary.

  - Documenting steps for every action taken when a report is received.

  - Determining how to remove the abuser from direct contact with vulnerable populations in the church. Consider if your church has any policies regarding the involvement of an abuser or sex offender in the congregation and when it would be appropriate to use these policies.

  - Planning how to get the full cooperation of church staff and leadership in investigations or legal proceedings.

  - Determining how to provide pastoral care for the victim, the family of the victim, and the abuser, whether from within the church itself or through a partner organization.

- As your policies and procedures come in to focus, ensure that they are meeting the needs identified by your team in the risk evaluation matrix and the ministry activity survey. Work to refine the policies and procedures until all identified needs have been addressed to the group's satisfaction.

Notes

> **These can be difficult scenarios and may often involve matters of discernment.**

_____

_____

_____

_____

_____

_____

_____

_____

_____

_____

_____

_____

Step Six—Formal Adoption of Policies and Procedures

- With a fresh, or freshly updated, set of policies and procedures in place that meet the ministry needs and goals of your congregation, it is now time for your team to present your work to the church council, or other approving group, for formal adoption. As you prepare for this step, ensure that you remember to state the *why* behind all of the work that your team has done to this point and include that statement as you present material to the church council.

- In anticipation of your presentation, consider sharing the contents of your new Safe Sanctuaries policies and procedures with the church council prior to the official meeting and final vote. This will give the council members time to prepare. Furthermore, if your team has been keeping up regular communication about your progress through each step until this point, then this step can be a formal moment of acceptance and celebration.

- Create an executive brief of three hundred words or less for the council to read over either before or during the meeting. Also, create a short presentation highlighting the *why* of your team's work, the risks and gaps identified by your research, the process used to create these new policies and procedures, and explain any major updates or changes to existing policies or practices. In this presentation, be sure to include a timeframe for periodic review of the new policies and procedures as well as the names of the parties responsible for this review.

> As you prepare for this step, ensure that you remember to state the *why* behind all of the work that your team has done to this point and include that statement as you present material to the church council.

Step Seven—Education and Buy-In from the Whole Congregation

- Once the new Safe Sanctuaries policies and procedures have been formally adopted, the Safe Sanctuaries team should work together with church leadership to create a coordinated effort to educate and create buy-in from the entire church regarding the new policies and procedures.

- There is no magic formula for creating a culture of awareness and support that will work in every context. Churches that have created buy-in from their entire congregation have used a variety of messaging techniques and a number of different processes to educate and generate investment from their communities. However, most of these successful efforts share two vital traits: 1) setting expectations and 2) focusing attention.

- Everyone agrees that abuse is bad. No one wants abuse to be present in their community. The issue is that many people in your community may not understand what this issue has to do with them or, more importantly, what they can do about it.

- To address the first issue, walk the congregation through the reasons behind the work you have done, the *why* that you highlighted in the previous step and that has guided your work since the beginning. Be sure to include both the active and preventative reasons for this work. You are not only working to prevent abuse in your congregation, but to create safe and healthy environments where everyone can thrive. Both of these are vital to getting people invested.

- To address the second issue, work with your congregation to build an understanding of the harm that abuse can cause, how to spot the potential signs of abuse, and then share with them the plan of action that your congregation has put in place if a member needs to report abuse. Lay out the basics of what is included in the Safe Sanctuaries policy adopted by your church and the expectations that are being set for everyone in the community to ensure the safety of all.

- This effort at education and creating buy-in also needs to be given adequate attention to find a place in the hearts of people. Consider offering educational opportunities about your church's Safe Sanctuaries policies through specific meetings, small groups, Sunday school gatherings, communications like emails and newsletters, bulletin inserts, information presented by leadership during worship times, the church's website and social media postings, and, of course, through the regular trainings you will offer those involved in ministering to vulnerable groups. These regular trainings can be done by members of your congregation or run by outside service providers or community partners who can provide accurate information and help to keep everyone in compliance with the policy in place at your church.

Step Eight—Review, Evaluate, and Repeat

- Once you've reached this step, take a moment to step back and consider all the work you've done. Take a breath. Celebrate! You have done a good thing by creating a new Safe Sanctuaries policy and inviting your whole congregation to be part of a supportive, knowledgeable, and healthy community. Good things are worthy of celebration and praise!

- At the same time, the work of building safer sanctuaries is never truly finished. Often, the best time to reflect on what you have learned through this planning process is within a month after the completion of steps one through seven. Take time with the team to analyze what went well, what you found challenging or even overwhelming, ideas for future work, and suggestions for future team members or church leadership to consider. A brief, written reflection will help the next team continue to do effective work regarding this important ministry.

- Create one final review that compares the initial ministry activity survey done prior to the creation/revision work with the final policy that you have

Notes

Good things are worthy of celebration and praise!

171

Notes

_____

_____

_____

_____

_____

_____

_____

_____

_____

_____

_____

_____

No matter how you go about this work, the most important considerations are always the safety of your community, the health of your ministries, and a humble attitude that embraces the idea that there is always more to learn.

adopted. Create a numbered list of additions, changes, and updates to the Safe Sanctuaries policy and note how many risk gaps have been addressed and if any remain or need to be revisited soon.

- Finally, work with church leadership and staff to identify a future date to review and update policies and trainings. Ideally, this would take place every one or two years and would not require the full amount of effort put forth for the initial rounds of policy creation.

As you embark on your own work of creating a new or revised Safe Sanctuaries policy with your team, remember that these are guidelines and helpful tips. If you discover something in your efforts that works better for your team than what we have recommended, then we encourage you to embrace these new practices and fit your work to the skills you have at your disposal. No matter how you go about this work, the most important considerations are always the safety of your community, the health of your ministries, and a humble attitude that embraces the idea that there is always more to learn. You are doing good work. Take heart and know that you are not alone in your efforts.

Visit **SaferSanctuaries.org** for more information on the **Safer Sanctuaries Online Guide**, your companion in the process of developing and implementing a Safe Sanctuaries policy for your church.

CHAPTER 22

Gaining Support and Creating a Culture of Protection

Kevin Johnson *and* Chris Wilterdink

Going All In

Creating buy-in among your congregation helps to shift the efforts of the Safe Sanctuaries team from policy creation into a movement that creates a culture of safety. This is a culture that acknowledges the reality that abuse can take place in any community, including theirs, but is also equipped to respond to this reality and protect the vulnerable among them. This is a culture that is empowered by education, that has learned to recognize abuse and knows how and when to report it. This is a culture that understands not only the *what* of Safe Sanctuaries policies, but also the *why* and is inspired to build a healthy, thriving community on a foundation of safety.

Developing a culture like this, a culture that respects and both proactively and innately creates safe spaces for ministry, can take time. But it is time worth taking, and these painstaking efforts will be worthwhile. Beyond this, keep in mind the old saying that "many hands make light work." The more buy-in you can foster in your congregation, the easier this task will be.

The first step to creating buy-in and creating this kind of culture lies in understanding how people think. People support and make space for things that add value to what they care about. With this in mind, framing the policies and procedures you've adopted in a way that emphasizes the new possibilities they create can be a positive way to encourage others to engage.

Similarly, when talking to the whole congregation, emphasize the ways that these policies and procedures empower them to actively respond to abuse. Abuse is a "when" proposition, not an "if," and having a plan for how to respond to allegations or incidents of abuse gives people a necessary framework for how they can help. Everyone should know what to do when abuse happens.

It is also important to emphasize the both/and motivations for having a Safe Sanctuaries policy. The policy protects both victims from abuse and staff and volunteers from unfounded accusations. Many in your congregation won't immediately realize that the policies are equally important to protect staff, volunteers, and potentially even themselves.

_____
_____
_____
_____
_____
_____
_____
_____
_____
_____
_____

Get student leadership engaged! Children and youth are among the vulnerable groups protected by effective abuse prevention policies.

Here are a few more steps that you and your Safe Sanctuaries team can take to gain buy-in from your entire congregation:

- As you work through the process of creating a new policy, periodically share policy drafts with select committees and teams for feedback in order to perfect your policy before adoption. Ask for evaluation and adaptation from these groups and show them how their input changed the final policy. Use your team of champions to create more champions.

- Get student leadership engaged! Children and youth are among the vulnerable groups protected by effective abuse prevention policies. Ensure that they are informed and meaningfully represented by any policy or language used in the church around Safe Sanctuaries. Yes, you will be training adult volunteers, but you should also consider what would it look like to do a training for children and youth to learn what is in your church's Safe Sanctuaries policy. You might even think about empowering some young leaders as accountability partners who can survey the different ministry activities they attend and provide feedback to adult leaders on whether Safe Sanctuaries procedures are being followed. Finally, consider inviting a representative student to talk about the Safe Sanctuaries policies used by the church and how these policies are creating a safe and welcoming environment for discipleship and growth. Look for examples of positive language throughout this resource for phrases you could use to encourage young people when they talk with the congregation.

- Request feedback from volunteers and parents, especially when specific needs arise. If you have trusted volunteers, ask them for feedback about the church's policy and how easy or hard it is to follow. Similarly, ask for feedback when conducting trainings and when evaluating how policies you have adopted are playing out in practice. If you have a new volunteer or parent, ask them to look at the policies and procedures with fresh eyes and ask, "Why do you think we do things this way?" Outside opinions and fresh insights can be very helpful!

- Remember, there will never be a perfect policy. However, that should not stop your team or church leaders from the work of perfecting the policies and procedures used in your ministry context. When something is this important, it deserves to be revisited and refined regularly to ensure that the church is providing spaces where the risk of abuse is minimal and any responses to abuse are well thought out and caring. Invite others into the planning and revision process, specifically using their areas of expertise or areas of passion.

- The approval process by a church council or church committee is another opportunity to create buy-in. It is a time to showcase why this ministry work is so important and how holistic adoption and support can strengthen the worshiping community. During the approval process, make sure that the *why* of the Safe Sanctuaries policies is coherent and connects with the *why* that motivates the ministry work of the entire church. Consider how

Safe Sanctuaries fits into the mission and vision of your church. Adopting a central Safe Sanctuaries policy can also ensure consistency across ministry areas. You will also want to ensure the legality of any policy you create by involving insurance providers and legal counsel. Those folks can be powerful allies and champions when they believe in the work of risk reduction.

An interactive process when creating policies and procedures for risk reduction in your church leads to an effective Safe Sanctuaries policy that will protect the vulnerable from high-risk situations and protect staff and volunteers from unfounded accusations. An interactive process also helps to encourage buy-in since more people are included in the effort and feel like they have a stake in the success of the policies that have been adopted. Effective Safe Sanctuaries policies protect the whole church and the ministries it offers.

Train Your Community

Regular trainings about your Safe Sanctuaries policies and procedures are another essential component of gathering support within your congregation and creating a healthy culture of protection. Staff members and volunteers should participate in trainings at least once a year to keep themselves up-to-date and to refresh their familiarity with the policies that you have adopted in your congregation. These seasoned veterans are also helpful in guiding new trainees through the Safe Sanctuaries process and can help with answering any questions.

It can also be useful to open up these trainings to the entire congregation, whether they are involved in the relevant ministries or not. This allows all members of the congregation, as well as parents, to become more knowledgeable about the policies in your church and the kind of culture that you are hoping to create. These church members can then become ambassadors to the rest of the congregation, helping them understand the mission of the Safe Sanctuaries ministry.

Similarly, consider inviting youth to join in these trainings, especially youth who are interested in one day volunteering in ministry themselves. This not only helps to train future generations of leaders, but also educates youth about the policies that are in place and allows them to hold church leaders, staff, and volunteers accountable for following through on the policies and procedures that have been adopted.

The scope of your training can be tailored to your particular context and the specific policies and procedures that you have put in place in your congregation. One template you may find useful is to follow the scope of this resource as a way to lay out your training and introduce your trainees to the ministry of Safe Sanctuaries.

If you choose to follow the scope and sequence of this resource, you can begin each training session by exploring the reasons why you are in attendance, the reasons why you have created Safe Sanctuaries policies, and the reasons why this ministry

Notes

These church members can then become ambassadors to the rest of the congregation, helping them understand the mission of the Safe Sanctuaries ministry.

175

is so essential to the church. From there, you can proceed to the reality of abuse, both in the world and in your particular context. This can include everything from statistics about abuse, stories from your own church's experience, how to recognize abuse, and the psychological impacts that abuse has on both victims and on the community where the abuse occurred.

Next, your training can move on to cover the basics of Safe Sanctuaries ministry and the essential principles that should be in place in every ministry. These principles can be summarized as honesty, communication, and accountability. Everything in Safe Sanctuaries eventually points back to one of these three principles. With these foundational elements in place, you may consider breaking trainees out into smaller groups based on the area of ministry where they will be serving. This allows for trainees to focus on the issues regarding Safe Sanctuaries that may be particular to their specific area of ministry.

Then, walk through the details of your policies and procedures. At this point, it may even be useful to take trainees through the eight step process that was used to create the policies that your church has adopted. This helps to highlight both the details of the policy and the reasoning behind why these policies were written.

Finally, as a group, celebrate the work that you have done together, affirm the work that those participating in the training will be doing, and send your trainees forth to do the work of ministry that they have been called to do.

Make This Work Worshipful

Another way to create buy-in and create a culture of safety that encourages healthy, thriving communities is to celebrate the work of Safe Sanctuaries together as a congregation. These policies and procedures are not only about avoiding damaging outcomes, they are also a work of ministry and pastoral care for the entire community.

When formally adopting your new Safe Sanctuaries policies and procedures, consider building a service around celebrating this adoption and the spirit of safety and protection within your community. A liturgy affirming the work of Safe Sanctuaries is included in this resource at the end of Chapter 28.

Beyond this service, regular reminders about the ministry of Safe Sanctuaries during times of worship can help to reinforce the important work being done in the community. Additionally, regularly including the work of Safe Sanctuaries in the prayers of the community is a way to support those who are implementing these policies while asking for God to bless the work of their hands. You are doing good work, and it is good to celebrate the work that you are doing in protecting all of God's children.

These policies and procedures are not only about avoiding damaging outcomes, they are also a work of ministry and pastoral care for the entire community.

Live the Policy and Do What You Say You Will Do

Ultimately, all of this work will bear fruit only if your team and the leaders in your church live out the policy you've created and do what you say you will do. The only way to truly build trust with a community is to be trustworthy and show people that your words are followed by actions. This is the last and most important way to build buy-in from your congregation. Everyone involved in this ministry must put forth the effort to create meaningful policies and then put them into practice. When you follow through, this attitude becomes infectious and begins to form the fabric of a faithful community that can endure beyond the work that you are doing today.

As you think back on the last few chapters and all that has been covered, let us highlight a few key points that bear repeating.

- Create a network of champions to help create the Safe Sanctuaries policies and procedures in your congregation. This is a communal effort and should be done in community. Never forget that the people in your community are your greatest resource in reducing the risk of abuse.

- Follow the policies that you create. Do thorough background checks, ensure that two adults are always present, and follow through when abuse is reported. You have put these policies in place for a reason. Trust the process you have created.

- Have regular trainings and embrace the practice of cross-training groups of volunteers alongside participants in ministry. Participants in ministry can help keep leaders accountable if they know the policies and procedures that are in place to keep everyone safe.

- Regularly update the entire congregation on educational opportunities, information regarding Safe Sanctuaries, and reminders about policies and procedures so that everyone knows what is appropriate and how to report potential abuse.

- Review the policies and procedures used by your congregation every one or two years. Pay particular attention to new ministries that have emerged or new gaps that have been created by scheduling, spacing issues, or the use of technology.

Everyone involved in this ministry must put forth the effort to create meaningful policies and then put them into practice.

CHAPTER 23

Recognizing Abuse, Defining Terms, and Policy Guidelines

Kevin Johnson *and* Chris Wilterdink

Every set of Safe Sanctuaries polices and procedures will be different based on the context of the congregation and the context of the ministry. There simply cannot be a one-size-fits-all policy. It is essential that you and your Safe Sanctuaries team do the work of putting together your own individualized policy.

However, it can also be difficult to work from an entirely blank slate. With that in mind, this chapter will include a handful of useful sections that can provide a template for your work and that may be useful to include within the policy you create. We encourage you to use these sections as a starting point or framework for your own policy creation process.

Definitions

It may seem like a simple task, but defining terms is an important part of putting together Safe Sanctuaries policy and communicating it staff, volunteers, and others. When we all work from a shared vocabulary, it helps us to communicate better and be more clear about the words that we are using. Below are a number of terms that are often used through the work of Safe Sanctuaries. Additionally, use the definitions for different types of abuse found in Chapter 9, "Forms of Abuse and the Basics of Our Legal Obligations" to help shape your work and create a shared vocabulary with your team.

- *Abuse* means harm or threatened harm to the health and welfare of a child, youth, or vulnerable adult by any person responsible for the health and welfare of that child, youth, or vulnerable adult.
- *Adult* means any person at least eighteen years of age.
- *Appropriate* means conduct that one understands would be acceptable and permissible by a child's parent or guardian.
- *Child* refers to a person under eighteen years of age.
- *Leader* means anyone personally responsible for supervising and overseeing a specific church-related function, event, or activity.

- *Parent or guardian* means any parent, stepparent, foster parent, grandparent, or appointed guardian with general responsibility for the health, education, or welfare of a child or vulnerable adult.
- *Sexual contact* means the intentional touching of the intimate parts or the clothing covering the intimate parts of a youth, child, or vulnerable adult.
- *Sexual exploitation* means allowing, permitting, or encouraging a vulnerable adult, child, or youth to engage in prostitution or photographing, filming, or creating electronic or computer-generated images depicting a child, youth, or vulnerable adult engaged in actual or suggestive sexual conduct.
- *Sexual harassment* means any sexual advance or demand, either verbal or physical, which is perceived by the recipient as demeaning, intimidating, or coercive.
- *Staff* means any employee of the ministry. This can include both paid and unpaid staff members, but is particularly used in reference to paid employees.
- *Volunteer* means a person who participates as a leader or assists a leader in activities relating to any event or ministry without compensation.
- **Vulnerable adult** are people eighteen years of age or older who are unable to protect themselves from abuse, neglect, or exploitation.
- *Youth* refers to a person between the ages of thirteen and seventeen.

Recognizing Abuse

Every Safe Sanctuaries policy and training should include information to help the congregation recognize signs of abuse, recognize abusers, or recognize abusive behavior.

Before we begin this discussion about the recognition of abuse, please note that the language and content discussed may have a triggering effect on you or those in your congregation. The following may contain sensitive material and covers topics like sexual assault, sexual violence, emotional abuse, neglect, and physical abuse, among others. Please be aware of the content and proceed with caution for both yourself and those in your pastoral care.

Additionally, it is important to remember that the presence of a single sign does not prove that abuse is occurring or has occurred. Instead, these signs should prompt a closer look at the situation, especially when signs appear repeatedly or in combination with one another. Finally, remember that this is not a complete list.

Signs a Child Has Been Physically Abused or Neglected

- The child exhibits sudden changes in behavior or school performance.
- The child receives no help for physical or medical problems that are brought to a parent's attention.

Notes

> Every Safe Sanctuaries policy and training should include information to help the congregation recognize signs of abuse, recognize abusers, or recognize abusive behavior.

_____

_____

_____

_____

_____

_____

_____

_____

_____

_____

_____

- The child lacks adult supervision.
- The child experiences learning problems or difficulty concentrating that cannot be attributed to a specific physical or psychological cause.
- The child appears to always be watchful or vigilant.
- The child is overly compliant, passive, or withdrawn.
- The child arrives at school or other activities early, stays late, and does not want to go home.

Recognizing Physically Abusive Behavior from an Adult

- The adult shows little concern for a child in their care.
- The adult denies the existence of or blames the child for the child's problems.
- The adult asks other caregivers to use harsh physical discipline if the child misbehaves.
- The adult expresses that the child is bad, worthless, or burdensome.
- The adult demands a level of physical or academic performance that the child cannot achieve.
- The adult looks primarily to the child for care, attention, and satisfaction of emotional needs.

Signs a Child Has Been Sexually Abused

- The child has difficulty walking or sitting.
- The child suddenly refuses to participate in physical activities.
- The child reports nightmares or bedwetting.
- The child experiences a sudden change in appetite.
- The child demonstrates bizarre, sophisticated, or unusual sexual knowledge or behavior.
- The child becomes pregnant or contracts a sexually-transmitted disease.
- The child runs away.
- The child reports sexual abuse.

Recognizing Sexually Abusive Behavior from an Adult

- The adult is unduly protective of the child in their care.
- The adult severely limits the child's contact with other children.
- The adult is secretive and isolated.
- The adult is jealous or controlling toward family members.

These signs should prompt a closer look at the situation, especially when signs appear repeatedly or in combination with one another.

Specific Policy Guidelines

If you've read through the rest of this resource, then much of what we will cover below will already be common knowledge. However, we feel that it will be helpful for you to have this information all in one place, laid out in a way similar to how it might be found in the Safe Sanctuaries policy that you and your team ultimately put together. Once again, remember that this is not a full policy. It is merely a template and a guideline to help you begin working on your own policy. You will want to flesh this out with your own policies that are tailored to your ministry context, your legal context, your resources, and the needs that you have discovered in your community.

Background Checks

Current background checks and yearly trainings should be required for all full-time staff, part-time staff, and volunteers who work with or come in contact with children, youth, or vulnerable adults.

All staff and volunteers must have a nationwide criminal background check completed and kept on file. It is standard that background checks be completed at least every two years. Often, the most helpful information to meet this standard can be found by running a county-level criminal background check.

An sample "Authorization and Request for Criminal Records Check" form can be found in the appendix on page 236.

Training Guidelines

Annual Safe Sanctuaries training is mandatory for all staff and volunteers. Proof of completion should be kept on file by both the church and the trainee and should be available to the conference upon request. There are several methods of training including in-person events, online training, and recorded videos. A church's Safe Sanctuaries coordinator should facilitate or organize speakers for these trainings. At minimum, training should include:

- A review of current policies and procedures
- A detailed overview about signs of abuse and local reporting laws
- Documentation of attendance and completion of training

These annual trainings can be made more useful by inviting guest speakers or by giving specific attention to topics unique to your context in addition to fulfilling the minimum guidelines.

Notes

> There are several methods of training including in-person events, online training, and recorded videos.

Supervision Guidelines

Safe Sanctuaries guidelines require that each local church provide adequate non-related adult supervision for ministries attended by children, youth, and/or vulnerable adults. A minimum of two non-related adults should be present at all relevant ministries.

With the exception of ministry involving vulnerable adults, a five-year difference in age between on-site supervisors and the oldest supervised participant is required. Persons closer in age to those supervised may assist the primary on-site supervisors.

Daycare programs hosted on the church campus, whether privately run or church affiliated, must follow all guidelines for non-related adult supervision.

Teacher to child ratios should be followed for all age-groups. When multiple age-groups gather together, the lowest ratio should be followed. The teacher to child ratios for different age-groups are as follows:

- Nursery (Birth to one year-old)—1 adult to 3 children
- Preschool (Two years old to five years old)—1 adult to 3 children
- Elementary (First to fifth grades)—1 adult to 5 children
- Middle school (Sixth to eighth grade)—1 adult to 6 children
- High school (Ninth to twelfth grade)—1 adult to 8 children

Contextual Guidelines

As previously mentioned, part of the work of your Safe Sanctuaries team involves taking the minimum standards for Safe Sanctuaries policies and fitting them to the needs of your local ministry context.

Local church policies should meet the following minimum standards:

- Educate the congregation on the definitions of abuse.
- Provide a copy of your Safe Sanctuaries policy in written form to the entire congregation. This policy should also be:
  - posted in easy-to-locate areas in each room.
  - available on the church website.
- Develop selection and screening criteria for church staff and volunteers that include background checks every two years for each person.
- Implement the two non-related adult rule.
- Annual Safe Sanctuaries training for all volunteers and paid staff.
- All internal windows should be uncovered in all rooms, doors should be left open, and all areas should have unobstructed views (hallways, shared areas, stairwells, playground, and so forth).

> **With the exception of ministry involving vulnerable adults, a five-year difference in age between on-site supervisors and the oldest supervised participant is required.**

- A sign-in and sign-out procedure should be implemented for nursery, pre-school, and elementary-age children. This means that:
  - Children must be signed in and out by a parent or legal guardian.
  - Youth activities should also have attendance policies or sign-in and sign-out procedures. The church can determine the appropriate age for youth to sign themselves in and out.
- A designated response protocol for allegations of abuse that follows state and federal law.

Additional Recommendations for Local Church Policies

- All counseling sessions should be conducted with open doors. Additionally, have a policy in place about when someone should be referred to a professional counselor, especially in response to abuse allegations.
- Provide advance written documentation notice to parents for off-campus activities, trips, and retreats.
- Maintain adequate insurance for the scope of your ministries, including coverage for transportation, camps, and on-site work.
- Maintain and update guidelines for church websites and social media platforms.
- Maintain and update transportation rules and guidelines. Transportation should also follow the two non-related adults rule.
- Implement a participation covenant for all participants and leaders that signals their awareness of all Safe Sanctuaries policies and procedures.
- Provide for first-aid and CPR-trained personnel to always be available and have access to adequate equipment.
- Provide annual parent and family Safe Sanctuaries training.

Vacation Bible School

Vacation Bible school (VBS) requires numerous volunteers over a short time period. Traditionally, VBS is offered as a week-long event. Significant effort should be given to include as many staff and approved volunteers as possible, and these leaders should be distributed so that at least one is in each specific area or grouping. In addition, a one-time orientation or training for VBS volunteers should be provided prior to the VBS event. As a part of this training, Safe Sanctuaries guidelines should be covered.

Notes

Vacation Bible school (VBS) requires numerous volunteers over a short time period.

183

_____

_____

_____

_____

_____

_____

_____

_____

_____

_____

_____

Care must be taken when planning these events so that leaders are as prepared as possible for unforeseen circumstances and are able to ensure the safety of all participants.

Preschool and Childcare Security Policies

Any preschool programs or licensed childcare centers hosted on the church property must have detailed, program-specific employee handbooks and security policies that are conscientiously followed and mandated by state guidelines. All teachers must follow the program-specific security policies and employee handbooks as well as the Safe Sanctuaries policy of the hosting church. Programs must always meet their state's staff-to-child ratios for these kinds of facilities.

Guidelines for Off-Campus Outings and Overnight Trips

Overnight trips and off-campus outings are important bonding experiences and help participants experience God in diverse ways. Care must be taken when planning these events so that leaders are as prepared as possible for unforeseen circumstances and are able to ensure the safety of all participants. It is the event coordinator's responsibility to understand the policies, accommodations, and available resources involved in planning a trip.

Policies for Off-Campus Outings

- An annual medical emergency information form should be required for participants of all off-site events. This must be signed by the parent or guardian of the participant. At a basic level, this includes emergency contact information, insurance information, allergies or medical conditions, as well as a permission to treat or seek treatment.

- Parents or legal guardians must also provide written permission for each ministry event in which the child or youth participates. Paper sign-in, digital sign-in, or online registration all indicate parental permission.

- Parents or legal guardians will receive at least forty-eight hours' notice with full information (including a predetermined start and finish time) about all events and activities in which their children or youth will participate. This should include a predetermined start and finish time.

- Emergency contact information for personnel leading an off-site activity must also be provided to parents or legal guardians in the event that a parent or legal guardian needs to contact the leaders or their child. This is also true for on-site events in which parents are off-site and may need to contact leaders.

- When youth are allowed to participate in activities out of sight of adult supervision, whether on-site or off-site, youth should be in groups of at least three. Adults must give youth a meet-up plan and instruct them to check-in with background-approved adults at given time increments.

Policies for On-Site Overnight Events

- In the event of an overnight event held on the church campus, gender-specific sleeping areas should be assigned with each gender sleeping in separate rooms that are supervised with a ratio of one adult per eight children or youth and at least two leaders. Any deviation from this procedure must include advance notice that includes the specific accommodation plan to parents, and parents must give their written consent. Note: A text message or email may suffice for permission at the discretion of the ministry director.

- For overnight events, normal activity ratios apply.

- Signed permission slips with emergency contacts must be obtained from a parent or legal guardian for each child or youth participant and should be turned in to a designated staff member prior to the event. Handwritten notes are not acceptable. Keep all forms on file for proper documentation.

- Appropriate sleeping attire must be worn by all adults, children, and youth, especially outside of the sleeping quarters (for instance, men should wear shirts).

Policies for Off-Site Overnight Events and Camping Events

- Selected hotels must have rooms that open to the interior of the building, and rooms should all be on the same hallway if possible.

- Genders must be separated during sleeping time.

- If two adults of the same gender as youth cannot be assigned to a room housing youth, the youth will be roomed separately from adults. However, children in sixth grade and below must have two adults in their room. If adjoining rooms are available with doors that can be left open, a single adult in each of the adjoining rooms is acceptable.

- An adult must never share a bed with a child or youth.

- When adults need to be assigned to separate rooms, it is recommended that adult rooms be dispersed between the rooms of other participants as much as possible.

- If room checks are needed, two adults should perform them together.

- When camping using tents, adults must sleep separately from children and youth. Doors to the tents of children or youth should face the doors of adult tents. Married adults may share a tent when accommodations allow.

- For private showers, bathers will dress and undress behind closed curtains or doors. Under no circumstances should two people share the same enclosed shower.

> Signed permission slips with emergency contacts must be obtained from a parent or legal guardian for each child or youth participant and should be turned in to a designated staff member prior to the event.

_____
_____
_____
_____
_____
_____
_____
_____
_____
_____
_____
_____

- If open showers are the only option, showers must be scheduled separately for unclothed children, youth, and adults. Bathing suits may be worn to help comply with Safe Sanctuaries practices.

- When children or youth are showering, adults will monitor activities from outside of the bathroom or shower facility.

- Every location is different, and it is the responsibility of the program director to ensure that arrangements comply with church policy.

- Children, youth, and vulnerable adults should have access to a telephone or cell phone during church-sponsored events that are held either on or off the church premises.

Transportation

Any person driving a church-owned vehicle or driving a personal vehicle on behalf of the church must consent to a motor vehicle record check and provide proof of current insurance coverage. When using charter buses or other contracted drivers, the carrier must provide certification that the driver has completed a recent background check. Keep in place the two non-related adult rule when providing transportation.

Transportation Guidelines

- All drivers for church events must provide proof of insurance and a driver's license for the local church to keep on file. Drivers must provide copies to the office whenever these documents are updated. Insurance must include the minimum insurance coverage for property damage and public liability as required by law. However, it is recommended that drivers have more than the minimum required.

- All drivers for any church event must be adults—as defined by this policy.

- Whenever possible, ministries should contract vehicles and drivers for events.

- All vehicles used for events must be in good working order and should contain a first-aid kit or be provided with one for a group trip.

- When transporting groups, copies of the entire group's emergency forms should be in each vehicle or available digitally. There should also be a copy of the emergency forms at the church or in the hands of a designated adult who will be available via phone for emergencies.

- When possible, it is a best practice that two non-related background-approved adults be in each vehicle.

- Drivers must not drive for more than ten hours per day. Breaks from driving must be taken at least every three hours.

- No youth should drive to an out-of-town event under any circumstances.

All drivers for church events must provide proof of insurance and a driver's license for the local church to keep on file.

Guidelines for Online Practice and Social Media

First and foremost, images and names of children and youth should not be posted online in any form without explicit consent.

Additionally, a social media covenant shall be adhered to by all participants and leaders. This covenant shall be kept on file alongside other Safe Sanctuary related documentation. It is recommended that this covenant include the following:

- Leaders shall never initiate a social media connection (for instance, friending, following, linking, and so forth).
- There must be boundaries regarding calling, texting, and private messaging between adults and children or youth.
- There must be specific boundaries regarding taking and distributing photos and videos.
- There must be specific boundaries regarding social media posts.
- Any posts made on a social media site, whether by you or others, will likely be seen by youth.
- No direct messages should be sent between adult staff or volunteers and children or youth.
- Texting should be limited to ministry-related communications and correspondence.

Guidelines for Third-Party or Outside Groups Using Church Facilities

A healthy church has solid partnerships with outside organizations and allows approved outside groups to use its facilities as a service to the community. This is a core belief for many congregations. When these service are provided to a third-party or outside group, the safety of children, youth, and vulnerable adults remains a priority. This includes the safety of children, youth, and vulnerable adults who are not members of your community or congregation. These third-party or outside groups should be required, at a minimum, to adhere to the Safe Sanctuaries policies and procedures of the congregation while on church property. Groups using church facilities must sign a covenant committing to follow the policies while on-site.

The church should provide outside organizations copies of all applicable policies and procedures governing the safety of children, youth, and vulnerable adults when such people will be present. In response, these groups must sign a covenant agreeing to abide by the policies provided.

Any allegation of non-compliance must be documented and reported for investigation to the staff member who coordinates outside events. Findings will be reviewed

Notes

> A healthy church has solid partnerships with outside organizations and allows approved outside groups to use its facilities as a service to the community.

_____

_____

_____

_____

_____

_____

_____

_____

_____

_____

The church can and should be a place for all. This affirms the dignity and worth of all people.

by a Safe Sanctuaries team who then will decide on appropriate action. If, at any time, an outside organization or individual fails to follow Safe Sanctuaries policies and procedures, the church reserves the right to terminate future use of its facilities to that group or individual.

Any allegations of abuse during an activity hosted by an outside group or individual on church campus should be reported, and the Safe Sanctuaries team should follow the reporting policy and response plan included in the Safe Sanctuaries policy.

Guidelines Regarding the Participation of a Registered Sex Offender

The church can and should be a place for all. This affirms the dignity and worth of all people. Those who have committed abusive acts in the past or who have been convicted of criminal acts of abuse also need a place to worship and participate in prayer. With proper guidance to protect the vulnerable, the church, and the offenders themselves, your church can be a place where registered sex offenders can have positive experiences with a faith community.

Discipleship Ministries offers resources about how to help church leadership work with registered sex offenders. These resources outline how and where these individuals can participate in the life of the church.[1] Registered sex offenders should not, however, be put into positions of leadership with or in positions that have direct contact with children, youth, or other vulnerable groups. Clear guidelines should be established that maintain the integrity of existing Safe Sanctuaries policies, protect vulnerable individuals, protect the registered sex offender, protect the church, and clearly outline when, where, and how the registered sex offender is present at church-organized and sponsored events or on church property.

Knowingly allowing an offender in the congregation could affect insurance coverage. Make sure you talk to the insurance carrier and secure written affirmation. A covenant agreement is helpful to show that the church did not participate in putting people in vulnerable positions for both insurance and court.

Regarding sexual offenders, ensure that the church has insurance coverage that acknowledges the following:

1. A registered sex offender is now a part of the congregation.
2. The church has the ability to provide resources for the affected party and not damage the ability of the church to continue mission.

We highly recommend reading and modifying the sample covenant from Discipleship Ministries to fit the specific situation your church faces. Church leadership and staff must determine the appropriate level of activity and supervision a registered sex offender may require as part of participation in the life of your church. We must also affirm the dignity and worth of any individuals in question, honor them by seeking to understand their case, history, and judgments, and help them to avoid situations that could encourage any repeat of their past offense.

Notes

1. "Safe Sanctuaries: Protection and Integration of Known Sexual Offenders," Discipleship Ministries, https://www.umcdiscipleship.org/articles/safe-sanctuaries-protection-and-integration-of-known-sexual-offenders.

A covenant agreement is helpful to show that the church did not participate in putting people in vulnerable positions for both insurance and court.

PART VI
THE RESPONSE

CHAPTER 24
When the Unthinkable Happens

Truman Brooks

No one imagines that abuse will take place in their church. No one goes into ministry thinking that someone will be hurt on their watch. Until it happens in our community, until we experience the hurt and sadness up close, the very idea of abuse in the church can feel distant. It can feel like one of those things that only happens at other churches to other people, but never to us and never in our community.

However, as we've explored throughout this book, abuse can happen anywhere. It can even happen in communities that do everything possible to reduce the risks and create a safe place for everyone. This is why we must not only prepare to prevent abuse, but also prepare for how we will respond if and when abuse happens in our congregations. When abuse occurs, we need to be prepared to respond appropriately. We need a plan to respond that is based on the clarity of our values, principles, and faith.

When abuse is discovered or when allegations of abuse are made against someone in our congregation, the emotions of the moment will be strong. These emotions may push us to ask questions that we would not ask otherwise, and the situation can be quite disorienting. In part two of this resource, we looked extensively at this kind of psychological turmoil when responding to abuse in a community. These strong emotions are one reason why it is essential for our communities to consider how we will respond to abuse before the situation ever arises. When we act, we want to act with compassionate care, respect, and support for the victim, openness and honesty with everyone involved, accountability for the congregation, and loving consideration for the perpetrators as they deal with the consequences of their actions.

Preparing the Answers

If we anticipate the possible questions that will arise, prepare our responses in advance, and set forward clear guidelines to follow in these difficult situations, then we will have a roadmap to follow during the chaotic and tumultuous moments that threaten to overwhelm us. While it is essential for each congregation to work through its own questions and prepare its own guidelines for responding to abuse, here are several questions that it will be important to consider in advance so that you can respond appropriately:

_____

_____

_____

_____

_____

_____

_____

_____

_____

_____

_____

_____

_____

> **Questions about privacy, in particular, can be difficult to puzzle out in the moment. It is important to state your congregation's values about privacy outside of a crisis situation.**

1. When should an incident be reported to law enforcement or child protective services? What legal requirements exist within your state? Who in your congregation is responsible for ensuring that reports are made and for following up with authorities when necessary?

2. What moral and ethical obligations does your congregation have beyond the legal requirements that exist within your state? How will your community respond to incidents that are not legal violations, but that do violate these community standards? Who in your community will be responsible for investigating and making decisions about these situations?

3. How much information should be shared with the wider congregation? How will you protect the privacy of the victim while being honest with the congregation and providing accountability to the community going forward?

4. If there is public interest beyond the congregation, who should speak on behalf of the church? What kind of information should be shared and what process should be used to prepare these statements?

5. If there is either a legal investigation or an internal investigation, what role should the alleged abuser have in the congregation while an investigation is ongoing?

These are only a few examples of questions that each congregation should work through on its own. Some, like questions about when to report to law enforcement and child protective services, will have clear answers that change based on the laws of each state. Others will require each congregation to find answers that work best to build a healthy, trusting community. Questions about privacy, in particular, can be difficult to puzzle out in the moment. It is important to state your congregation's values about privacy outside of a crisis situation. Privacy is often threatened by natural curiosity and concern from those outside the process. Balancing these concerns with the privacy of both the victim and the abuser or alleged abuser requires calm and thoughtfulness that may not be possible during a tumultuous time.

Transparency Is a Virtue

While it is uncomfortable to discuss, we must also address the very real threat to either cover up abuse or seek to minimize damage. This will always be a temptation in the moment, even if it is little more than a whisper in the back of our minds. There is always a temptation to maintain the status quo, to avoid rocking the boat, and to simply deny a painful reality. I want to remind you that such a temptation is not a moral failing, but it is a moment where we need to remember our values. It is a reminder to consider the goals and principles set forth by your congregation at a time when emotions were not driving the process. Cover-ups and efforts to contain or minimize damage only paper over a problem; they do not eliminate it. They are not healthy. Remember Jesus' words in Luke 12:2-23 (NRSVUE), "Nothing is covered up that will not be uncovered, and nothing secret that will not become known. Therefore whatever you have said in the dark will be heard in the light, and what you have whispered behind closed doors will be proclaimed from the housetops."

The only way out of a difficult situation is by moving through it, by confronting it and dealing with what comes next. Abuse is harmful; it causes pain not only to the victim, but also to the victim's loved ones and community. It even causes harm to the abuser, whether that person recognizes it or not. The only way to deal with this harm is by processing it and responding to it appropriately with honesty, open communication, and accountability. It will take time to heal the damage that comes from abuse, but these are the first steps.

As you work through your immediate response, transparency is also essential to begin the healing process. Though there are limits to transparency, as discussed earlier in this chapter, it is also a key virtue when responding to the wider community. Curiosity is natural, and many members of the community, parents for example, have a vested interest in knowing about safety risks. Revealing necessary facts, explaining a process for moving forward that protects both the victims and the alleged abuser as any investigations continue, allowing an open forum for questions or concerns, and surrounding the experience with prayer can help build trust within the community.

A Final Reminder

I know that all of this may seem obvious in the abstract. Everyone knows that it's bad to cover up abuse and that it's good to tell the truth, but in the moment, many of the obvious choices that we know we should make will be extremely painful and difficult. These situations may involve people who are our friends or our family, people who we simply can't believe would do the things they've been accused of doing. This is why it is so important to state clearly what we will do when an incident of abuse is either witnessed or reported. We must know how we will act before the stress of the moment overwhelms us. We do not want to respond to abuse or allegations of abuse on the fly. That is a recipe for mistakes, pain, and further damage to our communities.

Thankfully, there is one other thing that you should remember during these difficult times. You are not alone. Not only can you rely on others in your congregation, you can also rely on those outside of your congregation. Do not hesitate to reach out to denominational leadership for advice and counsel. Other churches have also worked through similar issues and can offer support and advice. There are so many resources for you to tap when a question seems impossible to answer, and there are so many people who would be happy to support you and your congregation as you seek to do the right thing in a trying situation.

Notes

The only way to deal with this harm is by processing it and responding to it appropriately with honesty, open communication, and accountability.

Finally, remember that responding to abuse is a long-term process. Much like responding to a natural disaster, there is so much attention paid to a crisis in the immediate aftermath that it may seem like everything has been resolved once the stress of the moment has died down. But once the moment has calmed, there is still long-term recovery work to do as well. We will discuss this in a later chapter, but I include it here as a reminder that we are not called to solve abuse in the moment; we are called to respond to it and to begin the process of healing. We don't have to do everything at once; we just have to do the next right thing.

There are so many people who would be happy to support you and your congregation as you seek to do the right thing in a trying situation.

CHAPTER 25

Immediate Steps

Truman Brooks

When abuse occurs in your congregation, it requires an immediate and appropriate response. As we discussed in the previous chapter, the first steps your congregation needs to take when responding to abuse should happen *before* an incident even arises. Prepare yourself for action in advance. Read about the reporting requirements in your state. Make sure that mandatory reporters know that they are mandatory reporters. Read the policies of your conference regarding abuse. You may even want to work on yourself so that you can be an open, non-judgmental, and calm presence when dealing with sensitive issues like abuse.

This is how you prepare. Know what you need to do. Know who needs to be informed, and know who will be responsible for putting your plan into action and taking care of each part. Hopefully, this abuse response plan is never necessary, but if it needs to be put into practice, you will be thankful that you prepared beforehand to respond in a timely and appropriate manner.

Reports of abuse can arise in any number of ways. They may start with an email or a phone call. Someone might request a private meeting with you where they pour out their experience, whether as someone who has witnessed abuse or been the victim. In other situations, a staff member or volunteer might come to you and share a story that a child or youth has passed. It's even possible that a report starts with a simple concern or suspicion raised by a staff member, volunteer, parent, student, or other member of the community. No matter how you initially become aware of an incident, the first step should always be the same: listen.

First and foremost, your job is to listen and to be supportive. Investigations and specifics are important and will come in time, but in the moment, we must listen to the person who is reporting the abuse or concern about abuse. We must be present and support the person who comes forward. This is particularly important when we are talking to people who are reporting abuse that they have experienced themselves. It is vital that we help people feel safe and remind them that they are not alone, that they have done the right thing, and that the situation will be handled swiftly and appropriately.

After listening to the report, it is essential to begin taking action immediately. This is true not only for legal reasons, but also to let victims know that we take their words seriously. When we respond to

Notes
_____
_____
_____
_____
_____
_____
_____
_____
_____
_____
_____
_____

allegations of abuse immediately, it helps build a culture where people feel comfortable coming forward when something has happened to them. They know that they will be believed. The following eight steps lay out how we should immediately respond to an incident or allegation of abuse:

1. Ensure the safety of the victim.
2. Remove the accused abuser from further involvement.
3. Notify the proper law enforcement and/or family services agency.
4. Notify denominational leadership, the church's insurance company, and the church's attorney.
5. Create a written record of the steps taken by the church.
6. Designate a spokesperson to make any necessary statements to the public.
7. Prepare a brief and honest statement for the congregation.
8. Cooperate fully with investigations from law enforcement or the department of family services.

1) Ensure the safety of the victim.

The first step when responding to abuse is to ensure that the victim is safe from the abuser and that abuse is no longer taking place. At a minimum, this means separating the victim from the abuser, but it can also include providing medical care or trauma counseling for the victim if the situation calls for it. When the victim is a minor, this first step is when you should notify the parents of the victim about the abuse and take any necessary steps to provide the family with support to care for their child. In the next chapter, we will talk more about designating a member of your congregation to provide pastoral care and walk alongside the victim and the family during this process. In any situation, the safety of the victim must be the church's primary concern.

In any situation, the safety of the victim must be the church's primary concern.

2) Remove the accused abuser from further involvement in any ministry.

Once you are confident that the victim is safe and cared for, turn your attention to the accused abuser. Do not confront the accused abuser with anger or hostility. It is important to treat the accused person with dignity, but also to immediately remove that person from further involvement in ministry, particularly ministry with youth or children. This is also an appropriate time to inform the accused of the reasons for his/her removal and to lay out the process that your congregation has in place.

Notify the proper law enforcement and/or family services agency.

When making a report to law enforcement, the report should be made by the person who directly witnessed the abuse, the person who suspects that abuse may be occurring, or the person who first heard about the abuse from the victim. It is also useful for this report to be made in the presence of a senior pastor, youth coordinator, or other church leader. This allows for both moral support and corroboration that a report was properly made. When creating your response plan, consider who this point person should be when making reports to law enforcement.

This is also the time when you will want to push for more specifics from the person reporting the abuse if that person did not provide these specifics initially. Remember that it is not your job at this point to determine the truth of the statements, but to record the statement as the individual reports it. There will be time for investigation and examination of the facts later in the process.

All staff and volunteers must know their state's requirements when reporting abuse to law enforcement and other governmental authorities. Each state has specific requirements, and you should consult a local attorney during your planning work to determine which requirements are applicable to those serving in your church.

In some states, all staff and volunteers who work with children and youth, whether paid or unpaid, are considered mandatory reporters and must report suspected cases of abuse they have a reasonable belief have occurred or are occurring. The same may be true for those working with vulnerable adults. However, this is not true in every state, so it is essential for everyone trained in Safe Sanctuaries ministries to be aware of the reporting requirements in the state.

Additionally, every state has statutory definitions of sexual abuse, child abuse, and elder abuse. Workers should also know these definitions and be able to recognize whether or not the behavior in question meets the statutory definition. This is another area where consulting with a local attorney can be useful. However, when in doubt about whether a situation should be reported, err on the side of making the report.

Furthermore, each set of state laws includes a reporting time limit. Once a person becomes aware of or suspects abuse, that person must report it to proper authorities within a set amount of time. In some states, this is as short as twenty-four hours. It is imperative that staff and volunteers be informed of these requirements. It is also essential that staff and volunteers know which law enforcement agencies need to receive a report, whether it is the city police, the sheriff's department, or another local law enforcement agency. Again, this is a question where a local attorney will be able to provide helpful information.

Finally, this information is always open to revision and change. Your church will want to keep up to date on state reporting procedures and the church's obligations. A local attorney, the local family services agency, and your church's insurance company can all help you gather this information and prepare a step-by-step plan.

Notes

Each state has specific requirements, and you should consult a local attorney during your planning work to determine which requirements are applicable to those serving in your church.

_____

_____

_____

_____

_____

_____

_____

_____

_____

_____

Documenting the steps taken by the church not only provides important evidence for legal questions down the line, but also provides a kind of checklist to ensure that the appropriate actions have been taken.

4) Notify denominational leadership, the church's insurance company, and the church's attorney.

Once you have informed the proper authorities, it is time to begin informing other interested parties so that they are aware of an ongoing situation. First, inform your denominational leadership about any allegations or reported abuse, then share with them the steps that you have already taken in responding to the situation, including how you have shown care for the victim, removed the abuser from his/her role, and made any reports to local law enforcement. This should allow denominational leadership to provide any additional logistical support that your congregation may need as they work through this situation.

Next, inform your church's attorney of the situation and all steps that you have taken. When working with your attorney, it is important to be open, honest, and clear about everything that has occurred so that your attorney can be positioned to respond appropriately and in the best interests of your congregation.

Once you have informed your attorney, contact your insurance company to let them know about the situation. When making this report, it may be helpful to have your attorney present to advise you.

5) Create a written record of the steps taken by the church.

When putting together your response plan, your team should assign a point person who will take on the role of documenting all the steps taken by the church as it begins to respond to any allegations or reports of abuse. You can find a sample form for reporting suspected incidents of abuse in the appendix of this resource.

Ideally, this documentation will take place at the same time as the preceding steps of ensuring the safety of the victim, removing the abuser, making a report to law enforcement, and informing other interested parties. However, it is important to place a reminder at this point in the step-by-step instructions to ensure that this documentation takes place.

Documenting the steps taken by the church not only provides important evidence for legal questions down the line, but also provides a kind of checklist to ensure that the appropriate actions have been taken.

6) Designate a spokesperson to make any necessary statements to the public.

In the event that an abusive incident will make the news, a congregation should assign a designated spokesperson to speak on behalf of the church. Again, this is a decision that can and should be made when creating your church's abuse response plan, but should be open to some flexibility depending on the context of the situation.

The designated spokesperson may be the pastor, another staff member, the church's attorney, or a lay member of the church, such as the chairperson of the board of trustees. Whoever is chosen should be capable of speaking calmly and thoughtfully and must be prepared to answer questions honestly without adding extra or unnecessary information. The designated spokesperson should be given permission to answer questions by saying, "We don't know at this time" or something similar.

The key goals of the spokesperson are to 1) protect the privacy of the victim, 2) express that the congregation is responding appropriately, and 3) provide any transparency possible about the ongoing response process. The spokesperson should be prepared to explain the church's policies and procedures for reducing the risk of abuse, the church's concern for the safety of the victim, and the steps the church will be taking to respond to the situation. It is a best practice for the spokesperson to have a prepared statement, or at least written notes, that have been checked by the church's attorney.

7) Prepare a brief and honest statement for the congregation.

When abuse occurs in a congregation, it does not only harm the victim, it also does damage to the very fabric of the community. The work of re-establishing trust and healing a community is not something that can be done in a day, and the damage cannot be fixed in the immediate aftermath of abuse allegations or reports. However, the first steps to healing can be taken.

Throughout this resource, writers have reinforced the principles of honesty, communication, and accountability over and over again as core elements for building safer sanctuaries. When informing your congregation about abuse that has occurred in your community, these three core principles are once again the fundamental ideals that should guide you. The first step in ministering to your congregation in the wake of abuse is telling the truth. This means engaging in honest communication about what has happened, but it does not mean engaging in gossip or speculation.

Notes

The first step in ministering to your congregation in the wake of abuse is telling the truth.

201

The best way to convey honest and forthright information to your congregation is generally with a letter that briefly explains the incident and the initial action taken by the church. This letter should avoid identifying either the victim or the accused abuser. It should, however, include information about actions taken to assure the congregation that the situation is being taken seriously, the victim is safe and supported, and that the accused abuser has been removed from any vulnerable situations. It should also work to assure your congregation that steps are being taken to safely continue the church's ministry. Finally, the congregation should be informed that there will be a congregational meeting after a set period of time where members of the community can ask questions and discuss the situation with church leadership.

People are naturally curious, and in a situation like this, that natural curiosity is mixed with a genuine need to know about the safety of their community. Therefore, the goal of this letter is to provide what information you can, while respecting the process and the privacy of those involved. This honest communication sets the stage for a healthy and productive dialogue that can help your community work through a painful situation.

8) Cooperate fully with investigations from law enforcement or the department of family services.

Your congregation can actively aid in the investigation by gathering any documentary evidence that may support allegations of abuse. This includes any emails, video recordings, sign-in sheets, or other evidence that could help to corroborate the victim's claims about what occurred. These can all be handed over to authorities who are investigating the situation.

In many ways, this final recommendation is a given, but it also a useful reminder. It is possible that interactions with authorities may become contentious at times, but it is important to remember that your role as a faithful community is to support the victim and to ascertain the truth, no matter how painful that might be.

Beyond Legal Requirements

To this point, we have largely focused on abuse that fits the legal definitions and that requires a formal legal process and investigation. However, the law is only the minimum bar for us as Christians. The commitments of our faith call us to far greater, and we must also prepare ourselves to respond to abusive actions that fall short of legal definitions.

In many ways, responding to these situations involves a similar process, although without the need to contact law enforcement, attorneys, or insurance companies.

This honest communication sets the stage for a healthy and productive dialogue that can help your community work through a painful situation.

If the issues in question do not rise to the level of a criminal offense, then the next step after removing the accused abuser and informing leadership will be to conduct an investigation and address the situation with the accused directly. While it should be understood, it is important to emphasize that the victim should not confront the accused directly or be present when you confront the accused abuser. Instead, have the pastor along with another designated member of your abuse response team talk to the person who has been accused.

In this conversation, the pastor and member of the abuse response team should be honest and direct. They should let the accused know that an allegation of misconduct has been brought against him/her and then the accused should be given the opportunity to present his/her side of the story. If the stories of the person bringing the allegation and the story of the accused do not agree, then do more investigation. It may be useful at this point to bring in an outside consultant or investigator depending on the situation, or you can create a designated team to handle such internal investigations as part of your abuse response plan.

These situations can be difficult to navigate, and it is important to conduct this process with honesty, open communication, and accountability for all involved. The steps should be clearly laid out so that everyone knows what will happen next and knows what the final decision-making process looks like.

When making final determinations in a difficult situation, remember your congregation's call to create a safe, thriving community and to care for everyone in the community. This may not make your decision easier, but these foundational principles can guide you as you seek to do justice.

Whether you are responding to a situation that requires the involvement of law enforcement or one that involves allegations that fall short of a crime, it is difficult to respond well to abuse. The best response will always be one that is planned in advance and that allows for those responding to keep calm and respond appropriately while showing care for the safety of the victim.

Notes

These situations can be difficult to navigate, and it is important to conduct this process with honesty, open communication, and accountability for all involved.

CHAPTER 26
Pastoring to All Involved

Truman Brooks

As a community of care, the church is called to walk alongside and provide care for both the victim and the abuser in the aftermath of abuse. This can be a difficult and complex process, but it is also a necessary one.

In the Social Principles, The United Methodist Church clearly states that,

> Family violence and abuse in all its forms—verbal, psychological, physical, sexual—is detrimental to the covenant of the human community. We encourage the Church to provide a safe environment, counsel, and support for the victim and to work with the abuser to understand the root causes and forms of abuse and to overcome such behaviors. Regardless of the cause or the abuse, both the victim and the abuser need the love of the Church. While we deplore the actions of the abuser, we affirm that person to be in need of God's redeeming love.[1]

When abuse occurs in our communities, the natural impulse is to try and help. This is a healthy impulse, but also one where we must understand the context and remember to focus on the needs of the person who was abused rather than our own needs to be helpful. Experiencing abuse, whether sexual, physical, or emotional, is incredibly disorienting. This is doubly true when the abuse takes place in a supposedly safe space like a church or when it is perpetrated by a trusted adult like a church leader or family member.

Supporting the Victim

With this in mind, the first and most important thing we can do as a community of care is to be present and available for the person who was abused. When people face this kind of pain, we must respond by showing our care, our love, and truly, genuinely listening to the people in need. This can be difficult, or even awkward, for those of us who seek to actively fix problems and alleviate pain, but there are no simple answers that will make things better. Presence is a powerful tool for showing that we care for one another, that we value one another, and that we will not abandon those in our community who are suffering. This is not only true for the victim, but for the victim's family as well. In addition to the person who has been abused, the family has also suffered a violation of trust and will need the support of the community.

It's important to note that this is not solely the responsibility of a congregation's pastor or staff, but of the entire church. In fact, a senior pastor may not be the best person to take on this task since the pastor's role can often be so wide-ranging and the victim and victim's family may need more focused support. As you put together your congregation's abuse response plan, think through what this process will look like and consider who will take on the role of showing pastoral care to those who suffer abuse. However, this is also an area where sensitivity and flexibility may be called for when the situation actually arises. For instance, you may assign someone to pastor to the victims and their families, but then realize that someone else in your community is better aligned to provide this kind of care in the moment. Be open for the Spirit to guide your work and your care for those in need, even if you have already made alternative plans.

While the direct support of the congregation is essential, it is also key to not limit your support of the victim or the victim's family to those within the church community. The person who experienced the abuse may need professional support, like counseling, and the church should use any connections it has to help the victim and the family receive the professional support they need. Smaller churches may even consider reaching out to conference or district staff for recommendations on professional support services for those who have been abused in their community. A pastor or other leader within the congregation can even serve as a liaison to help facilitate this support in order to rid the victim and family of any undue administrative barriers.

When assigning someone to provide pastoral care in these situations, it is important to be clear and honest with the victim and family. Have the assigned person explain that he/she has been assigned to support the victim and family as part of the congregation's response to the situation and that he/she will walk with the victim during this crisis. It should be clear that this person is not a counselor but a concerned friend and community member with whom the victim can talk. The assigned person will not judge the victim or be involved in any court proceedings or denominational/church investigations. The assigned person should be clear that he/she is there for the victim, to listen, to reflect, to offer resources, and to develop a caring relationship with healthy boundaries.

It is also possible that a victim or the family of a victim will not want the support offered from your church. This can be painful, but it is also understandable in many situations. In this scenario, the congregation should accept the wishes of the victim and family. The church should maintain an open, welcoming, and supportive stance so that those involved can reach out in the future if further assistance is needed. Remember, pastoral care is not only about taking care of someone's needs, it is about listening and respecting the person for whom we are showing care.

Similarly, a victim may not feel comfortable receiving care from the church where the abuse took place, but would accept support and pastoral care from a different congregation. If offers of support are rejected, consider partnering with a nearby congregation and offering to connect the victim and family to this neighboring

Notes

_____

_____

_____

_____

_____

_____

_____

_____

_____

Be open for the Spirit to guide your work and your care for those in need, even if you have already made alternative plans.

_____

_____

_____

_____

_____

_____

_____

_____

_____

_____

_____

community. Again, this situation can be painful, but it is important to prioritize the needs of the victim. If possible, make plans with another congregation about this potential situation while you are creating your response plan and offer your own congregation as a source of support in the event that a neighboring church has a similar situation arise. If you do connect the victim or the family with a second congregation, be sure to make introductions and connect them with a support person directly. Trust is essential in a crisis, and this helps to prevent a breakdown in communication.

Pastoring to the Abuser

The congregation is also responsible for pastoring to those who commit acts of abuse. This can be an incredibly difficult task, but it is also an important one. It generally cannot take place unless the perpetrators accept what they have done, confess to the harm they have caused, and genuinely begin to walk the path of reconciliation and restitution. Nevertheless, we know that Jesus calls us to love the outcast, the lost, the lonely, and those society deems the worst among us. This includes those who have committed abuse.

It is key here to say that ministering to the abuser is not the same as trying to reconcile the abuser with the victim. Instead, this is a path of reconciliation to God and to the wider church community. If the victim decides to seek reconciliation with the abuser, this should come only after much thought on the part of the victim and should be initiated only at the victim's request. The church should never push a victim to reconcile with an abuser. However, it is important that the church help perpetrators of abuse move forward to begin repairing the damage in their own lives.

In many cases, this healing work will need to take place in a new community. It is best for the abuser to be separated from the victim. If the victim and family choose to remain in the community, then it is typically in the best interests of all involved for the abuser to leave. It is useful in situations like this for churches to work together so that the original church can connect the perpetrator with a new community and inform the new community about the circumstances of the perpetrator's departure. This allows the new community to welcome the abuser with open eyes and open arms. This also allows the new community to establish healthy boundaries so that the new member does not abuse again.

The type of boundaries that need to be put in place will change depending on the type of abuse committed. The guidelines for these boundaries should be established by conversations held between church leadership, members of the Safe Sanctuaries team, and lay leaders. Ideally, these guidelines will be prepared in anticipation of an abuser eventually seeking to join the church so that the church is ready to respond.

The congregation is also responsible for pastoring to those who commit acts of abuse.

The United Methodist Church has made explicit recommendations about the steps to be taken when a registered sex offender seeks to be part of a church community. *The Book of Resolutions* states that three specific steps need to be taken by local churches in order to faithfully follow the church's commitment both to protect the community from abuse and to minister to abusers:

1. Hold discussions in the church council and in adult education settings about the possibility of facing the situation of a convicted sex offender returning to or joining the church. These discussions should be held and general agreements reached about actions to be taken should the church find itself in this circumstance.

2. Develop a carefully constructed and openly negotiated covenant between the offender and the church community. The covenant should include agreements in the following areas: participation in a professional counseling program for at least the entire time of church membership or participation; adult covenant partners to accompany the offender while on church property or attending church activities; areas of church facilities that are off-limits; restrictions on leadership in or on behalf of the church; no role in church that includes contact with children or youth; any additional conditions for presence or participation.

3. Assure that the covenant is maintained by having it written and signed by the offender, the pastors, and the chairperson of the church council. While confidentiality of victims should be respected, the covenant should not be secret. Monitoring of the covenant should be taken seriously as a permanent responsibility.[2]

It is important to hold these discussions not only so that your church can respond to abuse that happens within your community, but also so your church is prepared to offer pastoral care and assistance to those who have committed acts of abuse in other contexts. It is an act of mercy for a church to walk with perpetrators as they try to reform their life and work toward emotional health and wholeness.

It is also an act of mercy to prevent a perpetrator from holding a position of deep trust within the church again. The internal motivations that lead someone to commit acts of abuse are deep and complex. These urges are more often managed than they are cured. Abusers may need years of therapy programs and support groups before they can begin to be in a position to help others again. The church can help with resources, non-judgmental acceptance, words of kindness, and prayer. Through this process of ongoing confession, introspection, and acceptance of the pain they have caused others, true healing can take place.

It takes time to recover from abuse. Abuse hurts not only the victim, but also abusers who have lost a bit of themselves in their actions. It also hurts the whole community. Pastoral care is key when responding to these situations. Healing takes time. It takes patience. It takes focused effort and daily work to repair the wounds of a moment. But God is with us, and through God, all things are possible.

Notes

It is an act of mercy for a church to walk with perpetrators as they try to reform their life and work toward emotional health and wholeness.

Notes

1. 2016 United Methodist Social Principles, The Nurturing Community, "Family Violence and Abuse," *The Book of Discipline of The United Methodist Church, 2016* (The United Methodist Publishing House, 2016), ¶161, H.

2. "Church Participation by a Registered Sex Offender," *The Book of Resolutions of The United Methodist Church*, 2016 (The United Methodist Publishing House, 2016), Resolution #8014.

> **Healing takes time. It takes patience.**

CHAPTER 27

Moving Forward as a Community

Truman Brooks

Abuse most directly impacts those immediately involved and, to this point, that is where we have focused most of our attention. But abuse also permanently alters the community where it takes place. Abuse can shatter trust that has taken decades to build and can leave a church filled with doubt, uncertainty, anger, and fear. In the aftermath of abuse, we must also begin taking steps to heal the damage that this rupture of trust has caused in the community.

The work of healing a community also takes time. Think of it like responding to a natural disaster. In the days right after a hurricane or a flood, everyone springs into action, and there is so much work to do to clean up the devastation and get things functioning again. It's like a shot of adrenaline for the community. A crisis like this needs an immediate response. But there is also long-term work that needs to be done. There are deeper structural issues to tend to like infrastructure that needs to be repaired, houses that need to rebuilt, and people who need their lives restored. This takes planning, care, and determination. It takes work and dedication. The same is true when moving forward as a community after abuse is revealed. There will be lots of important and intense work to do in the immediate aftermath, but there will also be work that needs to be done long-term to repair the culture of a congregation and rebuild the trust of the community.

Immediate Response

The three core principles to keep in mind when communicating with the wider congregation about abuse are honesty, open communication, and accountability. When abuse happens in a community, the people of that community need to know. This is true not only so that people can protect their own loved ones, but can also help to limit the spread of harmful rumors and distrust.

As we discussed in Chapter 25 when covering the immediate steps to take after abuse is reported, the best way to share honest and open information with the congregation is often through a letter or brief statement to be shared with the entire community. This letter should be as forthcoming as possible without going into unnecessary details and should refrain from placing blame on the victim or revealing the

_____

_____

_____

_____

_____

_____

_____

_____

_____

_____

Invite church members to write out any questions or concerns they would like to see specifically addressed during the congregational meeting and submit these to church leaders in advance.

identities of those involved. This letter should also acknowledge the pain of abuse, the church's support for the victim, and the next steps that the church will be taking in the short-term.

At the same time, the congregation should also be informed that the church will begin taking steps to re-examine the policies and procedures that are in place to see if these need to be altered or improved in the light of what has occurred. Ideally, this announcement about the review of policies and procedures should also have a timeline attached so that the congregation can hold church leadership accountable to do the work that they have promised to do.

Finally, the church should announce that there will be a congregational meeting after a set period of time where members of the congregation can ask questions, share concerns, and discuss the situation with church leaders. Setting this meeting a few weeks after the initial announcement helps in several ways. First, it allows more information to come to light that can help the church collectively decide what to do in response. Second, it allows church leaders and community members time to reflect and gain much needed perspective outside of the stress of an immediate crisis. Third, scheduling the meeting for a set time in the near future allows members to choose whether or not they want to attend and allows for those who prioritize this conversation to arrange their schedules to participate. All of this helps set the stage for an honest, productive conversation.

Communication and Clarity

In the time between making an initial statement and the congregational meeting, continue to provide the community with necessary and timely updates about any review processes or internal investigations. Invite church members to write out any questions or concerns they would like to see specifically addressed during the congregational meeting and submit these to church leaders in advance. This will provide time for thoughtful reflection and make sure that topics that are important to the community are covered.

As you and your church navigate this situation, remember that it is easy to be defensive during times like this. It is also natural for community members to be both emotional or frustrated that they are not receiving more information. This is an area where you should prepare yourself emotionally and spiritually. Take time to breathe, take time to pray, both alone and with others on your team. Remind yourself regularly that you are responding to this situation with honesty, openness, and integrity. It is okay for people to be angry, to express their pain, and to express their frustration. However, you must also continue to do what you know is right while being open and accepting of their concerns. Listen to criticism if it is offered, but also remember that much of what you are hearing is threaded with emotion. Prayerfully consider it along with your team. Take what is valuable and leave what is not.

The Congregational Meeting

In preparation for your congregational meeting, work with your team and your church leadership to prepare a clear line of communication. Typically, this means that one person will be given the role of speaking on behalf of church leadership. This role will often fall to the lead pastor, but this is not required, and in many situations, it may be better for someone else to fill this role. Other leaders present may need to do little more than reinforce their support of the leadership during this crisis. This is a valuable contribution and should not be overlooked.

As mentioned above, your congregational meeting should be planned in advance with clear instructions about the location, time, and the format of the conversation. Preparation and planning for the event should involve a considerable amount of reflection and prayer on the part of church leadership and Safe Sanctuaries team. Select the leaders who will represent the congregation with intention. This will typically include the lead pastor and other staff members, but should also include lay leaders and representatives from the annual conference (a district superintendent would fill this role well).

Finally, your congregation may also consider having a qualified counselor on hand who is not a member of the congregation. A meeting like this will inevitably bring up strong feelings or past traumatic experiences. Every congregation likely has members who are survivors of abuse, and many survivors may be in attendance. A counselor who is present and available to all attendees can help support those who may need additional help processing the emotions this meeting brings up.

The format for a congregational meeting should include four core elements:

1. Fact sharing
2. Time for questions
3. Small-group sharing time
4. Reflection, prayer, and worship

We recommend that you open your time together with prayer. This helps to put the meeting into context as part of the healing work of the Holy Spirit. After opening the meeting with prayer, have the assigned leader walk through the facts that are available and appropriate. Any information that has been publicly reported should be considered public information and may be shared and discussed freely. However, if the identity of the victim and accused abuser are not public, refrain from identifying them at this time. This is also an opportunity to challenge misinformation and maintain boundaries. Explain to those in attendance why the answers to some of their questions may need to remain confidential. During this opening statement, you can also share the actions that the church has taken to this point and the actions that the church intends to take going forward.

> Your congregation may also consider having a qualified counselor on hand who is not a member of the congregation. A meeting like this will inevitably bring up strong feelings or past traumatic experiences.

Notes

_____

_____

_____

_____

_____

_____

_____

_____

_____

_____

_____

_____

As a congregation, acknowledge the pain of this situation and offer a final prayer for the church as you all work together to do justice for all involved and provide healing for those who are suffering.

After this initial time of sharing, set aside a specific period of time for open questions. At this time, take questions from those in attendance and also take time to respond to any questions that were submitted privately in advance of the meeting. While your team can prepare for many of the most common questions, it is also possible that you will receive questions that are uncomfortable, combative, or where you and your team simply do not know the answer. Prepare your team to respond to these questions with openness and honesty. Do not be afraid to answer questions by saying, "We don't know the answer to that yet."

After responding to the congregation's questions, invite the attendees to participate in a time of small-group sharing. This may be the most important part of the meeting. Divide those in attendance into groups of five or six and assign a prepared facilitator to each group. These facilitators will ideally be members of your staff, Safe Sanctuaries team members, or trained volunteers. The facilitators should let the group members know that this is an open time of sharing and that is acceptable to express any and all emotions within this small group. Everyone will be given time to share, and the group will not debate the feelings or emotions expressed. The goal of this time is to help those in attendance identify and share their feelings about what has happened in their community. It is not intended as a time to strategize about the church's response. Be prepared for this part of the meeting to take close to an hour.

When it is clear that the small groups are wrapping up, bring everyone back together. As a congregation, acknowledge the pain of this situation and offer a final prayer for the church as you all work together to do justice for all involved and provide healing for those who are suffering. Let the congregation know that healing will take time. Any investigations that are taking place may take months and could result in surprises, disappointments, or moments of deep sadness. However, when we work together and rely on Jesus and the Holy Spirit, we can overcome these dark times in the life of the church.

Reviewing Policies and Procedures

In the weeks and months that follow revelations of abuse, put together a team of lay leaders, volunteers, and church staff to review the Safe Sanctuaries policies and procedures that your church has put in place. This review should not only include the policies as they are written, but also the level of training provided and how well these policies are followed in every area of ministry.

Consider this an opportunity to dig deep into the culture of the church and see what the community could have done better to reduce the risk of abuse. Remind everyone involved in this review to do their best to avoid feelings of defensiveness and invite them to learn from failures in an effort to move forward and do better in the future. We cannot change the past, but we can change the future.

It is also possible that this review will reveal that there was little that could have been done differently. However, be cautious about allowing yourself to accept this answer as an easy out. Challenge your team to truly interrogate the system, be honest about where improvements could be made, and discover where the community can make systemic changes.

Once the review process is complete, have the team present their findings to church leadership and announce any recommendations and changes to the congregation as a whole. It is essential that your community rededicate itself to the work of providing safer sanctuaries for everyone. Maintaining strong policies and ongoing education is time consuming, but it is also imperative for a healthy and thriving congregation.

Rebuilding Trust

It is possible to rebuild trust in a community, but it will take time, and it is a process that cannot be rushed. Be honest with yourself about this and be honest with the members of your community. As you work through this process, normalize the fact that it will take time for healing to occur and that things may never be exactly the way that they were before. There will be twists and turns and unexpected consequences, but you can promote long-term healing.

The same is true when it comes to changing the culture in your congregation. It is possible to change the culture from an unhealthy, fearful one to a thriving culture full of support and openness. Again, this takes time, dedication, and buy-in from the community, but it is achievable.

All of this can feel quite overwhelming in the moment. Remember that you don't have to fix everything all at once. Every day, take a deep breath, have courage, and take the next step. Do the next right thing. You are not alone in this. You have a community of support behind you in your church, your denominational leadership, and the Holy Spirit. When we work together with God on our side, we can do wonderful things!

Notes

Maintaining strong policies and ongoing education is time consuming, but it is also imperative for a healthy and thriving congregation.

PART VII

THE AFFIRMATION

CHAPTER 28
Affirming Your Mission

Bishop Peggy Johnson

As we come to the end of our journey through this resource, I hope that you are filled with a sense of calling to engage in the work of making your community a safer sanctuary. I pray that you feel equipped by what you've read in these pages and that you feel inspired to incorporate what you've learned into your congregation's culture, into the very being of your church.

As you begin to practice and implement what you've learned, I want to remind you that we are not alone in this work. Ministry is something that we do together. Each part of the body of Christ has its own Spirit-inspired gift that can be used to help build a safe and thriving community. May you also remember that we are surrounded by a "great cloud of witnesses" who have gone before us and who laid the foundations for this work. It is now our turn to "run with perseverance the race that is set before us" (Heb. 12:1) and lead the church into an even brighter, safer future.

With this in mind, let us affirm the work that you and others in your community are about to undertake. It is my hope that both you and everyone who is engaged in Safe Sanctuaries ministry at your church take the time to engage in a solemn declaration of commitment at the end of your training event. This is an opportunity for both the trainers and the trainees to affirm their commitment to the work, acknowledge its importance, and promise to abide by its principles in tangible ways. This can take place privately, but can also take place publicly, thus allowing the entire church to bless the ministry you and your team will be leading.

Thanksgiving should always be a part of this affirmation as well. Linguists studying early Germanic languages have long seen a connection between the words "thank" and "think." These two words come from the same root and were sometimes used interchangeably. The idea seems to be that the more we think about some positive action, the more likely we would be to express our thanks.[1]

It is hard to underestimate the power of gratitude, both to God and to those serving on the team. At its core, giving thanks is an act of humility and wisdom. It gives us an opportunity to consider the blessings we have received from the labor of the community and the work of God. It allows us to acknowledge that we are not self-sufficient and reminds us that we are part of a community filled with the Holy Spirit.

Affirming the work of Safe Sanctuaries ministry should also include gratitude to those in leadership, A vast amount of work goes into building a safe, healthy, and thriving ministry. Those involved must answer the call to engage, undergo the necessary training, and work through numerous questions about building modifications, churchwide training events, insurance policy updates, extension ministry inclusion, and action plans in case of a violation. At times, creating a Safe Sanctuaries ministry can seem like a thousand-piece jigsaw puzzle. We all know what the final picture of a safe environment will look like, but it takes a lot of work to put all the pieces together.

It is vital that we give thanks to those involved in this work as we think back on the enormity of the task. Too often, those working in the church hear about all the problems, but are less likely to hear about the successes. Sometimes we just need to hear the words, "Thank you."

Gratitude is the oil that keeps the light of commitment burning bright. We lose leaders where their sacrifices are taken for granted and the hardships begin to outweigh the results. Thanksgiving, then, is an essential element of ministry.

As a country, we set aside one day a year to give thanks for everything we have received, but an attitude of giving thanks is not constrained by the calendar. It is not seasonal, but something we live out and show every day. Giving thanks is the way we show our appreciation to God for all our blessings, and it is the way we show appreciation to one another for all the blessings we have received from our community. We show in this in our words, but also in our actions. We give thanks by giving our money, our time, and our effort to help the work of God and the community.

As a community, pledge your support to those doing the good work of Safe Sanctuaries ministry. Do this in words, but also in tangible ways that will be felt for years to come. With affirmation and thanksgiving, we carry on this work and give thanks to God for this Spirit-inspired ministry. May our churches be a model for the world and a place of safety and grace for all!

> Sometimes we just need to hear the words, "Thank you."

Notes

1. Anatoly Liberman, "*Thought and Giving Thanks: Word Origins and How We Know Them,*" Oxford University Press's Academic Insights for the Thinking World, November 24, 2010, https://blog.oup.com/2010/11/giving.

A Service of Affirmation and Thanksgiving

Greeting: We have gathered as a sacred community, called to watch over one another in love. We gather to renew a covenant, to establish boundaries of respect for our beloved community. We are here to promise our shared trust and our watchfulness as we live together as the body of Christ in the world.

Hymn: "Come, Let Us Use the Grace Divine" (*The United Methodist Hymnal* #606)

Opening Prayer (said in unison)

Creator, Redeemer, and Sustainer, we gather in your name acknowledging there is evil in the world seeking to harm and destroy. We gather to remember our need to protect the vulnerability in all of us and establish safe spaces through the creation of personal boundaries. Every life has sacred worth, and you dwell within each one. Strengthen our resolve as we choose to covenant together in this act of solemn dedication. May you be glorified in the ways we care for one another. Amen.

Litany of Thanksgiving

One: Gracious God, we give you thanks for the many blessings we receive from our community. We thank you for the giftedness and wisdom passed onto us by those in the disability community. Help us respect one another and minister together as the body of Christ.

All: Grant that we might be your hands and feet, your eyes and ears, your comfort and presence.

One: We thank you for those who have grown to maturity among us. Thank you for the ways we can come alongside them. Thank you for trusted friends who are willing to lend a helping hand or give a kind word of encouragement. May the church be a haven of blessing for them.

All: **Grant that we might always be your hands and feet, your eyes and ears, your comfort and presence.**

One: We are grateful for the youth among us, so creative, so filled with questions, so filled with promise. Thank you for placing them within the protective environment of our community and for entrusting us to create a safe place for them to explore who they are and what they believe.

All: **Grant that we might always be your hands and feet, your eyes and ears, your comfort and presence.**

One: We praise you for new life, for the children among us, the most dependent, and the most vulnerable. Their lives bring us joy and hope. In their lives, we see dreams of a future not yet revealed. Thank you for entrusting them to our care, our protection, and our vigilance.

All: **Grant that we might always be your hands and feet, your eyes and ears, your comfort and presence, a constant blessing to their lives. Amen.**

One: We thank you for those who have answered the call to engage in leadership to provide safe protocols for our congregation that all may be secure.

All: **Grant that we might always be your hands and feet, your eyes and ears, your comfort and presence, a constant blessing to all. Amen.**

Affirmation and Commissioning of the Leadership Team

One: *(addressing the team)* Friends, God has called you to a ministry of safer sanctuaries in which you engage the entire church to work toward the end that all people are safe and protected in our buildings and in our ministries in the community. Do you affirm this call, which is in keeping with your baptismal covenant?

Team: **We accept our call to this ministry and reaffirm our baptismal promise to renounce the spiritual forces of wickedness, reject the evil powers of this world, and repent of our sin. We will use the freedom and power God gives us to resist evil, injustice, and oppression in whatever forms they present themselves.**

One: How will you accomplish your task?

Team: **We will do this through the power of Jesus Christ, who is our Savior, and we will trust in his grace to accomplish this work, which includes in its scope people of all ages, nations, and races. We will engage the help of the entire congregation that together, using our various gifts of the Spirit, we might empower ministry in safe and life-giving ways.**

One: *(addressing the congregation)* Members of this household of faith, I commend to you these persons who have been set aside for the work of the Safe Sanctuaries committee. Do all in your power to assist them that together this work may be an ongoing blessing to this congregation and the community.

All: We affirm the work of the Safe Sanctuaries committee with thanksgiving and pledge our support for this work. May God be glorified through this ministry.

One: Gracious God, bless this work that has been affirmed among us this day. Give your servants the strength and resources needed to accomplish the task and to serve in such a way that you receive the honor and the glory. This we pray in the name of Jesus Christ, our Lord. Amen.

Presentation of Certificates of Appreciation to Team Members

Hymn   "Take My Life, and Let it be Consecrated" (*The United Methodist Hymnal* #399)

Blessing   "Now to him who is able to keep you from falling, and to make you stand without blemish in the presence of his glory with rejoicing, to the only God our Savior, through Jesus Christ our Lord, be glory, majesty, power, and authority, before all time and now and forever. Amen. (Jude 1:24-25, NRSV)

A Service of Holy Communion

Invitation

One: Commit yourselves to Christ and to the care and protection of one another. Know that every life is sacred and precious. Every life is held in God's care. We are the presence of God for one another. Therefore, we commit ourselves to the calling of our baptism to resist evil, injustice, and oppression in whatever forms they present themselves. We will be watchful of others and encourage them to do the same. We will commit ourselves to our spiritual rule and practice to do no harm to anyone, to do good to everyone, and to live in perpetual fellowship with God.

    Let us go to the Trinity in prayer:

All: **Sacred Community of Three, we recognize that all people are entrusted to our care. We respond to your will for us to diligently watch over one another. Help us keep our eyes alert to dangers. Enable us to have attentive ears to even the silent cries for help. Let us be responsive to your restraining arms. Use our community to be a sure place of safety for all. Use our community to be a source of overflowing love and compassion. Use our community to be a haven of peace to those harassed by the world. Where we see danger, we will sound a warning. Where we see injury, we will seek aid. We will be involved and will ask questions. We will not walk away, because neither will you. Together we will make our world a safer place for everyone, the youngest, the oldest, the vulnerable, and those who have been deserted. Just like you, most Holy Trinity, we will never work alone but only with others in sacred community, now and always. Amen.**

One: Christ is the Good Shepherd. The Good Shepherd cares about the entire flock. If we go off on our own, Jesus goes after us to bring us back into community. Jesus never wants us to minister alone, and if we try, we know we will go astray. All ministry is community based, so we can watch over one another in love.

    Christ is the sheep pen. Jesus sets up boundaries to keep everyone safe from those who would seek to harm and destroy. Those who ignore gracious boundaries are not of Christ, no matter who they say they are.

Christ is the open gate. Jesus invites all to share in safe spaces where all can become the blessing God created them to be.

All: **Thank you for being our Good Shepherd and keeping us in community together for it is never your will that we minister alone. Thank you for setting up boundaries to keep us all safe. Thank you for being the open gate inviting us into a safe space. We promise to cooperate with you and with each other to hold this sacred space for all. Amen.**

Prayer of Confession (said in unison)

Dear Lord, you know that we have not watched over one another in love. We have failed to live accountable lives before you and our sisters and brothers. We have not respected the personal boundaries of others at times and have robbed them of peace. We have allowed others to serve you alone, without our support. Forgive us, we pray, and humble our hearts as we come before you. Give us a new and teachable spirit, that we might move away from our self-centered ways. Send us out two by two, to watch over one another and shield us from temptation. Shine your light upon all we do, and leave no secrets hidden. Let us be your servants with nothing to hide. Protect the world from our sins, so that they will not flee from your grace, provided by Jesus Christ our Lord. Amen.

Words of Assurance

One: "If we confess our sins, he who is faithful and just will forgive us our sins and cleanse us from all unrighteousness." (1 John 1:9, NRSV)

In the name of Jesus Christ, you are forgiven.

All: **In the name of Jesus Christ, you are forgiven. Thanks be to God.**

Passing the Peace of Christ

The Great Thanksgiving

One: As God has watched over us,

All: **We will watch over one another.**

One: We have found safety in the presence of God,

All: **We seek to extend that experience of safety to others.**

One: For God's loving kindness we are grateful,

All: **It fills our souls with music and dancing.**

One: God of peace that surpasses full understanding, you allow us to rest under the shadow of your wings. You allow us to breathe easy and rest in your care. We know that with you, we are safe. Your watchful eye never slumbers or sleeps. You are always alert to danger. Obedience to your guidance creates for us healthy boundaries. Your rules create a safe space where we can be free. Thank you that your care is not limited to us. Your desire is for all to be watched over with love. Your desire is for your tender care and concern to be extended to all. Your desire is for us to become your community of mindful grace.

In gratitude for our inclusion, we intentionally join your covenant community of watchful care. We join with those in our own church, with those in our community, with those throughout the world to be your eyes and ears, your hands, and feet, your very heart seeking to keep all safe from abuse and neglect. Together, we join with all your guardian angels in heaven, those who watch over their charges on earth, seeking to keep them from harm, and with them we worship around your throne saying:

All: **We love one another, because love is from God, and when we love, we are God's children and demonstrate that we know God, because God is love. We can love one another, because God saturates us with love. God is invisible, but we know that when we love one another, God's presence is visible in us and God is seen clearly in us.**

One: God is love and is seen perfectly in Jesus. Christ showed us that because of this love, we can be patient with one another, we can be humble and polite, we can be respectful of personal boundaries, and we will take no offense when corrected. Like Christ, we are empowered to give no space for evil, but create safe spaces where we rejoice in the truth and are free to expose any wrongdoing. Christ enables us to believe that the church can grow in grace. Christ empowers us to hope for a better future. Christ emboldens us to sacrifice ourselves to bring salvation to all.

No one was hopeless to Jesus. Jesus willingly knelt before anyone, no matter how evil their intentions, and washed their feet, seeking to redeem and to restore them. Jesus wants us to remember to love one another this way.

On the night that he was betrayed, Jesus took the bread of the Passover, which was used to keep us mindful of our vulnerability. Blessing this bread, Jesus broke it and gave it to his disciples saying, "Take and eat, this is my body broken and given for you." Jesus wants us to remember to love one another this way.

Later, Jesus took the cup of Passover wine, which was used to keep us mindful of the harm caused by our sins. Blessing this cup, Jesus passed it to all, saying, "Take and drink, this cup contains my blood, which is poured out freely in celebration of God's eternal covenant of grace, promising the forgiveness of our sins, and the sins of all others." Jesus wants us to remember to love one another this way.

We want to love like Christ, watching out for the vulnerable and caring for those who are in harm's way. In this holy mystery, we find Christ and we seek to proclaim to the world:

All: **Christ's death brought salvation. Christ's resurrection brought hope. Christ's coming again renews the face of the earth.**

One: Vigilant Protector, Watchful Care, transform these gifts of bread and wine for us into the body and blood of Christ.

Vigilant Protector, Watchful Care, transform the gift of our lives to become your church, the body and the bride of Christ.

Vigilant Protector, Watchful Care, we want to be like you. We want to love like you and forgive like you. We want to protect like you and encourage like you. We want to be involved like you to bless the lives of all. This privilege we ask through Christ, for Christ, and in Christ strengthened by the indwelling of your Spirit of love and grace. We are inspired by you, our creative God, who is always able to imagine the best for all of us. We sing our hymns of praise and worship before you forever. Amen.

One: Now as those united to our covenant God in Jesus Christ, let us pray as we were taught:

All: **Our Father who art in heaven, hallowed be thy name. Thy kingdom come; thy will be done on earth as it is in heaven. Give us this day our daily bread. Forgive us our trespasses, as we have forgiven those who have trespassed against us. And lead us not into temptation but deliver us from evil. For thine is the kingdom and the power and the glory forever. Amen.**

Receiving the Elements

The body of Christ given for all . . .

The blood of Christ shed for all . . .

Prayer after Communion (said in unison)

Thank you for sharing with us this holy mystery found in the sacrifice of Jesus Christ. You have opened your heart to us and have called us to join with you in watchful care. When we see something, we will say something. When we hear something, we will do something. Now send us out to share this grace with those in our church and community. Use us to keep people safe and share with all the grace we have found in you. Amen.

Benediction: Now let us work together. As the body of Christ, let us protect one another. Let us be one, as you are one, Father, Son and Holy Spirit. Amen.

PART VIII

SAMPLE FORMS AND APPENDICES

Safe Sanctuaries Task Force
for the Local Church

Pastor

Name: _____

Address: _____

Phone: _____

Member of Staff-Parish Committee

Name: _____

Address: _____

Phone: _____

Member of Board of Trustees

Name: _____

Address: _____

Phone: _____

Lay Leader

Name: _____

Address: _____

Phone: _____

Director of Youth Ministries/Youth Minister

Name: _____

Address: _____

Phone: _____

Director of Children's Ministries/Children's Minister

Name: _____

Address: _____

Phone: _____

Director of Weekday Program for Children (if applicable)

(This would include any daycares, preschools, or private schools that use church facilities during the week.)

Name: _____

Address: _____

Phone: _____

Representative of Each Ministry Working with Vulnerable Groups

(The number of members listed here will depend on the number of ministries in your congregation. For instance, children, youth, and so forth.)

Name: _____

Address: _____

Phone: _____

Name: _____

Address: _____

Phone: _____

Name: _____

Address: _____

Phone: _____

Sample Employment Application

This type of application should be completed by anyone who seeks any role that will involve the supervision and/or custody of children or youth. You should tailor the application to the specific circumstances in your congregation. At a minimum, this should include sections for personal identification, job qualifications, experience and background, references, and a waiver/consent to conduct a background check.

Name: _____
          (Last)   (First)   (Middle)

Preferred Pronouns: _____

Are you over the age of 18?   ❏ Yes   ❏ No

Present address: _____

City: _____State: _____ Zip Code: _____

Phone number: _____ Email Address: _____

Best method of contact: ❏ Email   ❏ Phone   ❏ Text message

Position applied for: _____

Date you are available to start: _____

Qualifications

Academic achievements (Schools attended, degrees earned, dates of completion)

_____

_____

_____

Continuing education (Courses taken, dates of completion)

_____

_____

_____

Professional organizations/other qualifications (List any additional relevant information)

_____

_____

_____

First aid training?   ❑ Yes   ❑ No

CPR training?   ❑ Yes   ❑ No

Previous Work Experience: Please list your previous employers from the past five years. Include the job title, a description of duties and responsibilities, the name of the company/employer, the name of your immediate supervisor, and the dates you were employed in each position.

_____

_____

_____

_____

_____

Previous Volunteer Experience: Please list any relevant volunteer positions you have held and list the duties you performed in each position, the name of your supervisor, the address and phone number of the volunteer organization, and the dates of your volunteer service.

_____

_____

_____

_____

_____

_____

Have you ever been convicted of or pled guilty to a crime, either a misdemeanor or a felony (including but not limited to drug-related charges, child abuse, other crimes of violence, theft, or motor vehicle violations)?   ❑ Yes   ❑ No

If yes, please explain:

_____

_____

References: Please list three individuals who are not related to you by blood or marriage as references. Please list people who have known you for at least three years.

Name: _____

Address: _____

Phone number: _____

Email address: _____

Length of time you have known reference: _____

Relationship to reference: _____

Name: _____

Address: _____

Phone number: _____

Email address: _____

Length of time you have known reference: _____

Relationship to reference: _____

Name: _____

Address: _____

Phone number: _____

Email address: _____

Length of time you have known reference: _____

Relationship to reference: _____

Waiver and Consent

I, _____, hereby certify that the information I have provided on this application for employment is true and correct. I authorize this church to verify the information I have provided on this application by contacting the references and employers I have listed, by conducting a criminal records check, or by other means, including contacting others whom I have not listed. I authorize the references and employers listed in this application to give you whatever information they may have regarding my character and fitness for the job for which I have applied. Furthermore, I waive any rights I may have to confidentiality.

In the event that my application is accepted and I become employed by _____, I agree to abide by and be bound by the policies of _____ and to refrain from inappropriate conduct in the performance of my duties on behalf of _____.

I have read this waiver and the entire application, and I am fully aware of its contents. I sign this consent freely and under no duress or coercion.

_____   _____
Signature of Applicant   Date

_____   _____
Witness   Date

Sample Volunteer Application

Name: _____
(Last)   (First)   (Middle)

Preferred Pronouns: _____

Address: _____

City: _____ State: _____ Zip Code: _____

Phone number: _____ Email Address: _____

Best method of contact: ❏ Email   ❏ Phone   ❏ Text message

Occupation: _____

Employer: _____

Current Job Responsibilities and Schedule: _____

_____

Previous relevant work experience: _____

Previous volunteer experience: _____

_____

Special interests, hobbies, and skills: _____

How many hours per week are you available to volunteer? _____

_____ Days   _____ Evenings   _____ Weekends

Can you make a one-year commitment to this volunteer role?_____

Do you have your own transportation? _____

Do you have a valid driver's license? _____

Do you have liability insurance? _____

Would you be available for periodic volunteer training sessions? ❏ Yes   ❏ No

Why would you like to volunteer as a worker with children and/or youth?

_____

_____

What qualities do you have that would help you work with children and/or youth?

_____

_____

Have you ever been charged, convicted of, or pled guilty to a crime, either a misdemeanor or a felony (including but not limited to drug-related charges, child abuse, other crimes of violence, theft, or motor vehicle violations)? ❑ Yes   ❑ No

If yes, please explain:

_____

_____

References: Please list three individuals who are not related to you by blood or marriage as references. Please list people who have known you for at least three years.

Name: _____

Address: _____

Phone number: _____

Email address: _____

Length of time you have known reference: _____

Relationship to reference: _____

Name: _____

Address: _____

Phone number: _____

Email address: _____

Length of time you have known reference: _____

Relationship to reference: _____

Name: _____

Address: _____

Phone number: _____

Email address: _____

Length of time you have known reference: _____

Relationship to reference: _____

_____   _____
Signature of Applicant   Date

Sample Authorization and Request for Criminal Records Check

I, _____, hereby authorize _____ to request the _____ police/sheriff's department to release information regarding any record of charges or convictions contained in its files, or in any criminal file maintained on me, whether said file is a local, state, or national file, and including but not limited to accusations and convictions for crimes committed against minors, to the fullest extent permitted by state and federal law. I do release said police/sheriff's department from all liability that may result from any such disclosure made in response to this request.

_____   _____
Signature of Applicant   Date

Applicant's full name: _____

All other names that have been used by applicant (if any): _____

_____

Date of birth: _____ Place of birth: _____

Social Security number: _____

Driver's license number: _____ State issuing license: _____

License expiration date: _____

Request sent to: _____

Name: _____

Address: _____

Phone number: _____

Email address: _____

This is a sample form. Your congregation may prefer to conduct criminal background checks on applicants through one of the many companies that provide this service. United Methodist Insurance has partnered with PeopleFacts (formerly TRAK-1) to help local congregations obtain these services. For more information, see uminsure.org/background-screenings.

Form for Reference Check

Applicant name: _____

Reference name: _____

Reference address: _____

Reference phone number: _____

Reference email address: _____

1. What is your relationship to the applicant?

2. How long have you known the applicant?

3. How well do you know the applicant?

4. How would you describe the applicant?

5. How would you describe the applicant's ability to relate to children and/or youth?

6. How would you describe the applicant's ability to relate to adults?

7. How would you describe the applicant's leadership abilities?

8. How would you feel about having the applicant as a volunteer worker with your child and/or youth?

9. Do you know of any characteristics that would negatively affect the applicant's ability to work with children and/or youth? If so, please describe.

10. Do you have any knowledge that the applicant has ever been convicted of a crime? If so, please describe.

11. Please list any other comments you would like to make.

Reference inquiry completed by: _____
                                         Signature   Date

Sample Volunteer Covenant Statement

The congregation of _____ is committed to providing a safe and secure environment for all children, youth, workers, and volunteers who participate in ministries and activities sponsored by the church. The following policy statements reflect our congregation's commitment to preserving this church as a holy place of safety and protection for all who would enter and as a place in which all people can experience the love of God through relationships with others.

1. No adult who has been convicted of child abuse (either sexual abuse, physical abuse, neglect, or emotional abuse) should volunteer to work with children or youth in any church-sponsored activity.

2. All adult volunteers involved with children or youth of our church must have been members of the congregation for at least six months before beginning a volunteer assignment.

3. Adult volunteers with children and youth shall observe the two-adult rule at all times so that no adult is left alone with children or youth on a routine basis.

4. Adult volunteers with children and youth shall attend regular training and educational events provided by the church to keep volunteers informed of church policies and state laws regarding child abuse.

5. Adult volunteers shall immediately report to their supervisor any behavior that seems abusive or inappropriate.

Place your initials next to the following statements to confirm your agreement.

1. As a volunteer in this congregation, I agree to observe and abide by all church policies regarding working in ministries with children and youth. ____

2. As a volunteer in this congregation, I agree to observe the two-adult rule at all times. ____

3. As a volunteer in this congregation, I agree to abide by the six-month rule before beginning a volunteer assignment. ____

4. As a volunteer in this congregation, I agree to participate in training and education events provided by the church related to my volunteer assignment. ____

5. As a volunteer in this congregation, I agree to promptly report abusive or inappropriate behavior to my supervisor. ____

6. As a volunteer in this congregation, I agree to inform a minister of this church if I have ever been convicted of child abuse. ____

I have read this volunteer covenant statement, and I agree to observe and abide by the policies set forth above.

_____

Signature of Volunteer   Date

_____

Print full name

Childcare Worker Position Description

Position: Childcare work in the church nursery

Reports to: Nursery supervisor/coordinator

General qualifications required:

1. All childcare staff members shall be of good character and be of the Christian faith.
2. All childcare staff members shall
   a. Be physically, mentally, and emotionally healthy.
   b. Have a basic understanding of children and their needs.
   c. Be adaptive to a variety of situations.
   d. Be willing to grow in their knowledge of children through periodic education and training events.
3. All childcare staff members shall have a physician's report stating that the staff member is in good health and has presented the result of a current tuberculin skin test.
4. _____ hires without regard to race, sex, or national origin.

Educational qualifications required:

1. All childcare staff members shall have completed the equivalent of a high school diploma.

Duties of childcare staff member:

1. Provide physical, emotional, and intellectual support and stimulation to each child in your care, as appropriate for the circumstances.
2. Provide appropriate guidance to each child in your care.
3. Develop a relationship of trust and continuity with the children in your care, which will enhance each child's development of a positive self-image.
4. Provide support and assistance to parents when they arrive with their child.

Performance expectations of a childcare staff member:

1. Be punctual. Notify the nursery supervisor in advance if you must be late.

2. Be reliable in your attendance. Notify the nursery supervisor in advance if you must be absent.

3. Attend periodic training and education events provided by the church.

4. Be polite, friendly, and courteous to others, both children and adults.

5. Do not engage in physical punishment or discipline of any child.

6. Cooperate with other childcare staff and with parents.

7. Abide by and apply the childcare policies of _____ at all times.

I have read the position description for childcare staff members at _____ and understand its contents. My signature below indicates my agreement and covenant to abide by the requirements set forth above.

_____

Signature of Applicant   Date

240

Report of Suspected Incident of Abuse

Name of worker (staff or volunteer) observing or receiving disclosure of abuse:

_____

Victim's name: _____

Victim's age/date of birth: _____

Victim's statement/detailed summary of observations: _____

_____

_____

_____

_____

Name of person accused as perpetrator: _____

Relationship of accused to victim (staff, volunteer, family member, other): _____

_____

Report to Pastor

Person making report: _____

Name of pastor: _____

Date/time: _____

Summary of report: _____

_____

_____

Report to Victim's Parent/Guardian

Person making report: _____

Name of parent/guardian: _____

Date/time: _____

Summary of report: _____

_____

_____

_____

Report to Local Children's Services/Family Services Agency

Person making report: _____

Spoke with: _____

Date/time: _____

Summary of report: _____

_____

_____

_____

Report to Law Enforcement Agency

Person making report: _____

Spoke with: _____

Date/time: _____

Summary of report: _____

_____

_____

_____

Other Contacts (list all other parties who have been informed of suspected incident of abuse)

Name: _____

Date/time: _____

Summary: _____

_____

_____

_____
Signature of Incident Reporter   Date

This is a sample form. Please tailor your congregation's form to comply with the reporting requirements of the laws of your state and your congregation's policies.

Sample Accident Report Form

Date of accident: _____ Time of accident: _____

Location of accident: _____

Name of child/youth injured: _____ Age: _____

Address of child/youth: _____

_____

Parent/guardian contacted: _____

Person(s) who witnessed the accident

Name: _____ Phone: _____

Name: _____ Phone: _____

Name: _____ Phone: _____

Describe the accident: _____

_____

_____

_____

_____

_____

_____
Signature of Accident Reporter   Date

Sample Policy for Social Networking, Blogging, and Internet Connection between Staff, Volunteers, and Students

This is a sample policy for staff members and volunteers regarding their online behavior. It is highly encouraged that each individual congregation adapt this policy to its particular guidelines, policies, and values.

In general, our congregation views social networking sites (such as Instagram, Snapchat, Facebook, and so forth) personal websites, and blogs in a positive light and respects the wishes of staff members and volunteers to use them as a medium for self-expression. If a paid staff member chooses to identify himself or herself as an employee of our congregation in these venues, we are aware that some readers may view this employee as a representative or spokesperson of the congregation. In light of this possibility, our congregation requires, as a condition of employment, that paid staff members observe the following guidelines when referring to the congregation, its programs and activities, its members, and other paid staff or volunteers, on social media, personal websites, or blogs. Furthermore, we highly recommend that volunteers at the congregation abide by these same guidelines.

1. Staff members must be respectful in all communications and blogs related to or referencing the congregation, its members, and other staff members or volunteers.

2. Staff members must not use obscenities, profanity, and vulgar language or images.

3. Staff members should not use social media, personal websites, or blogs to disparage the congregation, members, or other staff members or volunteers.

4. Staff members must not use social media, personal websites, or blogs to harass, bully, or intimidate others, particularly members of the congregation and other staff and volunteers. Behaviors that constitute harassment and bullying include, but are not limited to, comments that are derogatory with respect to race, religion, gender, sexual orientation, color, or disability; comments that are sexually suggestive, humiliating, or demeaning; and threats to stalk, haze, or physically injure another person.

5. Staff members must not use social media, personal websites, or blogs to discuss engaging in conduct that is prohibited by congregational policies, including, but not limited to, the inappropriate or illegal use of alcohol, the use of illegal drugs, sexual behavior, sexual harassment, and bullying.

6. Staff members must not post pictures of congregation members, other staff members, or volunteers without obtaining written permission.

Any employee found to be in violation of this policy will be subject to disciplinary action, up to and including dismissal.

Appendix: Opportunities for Flourishing for People with Disabilities

Whenever possible, congregational ministries and activities should be adapted so that everyone can participate together. Some ministries, however, respond to specialized needs. These require careful attention to safety. While they can be part of the solution, they can also be areas with higher potential for abuse. The following scenarios are each based on composite experiences of several churches.

Sensory Rooms

Anytown UMC is proud of their new sensory room set up by graduate students from a local occupational therapy program. The room has a ball pit, swing, bean bag pillows, tactile wall, fiber-optic display, and calm-down corner. Fidgets, weighted blankets, and noise-canceling headphones are available for use. The space allows children and youth to take sensory breaks to keep them focused and engaged in their age-appropriate classrooms. Parents appreciate a space to take overstimulated children during large, noisy all-church events.

Considerations:

- How will you ensure that participants remain visible and that the two-adults rule is followed when children use this space?
- What kind of specific training will you provide and who will teach it to your volunteers?
- How will you determine and monitor which activities are appropriate for each child?
- How can volunteers provide calming support within safe-touch boundaries?
- How will you disinfect soft surfaces and the ball pit, and who is responsible to do so?

Peer Support Groups and Classes

Central UMC offers a Sunday evening Bible study and fellowship time for socially isolated young adults with developmental and intellectual disabilities, some of whom live at home while others live in nearby group homes. After transitioning from high school, their options for employment and meaningful social participation are limited. Participants enjoy a chance to grow in faith and learn about the Bible and God in a setting where they are accepted and can be themselves. The curriculum includes a variety of engaging activities and is adult-oriented but at a reading level where no one feels excluded.

Considerations:

- How many volunteers do you need to provide successful interactions and support when the group is divided (for instance, for a restroom break) and while waiting for rides?
- If outside programs such as 12-step groups use the building at the same time, how do you handle potential interactions with adults who have not met safety standards?
- How do you support peer-to-peer friendships that may grow into relationships?
- What is your protocol if someone discloses abuse from the past or other settings?
- Do you have a procedure for drop-in visitors or members bringing friends along?

Respite Programs

First UMC has a history of hosting monthly respite evenings for individuals with disabilities. Having a few hours to themselves provides a welcome relief for parents whose schedules are full of therapy and medical appointments and whose children require close around-the-clock supervision.

Considerations:

- How do you ensure and track background checks and safety training for members of partner congregations from other denominations?
- How do you provide necessary health and support information to volunteers while keeping medical histories and diagnoses confidential?
- How will you meet the need for respite for all ages while separating children from youth and youth from adults?

- What volunteer-to-participant ratio is needed, and what happens if a volunteer cancels at the last minute?
- What logistics regarding food safety need to be worked out?

Notes

Off-Site Mission and Volunteer Opportunities

St. John's UMC has a strong outreach and mission-focused ministry. They routinely include a group of young adults with intellectual and developmental disabilities who are part of the congregation. Examples of their off-site volunteer work include packing weekend lunch kits for food-insecure children, cleaning up a local park, and performing a puppet show at a local nursing home.

Considerations:

- How will you manage safe transportation for the group?
- Who needs permission to participate and how will you obtain such permission?
- How do you provide adequate supervision in an uncontrolled environment outside the church where group members work alongside participants from other organizations?
- Are you prepared for potential injuries or medical issues?
- What is your protocol if a participant, despite your best efforts, is missing?

Overnight Camps and Retreats for People with Intellectual and Developmental Disabilities

Main Street UMC supports an annual week-long camp hosted by the conference camping ministry and held in a nearby conference-owned camp. Participants tend to return annually, citing the time at camp as the best week of their year. Volunteers also come year after year, although some of them are reaching a stage where they can no longer keep up as easily. Similarly, some participants have had changes in their mobility, health, and ability to care for themselves. Routines and schedules are similar each year to keep things predictable and repeat favorite experiences. Campers and counselors alike find they grow closer to God during the week.

Considerations:

- What system do you use to track medical information and permissions, both for routine care (medication administration) and in case of emergencies?

249

Notes

- What volunteer-to-camper ratio is needed for 24-hour support and supervision, including necessary volunteer breaks? How will you provide needed assistance with daily tasks that become evident during the week?

- What procedures are in place to ensure water and fire safety during typical camp activities? Are camp staff trained in working with campers with disabilities?

- How do you plan and offer inclusive but safe interactions with children and youth camps present during the same week?

- How do you address the danger of complacency and being less alert to risks when some volunteers have helped for many years and started before safety protocols were initiated?

Writing Team for Safer Sanctuaries

Bishop Peggy Johnson

Bishop Peggy A. Johnson is a native of Baltimore, Maryland, and is a retired bishop in The United Methodist Church. She served as the episcopal leader of the Philadelphia Area of The United Methodist Church, which includes the Eastern Pennsylvania Annual Conference and the Peninsula-Delaware Annual Conference, from 2008–2021. Bishop Johnson is currently the interim bishop of the New England Annual Conference. Prior to her service as a bishop, she served churches in the Baltimore Washington Conference, including the Christ UMC of the Deaf.

Angela Schaffner

Dr. Angela D. Schaffner is a licensed psychologist and owner of Schaffner Psychotherapy Services in Atlanta, GA. She authored two books, *Revealed: What the Bible Can Teach You About Yourself* and *Gather Us In: Leading Transformational Small Groups*. She is a third-degree black belt in taekwondo, and she enjoys playing tennis and spending time with friends and family.

Bonnie L. Bevers

Bonnie earned her master of divinity degree with a concentration in child advocacy from Garrett-Evangelical Theological Seminary. She also received her Certification in Youth Ministry from Perkins School of Theology. Bonnie has served as a youth pastor for nine years and as a volunteer for many years prior to that. Bonnie also serves as the Rio Texas Conference Youth Delegate Coordinator. Before serving in full-time ministry, Bonnie received a double master's degree in criminology and criminal justice, which led to her work with child advocacy centers across the United States. Bonnie has been a lifelong member of The United Methodist Church and is currently a certified candidate for ordination as a deacon in The United Methodist Church.

_____

_____

_____

_____

_____

_____

_____

_____

_____

_____

_____

_____

Leanne Hadley

Leanne Hadley is an advocate, speaker, consultant, and minister in The United Methodist Church. She received her master's in divinity and doctorate in ministry from United Theological Seminary. She is the author of several books and a speaker on children's spirituality and development. She is passionate about helping children and families grow in their relationship with Christ.

Brittany Sky

Brittany Sky is a writer, creator, and researcher who loves kids and the adults who care for them. She holds a BA and an MA in Christian education and an MBA for good measure. Brittany is the author of *Raising Good People*, the *Celebrate Wonder Bible Storybook*, the *Bible Basics Storybook*, the *Deep Blue Bible Storybook*, and countless curricula. Brittany lives on the land of the Cherokee (also known as Nashville, TN) with her partner, Michael, their toddler, Rowan, and two terriers, Charlie and Lily.

Kelly Peterson

Kelly Peterson has been involved with the work of Safe Sanctuaries for more than thirteen years. She was a trainer of trainers and developer of best practices as a part of the Safe Sanctuaries team for both the California-Nevada Annual Conference and the Division of Young People's Ministries for Discipleship Ministries. She participated in a focus group for the Centers for Disease Control and Prevention in their development of new policies around child-abuse prevention. She currently serves as executive director/CEO of Camp Fire Heart of Iowa, where she is helping implement new policies, training, and practices of national standards for the organization.

Lynn Swedberg

Deaconess Lynn Swedberg is an occupational therapist who has been part of the Disability Ministries Committee of The United Methodist Church since 2003, currently as consultant and newsletter editor. Her passion is improving accessibility to ensure that people with disabilities are fully and safely included in our faith communities and ministries. She co-developed The United Methodist Church accessibility audit and wrote the Leader's Guide for the Mission U study on "The Church and People with Disabilities." She is certified in ministry with people with disabilities through the United Methodist Board of General Education and Higher Ministry. Lynn also serves as adjunct faculty in the Accessibility Studies Program at Central Washington University.

Robyn Arab

Robyn Arab, BSW, CMC, has been working in the field of social work for more than thirty years in various roles. Her passion is working with seniors and their families to plan for the future by making wise and educated decisions.

Derrick Scott III

Derrick is a campus minister and United Methodist lay leader who has served college students and young adults in Jacksonville, St. Augustine, and throughout Northeast Florida for more than twenty years. He currently serves as digital campus minister and creative producer of Studio Wesley.

Jessica Gamaché

Jessica Gamaché is the association director for United Methodist Camp and Retreat Ministries. Her role is to guide the association and its members in resource development and member engagement. After earning her master's in recreation management from Slippery Rock University, Jessica served various camps and retreat centers in both the United Methodist and Lutheran connections. She believes that being immersed in the outdoors through a camp experience brings all people closer to God and one another.

Lynn Caterson

Lynn Caterson has been a practicing attorney for more than forty years and has her own law firm specializing in nonprofit law, which includes all types of religious organizations. She has served on the Judicial Council for eight years and was a delegate to General Conference from 2004 through 2019. She has been the chancellor to the Greater New Jersey Annual Conference since 2009. She has also held many positions in her local church and is now chair of the board of trustees.

Chris Wilterdink

Chris is the executive director of Congregational Vitality and International Discipleship and the director of Young People's Ministries at Discipleship Ministries of The United Methodist Church. His roles in ministry were based at the local church for more than twelve years where his undergraduate degree in English education and master's in nonprofit management shaped his approach to ministry. He is the father of two awesome kids, husband to an amazing wife, and an outdoor enthusiast. He has had several books published, including *Building Spiritual Muscle, Everyday Discipleship: Covenant Discipleship with Youth*, and most recently the eBook series, *Crash Courses in Youth Ministry*.

Notes

Kevin Johnson

Rev. Dr. Kevin Johnson is the Director, Children's Ministries for Congregational Vitality & Intentional Discipleship at Discipleship Ministries. Kevin's hero, Fred Rogers, suggests that we, "listen to the children, learn about them, learn from them. Think of the children first." This quote defines Rev. Kev's approach to ministry. Kevin, an ordained elder of the Kentucky Annual Conference, has more than twenty years of ministry experience in which he has thought of the children first. Prior to ministry, Kevin worked with children in the hospital setting and in group homes for emotionally and physically abused children. Kevin is married to Jennifer, and together they have three children, Braden, JonMarie, and Will.

Truman Brooks

Rev. Dr. Truman Brooks has served as a United Methodist pastor in urban, suburban, and county seat churches in Eastern Pennsylvania for more than forty years. He holds an M.Div. from Princeton Theological Seminary and a D.Min. from Palmer Seminary. For fifteen years, he has worked with churches that have experienced sexual misconduct by clergy, staff, and laity.

Continue the work of building safer sanctuaries with the *Safer Sanctuaries Online Guide*.

For many churches and related organizations, creating a Safe Sanctuaries policy can be a complex and overwhelming process. The **Safer Sanctuaries Online Guide** serves as a companion for your team as they work through the process of developing and implementing a Safe Sanctuaries policy.

The *Online Guide* supplements each section of this manual with video, reflection questions, and scenarios designed to deepen your understanding for successful implementation. The *Online Guide* will encourage and motivate your team to move from understanding the need for a Safe Sanctuaries policy to the creation of a policy unique to your setting.

Learn more at **SaferSanctuaries.org**.

Printed in the USA
CPSIA information can be obtained
at www.ICGtesting.com
LVHW081337180923
758473LV00029B/995

9 780881 779622